Christianity and the Kikuyu

American University Studies

Series IX
History

Vol. 45

PETER LANG
New York • Bern • Frankfurt am Main • Paris

David P. Sandgren

Christianity and the Kikuyu

Religious Divisions and Social Conflict

PETER LANG
New York • Bern • Frankfurt am Main • Paris

Library of Congress Cataloging-in-Publication Data

Sandgren, David P.
   Christianity and the Kikuyu : religious divisions and
social conflict / David P. Sandgren.
   p. cm. – (American university studies. Series IX,
History : vol. 45)
   Bibliography: p.
   Includes index.
   1. Kikuyu (African people) – Religion.   2. Kikuyu
(African people) – Missions.   3. Kenya – Church history –
20th century.   I. Title.   II. Series.
   BR1443.K4S26   1989   276.76'208'08996 – dc19   88-10092
   ISBN 0-8204-0732-1   CIP
   ISSN 0740-0462

CIP-Titelaufnahme der Deutschen Bibliothek

Sandgren, David P.:
Christianity and the Kikuyu : religious divisions
and social conflict / David P. Sandgren. – New
York; Bern, Frankfurt am Main; Paris: Lang,
1989.
   (American University Studies: Ser. 9,
   History; Vol. 45)
   ISBN 0-8204-0732-1

NE: American University Studies / 09

© Peter Lang Publishing, Inc., New York 1989

Printed by Weihert-Druck GmbH, Darmstadt, West Germany

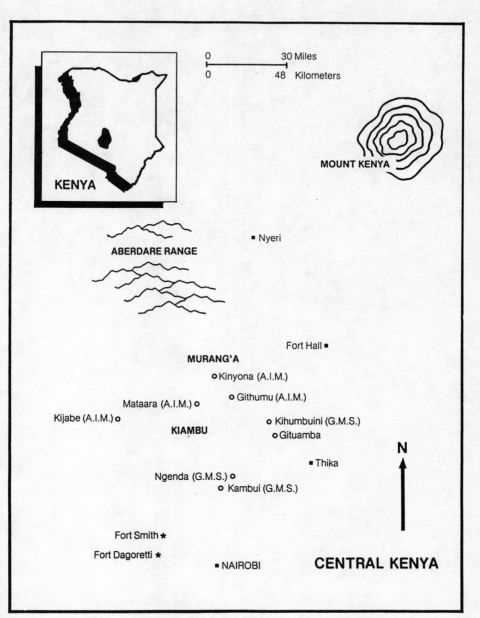

0   30 Miles

0   48   Kilometers

KENYA

MOUNT KENYA

ABERDARE RANGE

■ Nyeri

Fort Hall ■

MURANG'A

o Kinyona (A.I.M.)

Mataara (A.I.M.) o   o Githumu (A.I.M.)

Kijabe (A.I.M.) o   o Kihumbuini (G.M.S.)

KIAMBU   o Gituamba

■ Thika

Ngenda (G.M.S.) o

o Kambui (G.M.S.)

Fort Smith ★

Fort Dagoretti ★

■ NAIROBI   CENTRAL KENYA

N

ACKNOWLEDGMENTS

The seeds for this study were planted more than two decades ago when I took up residence in a small, rural Kikuyu high school. As a young teacher of history, I was soon introduced to local topics, first in a few student essays, and then more systematically when I organized history projects for students over their school holidays. They were encouraged to interview their families and friends about locally important topics and then report their findings in an essay to be handed in upon their return to school. But, what had started out as a strategy to improve student writing skills, soon developed for me into a fascinating introduction to local Kikuyu history. In a complete reversal of roles, these students and their families taught me a great deal about local historical topics of importance to them. There were often differing interpretations and hotly contested points of view, especially concerning the Mau Mau rebellion. This awareness of the local nuances of interpretation and opinion helped me in the collection and analysis of oral materials for the present study. Therefore, I wish to acknowledge my gratitude to the students from Giakanja Secondary School, in whose debt I remain.

To those who have taught me African history, I have an equal debt; these people include Philip Curtin and Jan Vansina, but especially Steven Feierman who, for twenty years, has shared with me his knowledge and expertise of East Africa and offered crucial and frequent guidance. Without his help, this book would not have been written.

I wish to express my gratitude to many institutions associated with my research: The Kenya Government for permission to pursue my research; and the Kenya National Archives for their great assistance; the Africa Inland Mission for the use of their archives, even before they were organized and catalogued for easy access; the Presbyterian Church of East Africa for use of their extensive archival holdings; and finally to Rhodes House Library for the generous help in the use of their manuscript collections and for their kind permission to use the following photographs: "Fort Smith, 1897" from Edward J.H. Russell, Diaries of an Assistant Commissioner, BEA Company, Mss. Afr. S.120, 1897; and "A Kikuyu Scene" from Sir Alfred Claud Hollis, Autobiography: East Africa Protectorate, Vol. III, Mss. Brit. Emp. S. 295.

To Concordia College, Moorhead, Minnesota, where I have taught since 1971, to the Department of History and to my collegues who have read all or part of the manuscript, especially, James Coomber, Carroll Engelhardt, Ralph Hoppe, Peter Hovde, Linda Johnson, and William Block, I offer my most sincere appreciation for their unfailing interest and support.

Thanks also go to John Lonsdale and Terence Ranger who gave thoughtful advice to my earliest ideas concerning this

interest and strong encouragement sustained me through the long
preparation of the manuscript. To Jo Engelhardt, who has
shepherded the manuscript through all its stages with unfailing
expertise and good humor, a special note of thanks is due.

Without the understanding and cooperation of many people
in Kenya, especially to those whose names appear in the footnotes as informants, this book would not have been possible.
To all of you I owe a debt that can never be paid. A special
note of thanks goes to Wakaba Kimani whose enthusiasm, guidance
and general encouragement, as my field research assistant,
enabled me to find and interview many dozens of people. None
of these institutions or people bears any responsibility for
the information or analysis found in this book; such responsibility is mine alone.

Finally, it is to my wife Ann, who has seen me through
this project with advice, good humor and encouragement, that I
wish to express my affectionate thanks and gratitude by dedi-
cating this book to her.

TABLE OF CONTENTS

LIST OF ILLUSTRATIONS

ABBREVIATIONS

ACC&S	Africa Christian Church and Schools
AIM	Africa Inland Mission
AIC	Africa Inland Church
CMS	Church Missionary Society
CSM	Church of Scotland Mission
GMS	Gospel Mission Society
IBEAC	Imperial British East Africa Company
KCA	Kikuyu Central Association
KNA	Kenya National Archives
KISA	Kenya Independent Schools Association
KPA	Kenya Provincial Association
PCEA	Presbyterian Church of East Africa

INTRODUCTION

The Kikuyu have had a rich, varied and much studied twentieth century history. Central to this history has been their encounter with European intruders, most particularly, a British colonial administration, resident white farmers and foreign missionaries. Of these three groups, it is the missionaries and the arrival of Christianity that are the focus. In particular, this study shows that the Kikuyu encounter with Christianity produced a series of rivalries which in time caused deep, serious and irreconcilable divisions among the Kikuyu. Though lasting for decades, these religiously and experientially based divisions have been unidentified by scholars.

The missionaries to which this study gives most attention were members of the Africa Inland Mission (AIM), a USA based nondenominational (though largely Baptist) society which came to Kenya at the end of the nineteenth century. The AIM and its offshoot--the Gospel Mission Society (GMS)--arrived among the Kikuyu a few years later and began their evangelistic efforts in Kiambu and Murang'a, two adjacent districts of colonial Kenya's central province. These mission societies are important because they provide us with the initial encounter of the Kikuyu with Christianity and they give geographical focus to the study. They set up the encounter and even give content to its initial pace and timing, but the missionaries are not the primary focus. Rather, it is the Kikuyu themselves and their grass roots interaction with Christianity that take center stage. It is their creativity and initiative that provide both form and content to their experience with missionaries and Christianity.

The study opens with a general description of Kikuyu society at the end of the nineteenth century and the intrusion of British Colonialism and white settler agriculture. Since this is a familiar story, little time is spent in description or analysis when the ground has been so ably covered by others. It is important to note, however, that the Kikuyu were remarkably adept at creating place for themselves in the colonial enterprise: they provisioned caravans on a large scale, hired themselves out for both official and private colonial armies, accepted and even lobbied for the first colonial appointments as the infant government administration began to spread its web across the southern Kikuyu frontier. The Kikuyu did not withdraw from the British but participated from the very beginning in the colonial enterprise, though at a subordinate level.

It was into this colonial context that the AIM (and GMS) appeared at the beginning of the twentieth century, first with the opening of the Kijabe and Kambui stations and then with several more sites during the following decade (see map). These American missionaries brought a great enthusiasm and optimism to their work among the Kikuyu. These qualities equipped them for the early years of isolation and physical hardship when few Kikuyu were interested in Christianity, but they were not sufficient to sustain the missionaries' enterprise when adherents grew in number and influence. They busied themselves in building and preaching and otherwise brought a very practical (and perhaps American) perspective to their activities. The AIM also took upon itself the right to define civilization for the Kikuyu and what was thought to be its automatic attendant--evangelism. The missionaries were neither calculating nor thoughtful in making these determinations but automatically assumed that they knew what was right for the Kikuyu. Those who inquired about Christianity were instructed to question the value of their society and culture and to accept without question the cultural merits of the west as well as its customs of dress and manners. Once baptized, adherents to the mission were strongly encouraged to stop all Kikuyu cultural practices. Offenders were disciplined and sometimes even expelled from the mission. In their zeal to promote and enforce western manners and morals, they were oblivious to their cultural arrogance even though they were repelled by such chauvinism when it was exhibited by the British colonial authorities. Indeed, the missionaries often congratulated themselves on being American and therefore did not identify with a country which participated in imperialism. Never did they identify their attitudes, ideas or behavior as being the religious equivalent of European nationalist imperialism.

Surprisingly, the Kikuyu did not chafe under the multiplicity of rules that the AIM laid down for their new adherents. They saw the mission station as a refuge from disagreeable aspects of their own society, and as a place where a plot of land could be obtained in a society where its availability had drastically declined under colonial rule. They were attracted to the literacy which the mission provided. The new colonial society prized such skills and awarded employment to those who possessed them. Finally, the AIM engaged the Kikuyu with the symbols and idioms of Christianity and the Kikuyu were influenced by them. Indeed, when asked about what brought them to the mission, informants often replied that it was the comforting word of the gospel message, or the presence of the preacher, or the melodies of the hymns that caught their attention.

While the central mission stations remained the primary centers of evangelism and the missionaries themselves the evangelists, their "straitjacket" approach to Christianity, as one scholar has tagged it,(1) prevailed. By 1920 or so, the first adherents began to leave the AIM and GMS stations, and thereafter it became increasingly difficult for either mission to practice their former vigilance or enforce their rules. In the next decade, outstations sprang up by the dozens around these central stations, often at some distance from them and under the direction of Kikuyu Christians themselves. It was not long before the center of Kikuyu Christianity had moved beyond the central station frontier and Kikuyu Christians became the prime agents of transmission.

In the last years of the 1920s and into the following decade, when the AIM had fully comprehended the slippage of their authority and loss of place, a nasty struggle ensued for control of these outstations, fueled by what has become known as the female circumcision crisis. This issue of whether adolescent Kikuyu girls could be circumcised and still considered Christians became so intense that it polarized all concerned into two bitter and antagonistic groups: one consisted of the AIM missionaries and a number of their first central station adherents who insisted that female circumcision was so antithetical to the faith that those who continued its practice should be thrown out of the church and barred from education in AIM schools. The other group, composed of AIM adherents, particularly the younger ones from the newly founded outstations, insisted that Kikuyu customs, such as female circumcision, were compatible with Christianity. From 1929-31 these two groups fought each other with the missionaries enlisting the aid of the colonial administration and the other side being aided by their non-Christian neighbors. Each side intimidated and occasionally physically abused the other; it was not uncommon for the colonial authorities to fine and even jail the combatants, mostly the outschool adherents. At the height of this struggle, Muthirigu, an abusive song containing many of the frustrations and resentments felt toward the AIM, was composed by the younger outstation adherents and used to taunt the missionaries and the Kirore, as their loyalist Kikuyu allies became known.

Ultimately it became apparent that a negotiated settlement with the AIM would not be possible--the only solution was a rupture in relations with the mission. This occurred when the Aregi, (those who refused AIM authority), withdrew from the mission and during the 1930s set about establishing their own independent system of churches and schools. The mission's authority was shattered and they withdrew to their central stations accompanied by their remaining Kirore adherents. From this time and for the next several decades, the cutting edge of the Kikuyu encounter with Christianity lay with the independent churches and schools; as a result, the AIM passed increasingly into the background.

The 1930s mark a turning point for the Aregi independents. Whereas the years immediately prior to this time were marked by frustration with and protest against the AIM, reaching its height during the time of Muthirigu, after their exodus and formal separation from the AIM, they turned their attention to the twin tasks of building a church and a school system. The AIM had become superfluous to their concerns. After several failed attempts to employ other missions to train their clergy, the independents secured the services of Daniel William Alexander, Archbishop of the African Orthodox Church of South Africa. He took up residence among the independents and generally helped to establish a sacramental and liturgical structure for them as well as to provide two years of instruction and to ordain eight Kikuyu clergy. Though these eight almost immediately divided themselves into two groups, each representing a separate church body (The African Orthodox Church and the African Independent Pentecostal Church) both remained close in doctrine and worship.

Since severing their ties with the AIM meant being excluded from the mission's network of schools as well, there was an immediate need for the Aregi to establish their own educational centers. This they did in 1932 when the Kikuyu Independent School Association (KISA) was launched. In time, a vast network of their schools covered the countryside, and stone buildings replaced the earlier wooden structures. By 1940 some schools had even received government grants, and many others enjoyed the praise of the Colony's Ministry of Education for their excellent buildings and quality teaching.

Where they could, the Aregi claimed former AIM outstation buildings as their own, for both church and school use. In doing so, they often had to battle with the Kirore, who also claimed ownership. Occasionally a shared use of the structures was successfully negotiated, if only for a while. Most often a bitter struggle ensued with each group sabotaging the other's attempt at church services or school lessons. The antagonism and rivalry which had characterized their behavior toward each other during Muthirigu, was now extended to their joint claim over common property. As a result the Aregi and Kirore religious divisions now forming in Kikuyu society became more acute.

While rejecting the AIM, the Kikuyu independents did not reject Christianity and their ecclesiastical structure closely paralleled that of mainstream missions: they wanted a trained and ordained clergy, catechumen instruction and baptism, and schools. Over time their worship patterns changed from the austerity of the American Baptists to more closely resemble the liturgical formality of Anglicanism. The church allowed as well individual members to decide the degree to which they wished to participate in Kikuyu cultural practices (female circumcision, for instance, was not forbidden). Nevertheless, they sought legitimacy and orthodoxy. Their separation from the AIM was more over the issue of mission authority than anything else.

It was also during the early 1930s that a second group of independents appeared among the Kikuyu--the Arathi or dreamers. A number of Arathi had been early AIM adherents or had become acquainted with Christianity through other missions or the influence of African Christian friends. Most Arathi, in identifying with the Aregi independents' concerns of mission arrogance and authority, had participated in Muthirigu and in the discussions which followed concerning the succession from the AIM and the establishment of an independent church and school system. This mutual identity with the Aregi came to an end by 1932-1933 when several Kikuyu, in response to their dreams, began to gather around themselves groups of people who professed their spiritual superiority to the <u>Aregi</u> independents. These <u>Arathi</u> increasingly secluded themselves in their own communities where they donned white garments and a turban headdress and rejected all things western as well as Kikuyu customs and traditions. In their place, they constructed an intricate set of rules concerning the maintenance of ritual cleanliness.

Finally in the late 1940s the last group of independents appeared, the <u>Kirore</u>, those Kikuyu Christians who had remained loyal to the AIM. In the twenty years since the earlier <u>Aregi</u> exodus, the <u>Kirore</u> had become completely disillusioned with the lack of AIM interest in their educational and spiritual needs. Their loyalty had neither produced an educated Kikuyu clergy who could minister to them within the mission or its infant indigenous church, the African Inland Church (AIC), nor did they feel that the mission's mediocre schools gave adequate attention to the education of their young people. The <u>Kirore</u> faulted the AIM for lack of leadership and vision; to them the mission had spent twenty years maintaining the status quo of missionary authority. In disgust, all Kikuyu adherents to the AIM, both the older <u>Kirore</u> and the newer members who had joined the mission since 1930, now left in one mass exodus. This move did not drive them into the arms of their rivals, the <u>Aregi</u> independents, however. Instead they built their own institutions, the African Christian Churches and Schools (ACC&S).

By 1950, then, the Kikuyu encounter with AIM Christianity had left the mission's churches and schools empty and in their place, three largely dissimilar independent church and school systems now existed. But the encounter with the AIM had not only produced this varied independence but also deep and significant religious divisions among the Kikuyu as well, such that in many communities, rival groups continually and regularly antagonized or shunned each other and generally made it difficult for all concerned.

. . .

There remains to discuss the extent to which this study complements or departs from current scholarship on the topic. One should first note that while a voluminous literature exists on the Kikuyu in the twentieth century (Kenya's Central Province is probably one of a dozen most researched regions of the continent), few studies directly examine Kikuyu Christian innovation. The classic account of the Kikuyu, by Carl Rosberg and John Nottingham (2) is an exception to this generalization. Their chapter on cultural nationalism was one of the first to give scholarly attention to the Kikuyu independents. At about the same time, Frederick Welborne's <u>East African Rebels</u>(3) introduced readers in detail to the African Orthodox

Orthodox Church and the African Independent Pentecostal Church.
Each of these pioneering works, however, is primarily concerned
with the protest nature of the Kikuyu independent churches.
Welborne thinks that the churches were a safe substitute for
political protest (you cannot be prosecuted for seceding from
the AIM) while Rosberg and Nottingham view them as a prelude or
training ground for future nationalistic activity. But in concentrating on the protest and proto-nationalist activity of
independents, they neglect the religious innovation and creativity taking place.

Two other accounts discuss the history of particular mission societies evangelizing among the Kikuyu. Robert Macpherson's, The PCEA in Kenya,(4) provides insight into the
Scottish mission history (CSM) in Kenya. Since the mission's
primary area of evangelism was Central Province, it is essentially a study of the CSM among the Kikuyu. Robert Strayer's
fine account of the Church Missionary Society in Kenya (5) also
gives much attention to the Kikuyu. Though Strayer takes a
mission centered approach as well, he departs from Macpherson
by concentrating his description and analysis on the Kikuyu
community that emerged from the mission's proselytizing.
Throughout his account there is a good balance between emphasis
on CMS policy makers and the Kikuyu recipients of that policy.
But, since his focus is on those Kikuyu who stayed with the
mission (which for the CMS was the majority), he says little
about the Kikuyu independents.

Jocelyn Murray has provided us with a shorter account of
Kikuyu religious history concerning the Arathi or spirit
churches as she calls them.(6) Murray's research is comprehensive and she provides valuable information and analysis on this
topic. However, her discussion of the Arathi is isolated from
the other currents of independency taking place among the
Kikuyu.

Finally, Valeer Neckebrouck has written two recent
accounts concerning religious and cultural history in central
Kenya.(7) His Le Onzieme Commandement, in particular, gives a
careful analysis of the African Independent Pentecostal Church
(AIPC) and the book more generally has made a great contribution to the historiography of independent churches in Kenya.
But, Neckebrouck gives very little attention to the Aregi-
Kirore conflict which I find so central to the development and
growth of the AIPC.

My own study of the Kikuyu encounter with Christianity
departs from those described above in several ways. First,
though I give attention to the AIM and almost exclusively to
the Kikuyu area that they claimed for evangelism, it is not a
mission study. This discussion does not focus primarily on
mission policy and Kikuyu reaction nor does it place mission
activity in the forefront. Rather the Kikuyu themselves are
examined as they innovate and create their inquiry into Christianity. Some of their initiatives concern the AIM, many of

them do not.   Second, while this study does make use of archival materials, private papers and secondary sources, (as do the
other studies mentioned), the bulk of the research material
consists of oral evidence.   With perhaps the exception of
Murray and Neckebrouck, no other research among the Kikuyu on
this topic has depended so heavily upon the location and inter-
viewing of Kikuyu people themselves about their experiences
with Christianity; the reconstruction of the religious dramas
of the 1920s, 1930s and 1940s and the conclusions which have
been drawn from them have been guided most by Kikuyu testimony.
As a result, my study has taken me into the areas where government or mission documents are silent.   Even on topics where
archival material is available, the oral evidence and documents
located in the field has enabled this study to explore with
more detail and specificity, and at a much more localized
level, one that is found only in a very small portion of the
literature.

8

END NOTES

1. Adrian Hastings, A History of Christianity 1950-1975 (London: Cambridge University Press, 1979).
2. Carl Rosberg, Jr. and John Nottingham, The Myth of Mau Mau: Nationalism in Kenya (New York: Paul Mall Press, 1966).
3. Frederick B. Welbourn, East African Rebels (London: SCM Press, 1961).
4. Robert MacPherson, The Presbyterian Church in Kenya (Nairobi: PCEA, 1970).
5. Robert W. Strayer, The Making of Mission Communities in East Africa: Anglicans and Africans in Colonial Kenya 1875-1935 (London: Heinemann, 1978).
6. Jocelyn Murray, "The Kikuyu Spirit Churches," Journal of Religion in Africa, 5, No. 3 (1974), 198-234.
7. Valeer Neckebrouck, Le Onzieme Commandement: Etiologie d'une eglise independente an pied du mont Kenya (Immensee, 1978); Le Peuple Afflige: Les Determinants de la Fissiparite dans un Nouveau Mouvement Religieux an Kenya Central (Immensee, 1983).

Chapter 1

Kikuyu Society and the Colonial/Mission Intrusion

Kikuyu Society Before 1900

The area occupied by the Kikuyu at the beginning of the twentieth-century was something of a paradise: high, forest-covered ridges and valleys running parallel to each other, more than adequate rainfall for successful agriculture, and temperatures that rarely dipped below 50 degrees or climbed past 75 degrees.(1)

The Kikuyu took up occupation of this highland area at some time in the past, slowly moving north and south along the spine of the Aberdere Range. Normally, the pioneer and his family moved along the valley bottom in their exploration of the area. When a suitable place was found, the family settled upon the top of the ridge for defense purposes and began to clear the forest for cultivation. The pioneers of such settlements came to be thought of as founders of the Mbari or descent group.(2)

Each Mbari worked as a corporate unit, expanding its area of cultivation and developing in relative isolation to other Mbari. This isolation led to a feeling of exclusiveness as each Mbari came to depend upon its own resources for solving the frontier problems of economic advancement and protection. The highland geography encouraged such parochialism since each Mbari was often separated from its neighbors by swiftly moving rivers and steep-sided valleys.

Gradually much of the land originally claimed by the pioneers became occupied and cultivated as the Mbari numerically expanded over time. In five or six generations a land shortage was felt and the way paved for a new pioneer and his family to leave the Mbari, set out for the frontier and establish a new Mbari isolated from the old one and the others as well. The Mbari fission became a common means of propelling the migration throughout the highlands.

In some circumstances, descent groups overcame their parochialism and isolation. Neighboring Mbari sometimes found it desirable to cooperate in defense and profitable to undertake joint trading expeditions. Sacrificial worship and the settlement of disputes might also take place at the neighborhood level. Occasionally coordination of Kikuyu activities took place on an even wider level, such as Miaka, a group of neighborhoods, or the Bururi, which best translates as a district and would involve a number of continuous ridges and many Mbari.

Clans or Mihiriga also promote some solidarity, though this seems particularly true before the Kikuyu dispersed throughout the highlands. With the increase in population once the Kikuyu reached the highlands, and with the Mbari fission

which ensued, Mihiriga became dispersed throughout the
plateau, and corporate action became much harder to achieve.

But above all it was the Mariika (sing. Riika), or age
associations, which countered the isolation and parochialism on
the Kikuyu frontier.   Those young men who reached late adolescence together, were initiated together. The association thus
formed cut across all kinship and territorial lines; it put
people, primarily men, though women had their age associations
too, together for life irrespective of their membership in
different clans, descent groups, or locale. The ties of com-
radeship which were formed lasted a lifetime and became the
basis for such informal tasks as self-help work projects,
dancing groups, and such formal obligations as the military and
judicial system.

Leadership among Kikuyu was limited to the Muramati or
Mbari leader, whose primary responsibility was to allocate and
administer land; and, within the Kiama or elders' council, to
the Muthamaki (pl. Athamaki) or spokesman.(3) The Muthamaki
was a leader in the sense that, within his locale, he was
recognized as being particularly gifted in wisdom, tact, self-
control, and public speaking. He led Kiama discussions and
proclaimed Kiama decisions. Other Athamaki might be particularly gifted in religious matters and therefore they special-
ized in sacrifices and prayers, an area that will be mentioned
shortly.

The Kikuyu had no kings or chiefs, then, nor did they have
self-appointed or elected leaders who could dictate decisions
to the people. Rather, each of the regiments and the various
Kiama had men with recognized leadership qualities who took
part in the most important decisions of these groups and then
had the authority to proclaim the decisions to others. They
were spokesmen.

Kikuyu religious conceptions can be divided into two separate but related areas.(4) The first was belief in Ngai, the
high god of the Kikuyu. Numerous texts depicted Ngai as the
supreme power in the Kikuyu universe; thus, by implication,
Ngai controlled all power in the world. He was the creator and
sustainer of all things, and while the Kikuyu recognized that
Ngai was the god of their neighbors as well, they believed that
he had a special relationship with them.(5)

The dwelling place of Ngai was thought generally to be in
the sky but his presence was particularly associated with Kiri-
Nyaga (Mt. Kenya), and to a lesser extent with three other
land masses along the perimeter of Kikuyuland.(6) Ngai was
also associated with a few particular trees in each locale,
normally a type of fig tree known as Mugumo. Certain other
natural phenomena, such as the sun, moon, stars, lightning, and
rain were all associated with the authority and general majesty
of Ngai.

Ancestors formed the second area of Kikuyu religious conceptions. Though dead, ancestors continued to have an influence upon the living through their Ngoma, or spirit. The

Kikuyu distinguished between three different types of ancestral spirits: Ngoma Cia Aciari, ancestors of the Mbari; Ngoma Cia Muhiriga, clan ancestors; and Ngoma Cia Riika, age-group ancestors.(7)   Relationships among Kikuyu began with the living and stretched into the past to include the dead as well. Death was not thought a barrier to this relationship nor was it considered a hindrance to the continued action in the presence of one's ancestors.   Mbiti accurately described ancestors as the "living dead."(8) They were to be consulted and obeyed after death as they had been while living.

The Mbari, the primary descent group under the leadership of its Muramati, was the basic religious unit as well.   The Muramati's major concern was for the well-being of his descent group and this included their religious health.   He was alert to the transgression of traditional taboos, for they could not only harm the transgressor but the entire descent group, rendering them ritually impure or having Thahu.   It was commonly believed that if disease was infecting people or livestock, or if crops were not prospering, someone had broken the social code and upset the balance between society and the universe. The Muramati would then call in the services of a Mundo Mugo, a religious specialist.   In times of crisis, of particular concern to the Muramati was the relationship of his Mbari to their Ngoma.   A Mundo Mugo would try to discern what in particular had caused the wrath of the Ngoma.

Kikuyu worship did not only center on crises.   The Muramati conducted sacrifices for his Mbari at times of birth, circumcision, marriage and death.   At these times, as well as during the planting and harvest seasons, Ngoma would be beseeched for future good fortune, and thanksgiving would be offered to them for past times of plenty.

Ngai was not forgotten.   The Mbari offered to him periodic sacrifices of praise and thanksgiving for the prospering of their families and livestock.   But one did not trifle with Ngai: the text, "Ngai is not to be pestered," made this quite clear.   He was not concerned with individuals; that was the task of the Muramati.   The Kikuyu approach to Ngai was entirely different from their regard for Ngoma: one "beseeched" or "worshipped" Ngai but was in "communion" with the ancestors.(9) Ngai would only be approached when all other ritual avenues had been exhausted.   Then those Athamaki considered religious specialists would gather at a sacred Mugumo tree and beseech Ngai, with the Mbari or even the entire neighborhood in attendance. The Athamaki would make a sacrifice, and offer prayers, for rain, for example, and, in the words of one informant, "rain would fall even before we returned home."(10)

Mbari members were bound together by common descent, corporate land ownership and collective worship.   Each of these would be threatened by the colonial government and mission intrusions.

Colonial Intrusion and the Kikuyu Response

The official British presence in East Africa had been limited up to the last quarter of the nineteenth century to indirect influence through the Sultan of Zanzibar. Over the decades, Britain had pressured the Sultan, through a number of treaties, to stop his slave trading on the mainland. But Britain had been very reluctant to become more directly involved in East Africa. Reluctance vanished, however, when Germany began to talk of establishing an East African colony. In a pair of Anglo-German treaties (1886 and 1890), Britain quickly limited Germany to the southern portion of East Africa, later known as Tanganyika, and kept the northern part for itself, together with access to the recently discovered Nile headwaters in Lake Victoria. In a parallel move, which eventually brought administrative commitment, Britain granted a charter to the Imperial British East Africa Company (IBEA) to operate within that part of Britain's sphere later known as Kenya.(11)

The IBEA quickly set about establishing a series of posts along one of the routes from the coast to the interior, linking the trading entrepot of Mombasa to Lake Victoria, six hundred miles inland. Of the string of posts that linked IBEA headquarters in Mombasa with the interior, one was established among the Kikuyu. It is certainly not surprising that a trading post should have been established here, for the Kikuyu were located on the first fertile island that existed between their area and the coast. Kikuyuland became a refreshing stop, providing weary travelers and traders with a chance for rest and recuperation before setting out on the second half of their journey. It also provided all the food supplies needed to keep a caravan going over the next stretch of inhospitable country, an area where provisions were not readily available. Several travelers noted the abundance of the Kikuyu farms. MacDonald wrote:

> As agriculturalists the Wakikuyu are very enterprising, as is shown by the miles of potato plantations, which far ex-ceed their own requirements. New clearings are daily being made with fire and axe in the surrounding forest.(12)

The Kikuyu had a surplus of other goods, too; more importantly these were available for purchase by foreigners, as noted by another traveler:

> . . . astonishing fertility is everywhere seen. . . . Enormous quantities of sweet potatoes, yams, cassava, sugar cane, Indian corn, millet, etc. are raised, and the supply seems to be inexhaustible. On my return I found

a caravan of over 1,500 men staying at
Ngongo [southwest Kikuyuland] who remained
there a month, and carried away little short
of three month's provisions, yet it did not
seem perceptibly to affect the supply or raise
the ridiculously low prices. Extremely fat
sheep and goats [are] about, while they have
cattle in considerable numbers.(13)

The strategic location of the Kikuyu and their surplus of
goods accounts for the IBEA's efforts to establish formal
contact with the Kikuyu. When the first official caravan, led
by Frederick Jackson, came through in 1889, he gave one of the
local Muthamaki a company flag and agreed to submit to a blood
brotherhood ceremony with him.(14) It is upon this foundation
that Frederick Lugard built the first trading post and fort
among the Kikuyu the following year. This closer contact was
to cause friction between these foreigners and the Kikuyu.
It is clear that Lugard did not foresee this turn of
events. Indeed, his month among the Kikuyu was marked by very
cordial relations. From the beginning, Lugard operated from a
position of respect for the Kikuyu. He was determined that the
Company should not infringe upon the Kikuyu territory. Therefore, he located the plot for the new fort at Dagoretti, some
distance from Kikuyu cultivation. He included the local
Muthamaki, Waiyaki, in this decision and made payment to him
for the land taken.(15)
Engendered by an atmosphere of cooperation and goodwill,
the fort was built within a month, and Lugard departed
praising the Kikuyu:

The Wa-Kikuyu are a fine, intelligent-looking
race. . . . I lived among them for close
to a month, and I was more favorably
impressed by them than any other tribe I had
yet met in Africa. . . . I had no hesitation
in trusting myself almost alone among them,
even at considerable distances from camp. . . .
I had very little trouble of any sort
among them. . . . They were extremely intelligent, good mannered, and mostly friendly.(16)

Wilson, a European assistant, with thirty askaris (soldiers)
remained among the Kikuyu.
During Lugard's two-year absence, IBEA relations with the
Kikuyu changed for the worse. Where before mutual respect and
tranquillity prevailed, now anyone staying outside the fort was
considered fair game by the Kikuyu; as many as forty company
employees had lost their lives in this way.(17) Mail runners
had been repeatedly attacked and, with food at the fort in
short supply, foraging parties were going out only under heavy

armed protection. Several caravans had also been attacked as
they neared the fort, including one transporting from the coast
a steel boat for company use on Lake Victoria. The boat had to
be abandoned and was subsequently destroyed by the Kikuyu.
Indeed, the station was no longer so much a trading center as
an armed camp.(18)

This state of affairs was partly caused by the increased
caravan traffic along the frontier in the vicinity of the
Lugard fort. Not only IBEA caravans paused there, but now all
caravans stopped over at Dagoretti. The fort provided some
comforts (19) after nearly 300 miles of trekking and served as
a place to secure provisions for the next part of the journey.
The Company not only provided for its own caravans, but it
stockpiled food-stuffs at the fort for future sale to others.
By providing this service, the company directly encouraged an
increase in caravan traffic in the Dagoretti area; this might
well have been the root of the events which followed. When
local provisions were insufficient to meet caravan needs, some
pilfering took place in Kikuyu gardens. In the past, the
Kikuyu seemed prepared to overlook this, but now increasing
caravan traffic led to an increase in theft on a scale that the
Kikuyu could no longer ignore. Early in 1891, they retaliated
for the first time, murdering several pilfering caravan
men.(20) After that the Kikuyu became increasingly aggressive
towards the company, and the IBEA began to fire upon any Kikuyu
who came within rifle shot of the fort. The climax to this
round of events was soon reached when the Company garrison
abandoned Dagoretti fort, in the middle of the night, apparently for lack of ammunition. The next day the Kikuyu burned
the fort to the ground.(21)

The increasing number of caravans and rising incidence of
theft in Kikuyu gardens gives partial explanation to this IBEA-
Kikuyu warfare. The need for the company to tighten up finan-
cially was also to blame.

Mrs. De Kiewiet Hemphill noted that the IBEA was in
trouble from the very beginning: "The IBEA Company was by all
odds the least distinguished of the African Chartered compa-
nies. Poorly conceived, badly managed, and grossly undercapi-
talized, the company was destined from the start to short
existence."(22) Even though the founders managed to raise among
themselves personal subscriptions totaling 240,000 shillings,
the Company never enjoyed any financial security. The direc-
tors had continual problems in raising further money, and they
never commanded more than half a million pounds sterling in
working capital. Set against the Company's commitment to
administer 200,000 square miles,(23) the result was gross
undercapitalization.

In addition to undercapitalization, there were other problems that prevented the company from achieving financial
success. The nature of East Africa itself with its limited
range of immediately exportable produce and its lack of navi-
gable water routes from the coast into the interior was an

obstacle to the Company. Since the high incidence of the Tse-
Tse fly ruled out the use of draft animals, everything had to
be moved by human portage.   The only exportable commodity that
could pay its own way was ivory. Since taxation was simply not
yet feasible in the interior, the company was extremely limited
in its means to raise revenue.

It is not surprising then that this situation soon placed
the company in a position of financial exigency and orders were
issued to tighten up on expenditures.   This meant that Fort
Smith had to become self-sufficient.   Kikuyu gardens were
raided with more frequency, and generally the maintenance of
good Company-Kikuyu relationships was increasingly sacrificed
to the higher priority of the balance sheet.(24)

But to characterize the European-Kikuyu encounter solely
in terms of Company insensitivity and Kikuyu hostility is to
see only part of the dynamics of the situation.   For, if the
arrival of Europeans was a nuisance to the Kikuyu, it was also
certainly an opportunity.   They could exchange garden produce
and perhaps ivory with the Europeans for trade goods as they
had been doing with the Swahili traders for some time.   This
clearly seems to be the motivation of Waiyaki, a local
Muthamaki, when he sought to have the first IBEA fort built
near his home area.   When Lugard decided to locate the fort at
Dagoretti, some distance away,(25) Waiyaki undoubtedly resented
this decision. Some of the attacks which were made on the fort
in the following months may have been motivated by this resentment.   Waiyaki finally had his way for he successfully enticed
Major Smith to rebuild the fort in 1892 on the site which he
had originally proposed to Lugard.   Waiyaki was now satisfied
because his kinsmen and neighbors profited by the monopoly they
had on the sale of produce to the Company and to passing caravans, until Purkiss, the commander at Fort Smith, began to
stockpile the station with cheaper produce from further afield.
This new turn in events obviously threatened Waiyaki's monopoly, and he might well have been at least partly responsible
for the series of raids the Kikuyu now conducted against the
Europeans in 1892; company caravans were attacked, equipment
was destroyed and several mail runners and other isolated
company employees were murdered.(26)

Into this complicated situation we must add an apparent
rivalry between Waiyaki and a neighboring Muthamaki, Kinyanjui.
Kinyanjui entertained ideas of making use of the Company for
his own purposes too, for we find that when Waiyaki and others
attacked the first Dagoretti fort, it was Kinyanjui who helped
the company retreat to Machakos.(27) We know that he also
guided a combined Company and railway survey attack on Ndorobo
allies of the Kikuyu the next year.   It seems that Waiyaki's
moves were being countered by Kinyanjui. It is not surprising,
then, that with the deportation of Waiyaki, Kinyanjui became
the first European appointed "chief" among the Kikuyu.(28)

The Kikuyu saw other ways to use the Europeans too. If Europeans could be used to promote prosperity and to limit local rivals, perhaps they would make a good counter-weight against the Maasai. The Kikuyu had had a long-standing relationship of trade and warfare with these neighbors. While the Maasai may have had the upper hand in the past--often defeating the Kikuyu on the plains and forcing them into the surrounding protective forests--more recently, the Kikuyu had attempted to equalize the raiding situation by borrowing significant aspects of the Maasai military system.(29) Using the Europeans now as allies might well have been an extension of this earlier strategy. Fort Smith had only just been finished when Waiyaki approached Purkiss, the officer in charge, with a request for help against a recent Maasai invasion of several thousand. Purkiss agreed to Waiyaki's request, and the entire Company garrison and five thousand Kikuyu dispatched the Maasai and then shared the captured livestock among themselves.(30)

This initial success, however, turned to defeat several years later when the Company decided to use the Maasai as a means to control Kikuyu aggression. Each Kikuyu attack was met with a Company-Maasai counterattack and a follow-up punitive expedition. The heavily fortified frontier settlements of the Kikuyu were penetrated, perhaps more successfully now by the Maasai. The Kikuyu suffered repeated attack, confiscation of crops and livestock, and, of course, many lost their lives. In the course of the next few years, this pattern of warfare eventually wore down the Kikuyu so that they either capitulated or were pushed back. By 1895, a relatively safe area, ten to fifteen miles in radius, had been created around the fort. It was within this safe zone that the newly appointed chiefs and their assistants began to operate.(31)

The appointment of chiefs like Kinyanjui served a very practical purpose for the company; it needed friendly contacts in an otherwise hostile population. With the pacification of larger and larger areas around the fort, these chiefs and a growing number of assistants--now called "friendlies"--began to assume greater responsibility for provisioning caravans. Kinyanjui contracted with the company to supply all passing caravans. He accomplished this by establishing a network of agents both within and without the safe zone to buy and transport foodstuffs to the fort. These agents also brought in men who were willing to serve as porters for the company, and the group of "friendlies" continued to expand. Later, when the company deemed it safe to build a road from Fort Smith to the Machakos station forty miles to the southeast, a group of friendly Kikuyu porters and laborers were hired, most probably by Kinyanjiu and his contacts.(32) By the late 1890s, these laborers had been used for a multitude of tasks, for we find that Fort Smith had grown into something of an urban center. Several retail shops were to be found together with a few

European residences, a large Kikuyu market and several rows of African houses.(33)

It is not surprising that some Kikuyu should be drawn in to this kind of association with the Europeans. Certainly the selling of their surplus produce was attractive. To others, employment for even a limited time was paid in trade goods, and some Kikuyu definitely wanted to acquire foreign-made articles. More than this, however, the very nature of the Kikuyu social system contributed to the making of this group of "friendly" Kikuyu.

As mentioned above, not all Kikuyu resistance was based simply on the intruding Europeans and their increasing demands. Some Kikuyu, notably the Athamaki leaders, were loath to lose their positions of leadership for which they had successfully competed. Since the Athamaki position was largely based upon merit or achievement, rivalry was common among claimants. A possible way to insure it against loss to other candidates, or even to the Europeans themselves, was to establish connections with these intruding foreigners. Waiyaki's increasing contacts with the commander of Fort Smith might well have been a strategy for retaining his leadership position. There was yet another Kikuyu group that was attracted to the Europeans. These were the losers in the struggle for the leadership positions, the men who had failed to become Athamaki. The arrival of the Europeans now gave them another chance for power.

This collaboration with Europeans was not without its cost. While these Kikuyu "friendlies" tried to turn the Company intrusion to their advantage, they accomplished this at the expense of other Kikuyu. Waiyaki, by encouraging the Company to locate its station near his homestead, had earned the displeasure of his neighbors. Later, when Kinyanjui collaborated with the company on punitive expeditions, he earned the wrath of many frontier Kikuyu.

The European intrusion brought not only conflict, repression and even death to the Kikuyu, but also new opportunities of prosperity and leadership--complete with rewards and dangers --which created divisions among some Kikuyu. Other divisions were to occur with the arrival of a second group of intruders-- the missionaries.

The Africa Inland Mission

The beginning and early development of the Africa Inland Mission (AIM) came through the work of two men--Peter Cameron Scott and Charles Hurlburt. Any account of the AIM must start with them, for they dominated and directed its organization and generally set the character and mood of the mission during its first quarter-century.

Peter Cameron Scott was born in Glasgow, Scotland, but emigrated in 1879 with his parents to the United States at the age of twelve. The family settled in Philadelphia. Young Scott suffered from chronic ill health throughout his adolescence, and at eighteen he was forced back to Scotland for convalescence at doctor's orders. There, according to Catherine Miller, his biographer, he made a pact with God: "weary, ill and discouraged, he knelt at the grave of a little sister in Janeville Cemetery, and promised God that, if his life was spared, he would dedicate it to the Lord for His service."(34) The following year he was well enough to return to Philadelphia, where he became interested in joining the chorus of the local opera. But on his way to the audition, he had a type of spiritual experience that was later to become typical of many AIM missionaries:

> As he ascended the steps of the Opera House, a voice within whispered, "Are you going to glorify God by going in there?" Irresolute, he paused, then went on. Again, the voice spoke, and with the conviction that it was the Lord who spoke to him, he turned abruptly and retraced his steps, saying "No, Lord, I will never go there again!" Walking rapidly home, he threw himself on his knees in his room. It was a moment of absolute surrender to the Lord for his body as well as for his soul . . . a peace that passed all understanding filled his heart. With that peace came the remembrance of the vow made in the far away Scottish cemetery. . . .(35)

Scott was not yet a missionary, but after this experience, events rapidly moved in that direction. During the next year Scott worked to support himself in a printing shop but spent most of his time as an itinerant evangelist. As the months passed, he became increasingly convinced that God had called him as a missionary to Africa. His application to the Christian and Missionary Alliance was accepted in 1890. He sailed to Banana at the mouth of the Congo River and his brother joined him later. In two years his brother had died, and Scott had become so ill that he was not expected to survive the trip back to the United States.(36)

Scott did live, however, and he began to make plans to return to Africa, where he hoped to build a chain of highland mission stations, free from disease, and stretching from east to west across the continent. Unable to find support from his church--Presbyterian--he began to discuss this vision with a group of Philadelphia men interested in mission work. These men, including Charles Hurlburt, formed the Philadelphia Mission Council in 1895, a non-denominational society pledged to evangelize the world, and they agreed to sponsor Scott's venture to begin a chain of mission stations in East Africa.(37)

The AIM took shape throughout the winter and early spring in a series of meetings between Scott and the Philadelphia Missionary Council. The Council recognized Scott as founder and director of the mission. They decided to trust God for all financial support; no funds would be publicly solicited but all contributions would be gratefully accepted. The mission's principle aim was African evangelism, not education: "In view of the many untouched millions, we feel called to do a thorough evangelistic work, rather than to build up strong educational centers."(38) Finally, The Philadelphia Mission Council would accept missionaries from all denominations that agreed with these conservative doctrines and the Council would act as the United States parent body to the AIM.

By August, 1896, Scott had successfully recruited six missionaries, including his sister. They sailed together first to London, where another missionary joined the party, and then to Kenya, where they arrived in October. By the end of the year, they had established a station 300 miles in the interior.(39)

The AIM was one of the first missions to venture past Kenya's coast. Scott considered his work "inland," hence the name of the mission. He and his co-workers built their first station among the Kamba, an agricultural and pastoral people living between Kenya's fertile highlands and the dry Nyika wasteland nearer the coast. During 1896 Scott established three other stations among the Kamba, and a second party, consisting of Scott's parents and his younger sister, joined the original mission group. Tragedy struck at the end of the year, however, when Scott, barely thirty years old, unexpectedly died.(40)

For the next three years the work of the AIM steadily declined and nearly collapsed. So much of the whole mission venture had been Scott's vision that his death caused confusion and disorder both to the Council in Philadelphia and in the field. Most of the missionaries returned to the United States in 1897 and 1898, driven home by lack of finances and ill health. A few stayed in Kenya in other capacities: Scott's older sister married John Ainsworth, the government administrative officer among the Kamba; another took up land in Kiambu as a settler; and at least one other went to work for the Kenya government. By mid-1898 only one of the original party remained, and he soon left to establish a Quaker mission in Nyanza Province of Western Kenya.

Scott's death and the ensuing disorder brought Charles Hurlburt to the forefront of the AIM. Hurlburt was a man of great energy and determination. Like Scott, he had had several emotional religious experiences, and these had led him to choose a career of Christian work, first with the YMCA and then at the Pennsylvania Bible Institute. At age thirty-six he was president of the Institute when Scott died.(41)

Hurlburt had been active in the formation of the Philadelphia Missionary Council. It had in fact grown out of a prayer and Bible study meeting held in his home. He had encouraged and supported Scott's missionary plan for Africa. He had helped to organize the party of missionaries that left with Scott for East Africa. After Scott's departure, he helped interview and send several other missionaries out to the Kenya field, and he had offered the facilities of the Bible Institute for the meetings of the Missionary Council. It was quite natural that the other members should look to Hurlburt after Scott's death for the future direction of the AIM.

Early in 1897, Hurlburt set about drawing up a more formal organization for the AIM than had existed under Scott. The resignations in the field led to constant recruiting and the appointment of a new field director. The surviving records of this period reveal that Hurlburt was clearly managing the affairs of the AIM, and in recognition of his leadership, the Philadelphia Missionary Council, now the home council of the AIM, made Hurlburt their general director.

Immediately upon his appointment as general director, he went out to Kenya to acquaint himself with local conditions. Upon his return two months later, he gathered together more than a dozen missionary recruits and announced his decision to the home council that he could best serve the AIM by returning to East Africa.(42)

For the next quarter-century, until his resignation in 1926, Hurlburt worked tirelessly for AIM expansion and success. As none of the four Kamba stations were near the new government built railroad, he established another station at Kijabe. This station was located just north of Nairobi on the Rift Valley escarpment, and within two miles of the railway line. Kijabe was at first used almost exclusively for the evangelism of the nearby Kikuyu and Maasai, but in time it became a transition and service center for missionaries. Here language study was undertaken, and a hospital, printing press, Bible college and a school for missionary children were established. In seventy years it grew from Hurlburt's house and a few others to several hundred buildings and more than one hundred missionaries--the largest mission station in the world.

Kijabe was also Hurlburt's base for AIM expansion, first into other parts of Kenya and then to other East African colonies: Tanganyika (1908), Congo (1912), Uganda (1923), Central African Republic (1924), and, after Hulburt's death, Sudan (1951). Hurlburt pioneered several mission stations himself and directed the establishment of many more. His enthusiasm and energy inspired many to donate money to the AIM or to volunteer their services as missionaries. During his lifetime the AIM grew from the four Scott stations in Ukambani to more than two dozen mission stations and ten dozen missionaries. By 1960, the AIM was one of the largest mission societies in Africa, with more than 600 missionaries in five different countries.(43)

But the great missionary venture of the AIM was clouded from the outset by a number of problems. The rapid expansion of the mission under Hurlburt created the need for more missionaries, and his frequent tours of the United States and Britain brought a flood of missionaries to East Africa. Many of these church workers came without any preparation or adequate financial support. Mission policy directed missionaries to find their own support. In the euphoria of being accepted by the AIM, some missionaries considered adequate support a one-way steamship ticket to Mombasa and a few dollars left in their pocket. Soon after their arrival in the field such people had to concentrate all their efforts upon surviving without adequate means. Many became a burden to other missionaries and hindered their missionary activities.(44)

The informal mission organization during these pioneer years was slow to correct this problem. A directive from Hurlburt in 1915 finally stated that all missionaries must have at least three months support before they set out for East Africa. This did little to help, for the home council soon created a general fund for all undesignated gifts given to the AIM. From this fund unsupported missionaries were paid. But this solution resulted in two other problems. Missionaries supported by the general fund had to reimburse the mission for the total amount of money paid to them if they left the AIM before serving five years.(45) This prevented people unsuited for mission work from leaving before their five year contract was completed. It also led to the "pooling" of all gifts by the AIM. Apparently, the demand upon the general fund became so great that even designated gifts were diverted into the general pool, and they failed to reach the people and projects for which they were intended. One missionary woman on furlough raised money for the Kijabe girls' home. But upon returning to Kijabe, she found that the mission hierarchy had decided to use this money for other purposes and that her request for the girls' home had been ignored:

I came here to find all the children in rags--
with half a cotton blanket; some even farmed
out to the natives to earn their living--when
all the time I was at home I saw to it that
these children had support. I had such
faith in our declared principle that "all
monies contributed are used only for the
purpose for which they are given." How many,
many times have I been told at home that the
AIM is not true to this principle and that
money sent for certain individuals or natives
under them, had never reached the people
for whom it was sent. I have always denied
this and encouraged people to send to the
office . . . can you imagine how I feel now? I

> have been a _liar_ to these people--none of the
> money sent out ever reached Kijabe. . . .(46)

The ill-feeling that "pooling" caused among missionaries led some even to terminate their career with the AIM,(47) and the hardship it brought to Africans was hardly conducive to producing harmony in the AIM mission venture.

AIM peculiarities were also apparent in their candidate selection process. When the AIM was founded at the end of the 19th century, it believed that religious conviction rather than the mere observance of rituals and practices was the mark of being a Christian. The candidate application papers reveal that the AIM was vitally interested in this "inner life" of prospective missionaries. A number of questions were aimed at probing their conversion and "call from God" to be missionaries. Candidates were also instructed to compose an autobiographical sketch in which they had to document "[their] victorious struggle over Satan."(48) Later, when the AIM interviewed the candidate, particular emphasis was placed upon these materials.(49)

One consequence that followed this selection of missionaries was that it sent out to East Africa a group of strong-willed individuals who felt themselves personally directed by God and answerable only to Him. Two Kikuyu stations, Kambui and Ngenda, which had been opened after Kijabe, seceded from the AIM in 1913 because their missionaries, Mr. and Mrs. William Knapp and Dr. John Henderson were unable to accept the authoritarian nature of AIM leadership, the mission's narrow theology and its racial attitudes discussed below. In the same year, the Knapps and Dr. Henderson began a mission of their own, the Gospel Mission Society (GMS).(50)

A somewhat similar situation occurred in 1924, when George Rhoad, an AIM missionary among the Kamba for twenty years, left the AIM over sharp personal disagreement with another missionary. After some years in the United States, he returned to Ukambani with his own society, the Gospel Furthering Fellowship (GFF). Great opportunities existed for cooperation between the two groups as they were the only Protestant mission societies among the Kamba. But for the next decade, they waged verbal war in the United States and in Kenya. Each was critical of the other's policies and practices, and their disagreements were even carried into Bible translation: both societies refused to share their linguistic expertise with the result that a new translation of the Kamba Bible was delayed for years. Each society considered its actions motivated and sanctioned by God.(51)

The AIM was generally distrustful of other mission societies and of the Kenya Government. When the chief Protestant missions joined together to form the Kenya Missionary Council, (KMC) a body devoted to mediating between the colonial government and missions, the AIM reluctantly joined and repeatedly threatened to quit.(52) The AIM felt it had to be vigilant against government control and the diluting of its commitment to evangelism. In the late 1940s the AIM nearly did quit the Christian Council of Kenya, successor to the KMC, over the issue of the Council's intended affiliation with the World Council of Churches. The AIM considered this body's emphasis on ecumenical and social development a threat to evangelism.(53)

Nowhere is the exclusive passion for evangelism seen more clearly than in the neglect by the AIM of African education and medical care. Few missionaries were trained teachers; rarely did an AIM school go beyond the second or third grade. Some missionaries even claimed that this meager education detracted from evangelism and might lead to government control. An early missionary had this to say about evangelism and education:

> I believe the Government should control education, and lay down the exact order that should be followed, and that our schools should faithfully follow that order but if we find we cannot do so . . . then it would be better to drop educational work altogether. In fact I could never quite see why we should do what I think all would agree is of secondary importance.(54)

These ideas persisted and there was no serious discussion of upgrading the educational program until the government forced the AIM to do so in the 1950s.(55) Medicine shared a similar fate. Few hospitals were built and little medical training was given to Africans. Nor were the medical resources of the AIM fully utilized. Dr. Virginia Blakeslee, an osteopath, spent forty years as a missionary among the Kikuyu and seldom used her medical skills.(56)

Education and medicine were considered only a means to the desired end of Christian conversion. AIM schools taught the fundamentals of education so that school attenders could read the Bible. AIM doctors conducted daily worship services among their patients, and led patients to believe that attendance at services was a prerequisite for treatment.(57) The AIM considered that "the church does not engage in social reform. . . . [The church] should not use their influence collectively for further social and economic progress."(58) A theology of the whole person was not operative among the AIM; they were interested in African souls, not in the conduct of their minds or bodies. Emphasis on evangelism and conversion fostered great insensitivity to East African culture and society. Missionaries received little cultural preparation for life among Africans, nor were they encouraged to learn about local customs and practices once they arrived at their station. Missionaries were to concentrate wholly on the Africans' inner spiritual condition. Kikuyu young women who attended school at Kijabe were called "wild, black girls of the bush . . . thoroughly chained and enslaved by the dark customs and superstitions of their tribal life."(59) Elsewhere, AIM missionaries forced those interested in becoming Christians to discard all bead and copper ornaments and their skin garments as well. Nor were pierced ears permitted among Christians; prior to baptismal ceremonies, AIM doctors did a brisk business in stitching them up.(60) It was not long before the AIM began to think of all African society as evil. A 1915 letter from Kinyona station described mission work there as "a battle line . . . working against the rulers of darkness of this world, against spiritual wickedness." Missionaries credited the persistence of African customs and the lack of interest in Christianity among Kinyona people to the work of Satan. He was "fiercely counterattacking . . . and assaulting every point" of the mission enterprise and "Satan's forces were strong."(61)

The AIM assimilated the racism of colonial society. African people were seen as subordinates or helpers and seldom as equals. Specific instructions to new missionaries on AIM stations encouraged the growth of servile status for Africans.

> Every [new] missionary should get from one of
> the workers information as to what his
> attitude towards the natives should be. . . .
> Deal kindly with them before reproving them.
> . . . Do not be too lax with native helpers
> and so spoil them . . . . As soon as possible
> have a native boy or boys, girl or girls to
> look after. . . . Let them do what work they
> can for you, caring for your room . . .
> cooking, washing, housecleaning, sewing,
> planting, under your direction, [sic] your
> time can be given to something else.(62)

Many early adherents complained that their interest in education was countered by missionary interest in their labor. Young men and women spent long hours building and maintaining AIM stations. At Kijabe all school attenders were required to work a half day in the station garden, a huge plot from which the mission made a profit by selling produce to hotels in Nairobi. Girls at the same station were anxious to learn reading and writing but found that much of their time was spent learning skills of western housekeeping, after which they were encouraged to become house servants of missionaries.(63)

The AIM also practiced the color bar. Kijabe had separate worship services for missionaries and African Christians. At the mission's Theological Training Center at Machakos, two Bible studies were held during the week: one for white teachers and the other for students and other African personnel. The Rift Valley Academy (RVA), a fully equipped school at Kijabe, was kept exclusively for missionary children and other

white children in East Africa. The AIM rationalized its
"whites only" rule by stating that:

> . . . mission children lived in great isolation
> --only having contact with Africans and [mis-
> sion children] are learning things which they
> will later wish that they hadn't. RVA
> provides contacts only with other white child-
> ren.(64)

The color bar was even extended to mission homes. In a 1938
memorandum concerning missionary conduct, the following paragraph was found:

> That the missionary's home should, as far as
> possible not be used for the routine life of
> the station, particularly in that part of
> station activity which necessitates the coming
> and going of natives.(65)

AIM problems, then, not only included a conversion bound
theology, strong willed missionaries and authoritarian leadership, but also an arrogance and a cultural chauvinism that gave
second place to African people. While the first set of
problems may have hampered or prevented a completely successful
mission enterprise, the active subordination of Africans doomed
the AIM to complete disaster among the Kikuyu. In the chapters
that follow, it will be shown that missionary insensitivity and
their general "lack of love" for the Kikuyu, as a recent
observer states,(65) led to a bitter end for the AIM: first,
Kikuyu resistance and protest, then outright secession from the
mission.

26

END NOTES

1. S.J.K. Baker, "The East African Environment," in Roland Oliver and Gervase Mathew (eds.), History of East Africa, I (Oxford: Clarendon Press, 1963), Chapter one.

2. I am indebted to Godfrey Muriuki of the University of Nairobi for the reconstruction of pre-twentieth-century Kikuyu history which follows. He generously gave of his time and permitted me to read his thesis, the only comprehensive and systematic collection of Kikuyu traditions: "A History of the Kikuyu to 1904," Diss. University of London, 1969, later published as, A History of the Kikuyu 1500-1900 (Nairobi: Oxford University Press, 1974).

3. For the section on leadership which follows, Muriuki depends heavily upon the following sources: H.E. Lambert, Kikuyu Social and Political Institutions (London: Oxford University Press, 1956), pp. 100-06; W. Soresby Routledge, With A Prehistoric People (London: Edward Arnold, 1910), p. 195; C. Cagnolo, The Akikuyu, Their Customs, Their Traditions and Folklore (Nyeri: Mission Printing School, 1933), p. 24; C. Dundas, "The Organization and Laws of Some Bantu Tribes in East Africa" (Kamba, Kikuyu, Tharaka), Journal of the Royal Anthropological Institute, 45 (1915), 238.

4. Muriuki says little about Kikuyu religion and there are no other comprehensive or systematic collections of Kikuyu religious traditions though several published works give it some attention. Jomo Kenyatta devotes a chapter to religion in Facing Mt. Kenya (London: Vintage, 1962) as does L.S.B. Leakey in Mau Mau and the Kikuyu (London: Methuen, 1952). The best account by a missionary is found in R. Macpherson, The Presbyterian Church in Kenya (Nairobi: PCEA, 1970), Chapter one. There are several useful unpublished accounts of Kikuyu religion: Samuel G. Kibicho, "Theory and Practice in Church Life and Growth," Proceedings of the Interdisciplinary workshop in Research on Religion in Africa, June 1966-1968, Nairobi, Kenya, pp. 381-394; Ephantus G. Macharia, "Traditional Religion Among the Kikuyu." Seminar paper, Kenyatta University College, n.d.: and J.H. Mwangi, "Worship of Ngai in Gikuyu," seminar paper, St. Paul's Theological College, n.d.

5. Macpherson, Presbyterian Church in Kenya, p. 10.

6. Kia Nyahi (Donyo Sabuk), Kia Nyandarya (Aberdare Mountains) and Kia Mbiruiru (Ngong Hills), Kibicho, "Interaction of Kikuyu Concept of God with the Biblical Concept," p. 385.

7. Macharia, "Traditional Religion Among the Kikuyu," p. 2.

8. John Mbiti, African Religion and Philosophy (London: Heinemann, 1969), p. 25.

9. Kenyatta, Facing Mt. Kenya, p. 223.

10. Oral Evidence: Karanja Kamunya, February 15, 1971.

11. For more details, see R. Coupland, The Exploitation of East Africa, 1856-1890 (Oxford: University Press, 1939), Chapter 15; and more recently, John Flint, "The Wider Background to the Partition and Colonial Occupation," in Roland Oliver (ed.) History of East Africa (Oxford: Clarendon Press, 1963), pp. 352-390; William Langer, Diplomacy of Imperialism (New York: Macmillan, 1935, reprinted in 1960), pp. 101-144B; Roland Oliver, Missionary Factor in East Africa (London: Longmans, 1952), Chapters 1 and 2.

12. Major James R.L. MacDonald, Soldiering and Surveying in British East Africa (London: Edward Arnold, 1897), p. 109.

13. Joseph Thomson, Through Masailand (London: Sampson, Low, Searle, and Rwington, 1885), p. 307.

14. Sir Frederick Jackson, Early Days in East Africa (London: Edward Arnold, 1930), p. 170.

15. Margery Perham, (ed.) Diaries of Lugard, I (London: Faber and Faber, 1958), p. 338.

16. Capt. F.D. Lugard, The Rise of Our East African Empire, I (Edinburgh: Blackwood, 1893), pp. 326-27.

17. Lugard, East African Empire, II, p. 537.

18. George Francis Hall, "Letters, Papers and Diaries of a D.O. (with typed) calendar of correspondence 1880-1901," II, Rhodes House Archives. MSS Afr. S. 54-62, 42.

19. The station commander offered hospitality to passing Europeans in the form of produce from his vegetable garden and a good night's sleep between fresh sheets on something more comfortable than a camp bed. Rachel Stuart-Watt. In the Heart of Savagedom (Glasgow: Pickings and Inglis, n.d.), Chapter 15.

20. George Portal, The British Mission to Uganda in 1893 (London: Edward Arnold, 1884), p. 92; Lugard, East African Empire, II, 535.

21. Ibid.

22. Marie de Kiewiet Hemphill, "The British Sphere, 1884-1894" in R. Oliver and G. Mathew, History of East Africa, I (Oxford: Clarendon Press, 1963), p. 393. Oliver called it "a sickly child." Roland Oliver, Sir Harry Johnson (London: Chatto and Windus, 1957), p. 86.

23. J. Scott Keltie, The Partition of Africa, 2nd ed. (London: Edward Stanford, 1895), pp. 348, 350.

24. de Kiewiet Hemphill, "The British Sphere," pp. 409-410.

25. Perham, Lugard Diaries, III, 379.

26. H.H. Austin, "The Passing of Waiyaki," The London Times, November, 1922; Hall Papers, p. 42 Rhodes House Archives.

27. W. McGregor Ross, Kenya From Within (London: Allen & Unwin, 1927), p. 57.

28. Austin, "Passing of Waiyaki," pp. 4-6.

29. William L. Lawren, "Maasai and Kikuyu: An Historical Analysis of Culture Transmission," Journal of African History 9, No. 4 (1968), 571-583.

30. Austin, "The Passing of Waiyaki," pp. 2-3.
31. G. F. Scott Eliot, A Naturalist in Mid-Africa (London: A.D. Innes, 1896), p. 19; P.L. McDermott, British East Africa, A History of the Formation and Work of the Imperial British East Africa Company (London: Champman & Hall, 1895), p. 424.
32. Hall Papers II, 73, Rhodes House Archives.
33. Major Herbert H. Austin, With MacDonald in Uganda (London: Edward Arnold, 1903), p. 25.
34. Catherine S. Miller, Peter Cameron Scott, The Unlocked Door (London: Perry Jackman Limited, 1955), pp. 16-18.
35. Ibid., pp. 18-19.
36. "Draft of Mr. Hess' Comments Concerning the Beginnings of the AIM," Manuscript found in historical files, AIM, New York.
37. "Excerpts of Minutes of the First Council Meetings of the AIM Compliled in November 19, 1942," found in files marked "Early history of the AIM," AIM, New York.
38. Excerpts . . . of Council Meetings. . . . May 6, 1895, AIM New York.
39. Excerpts . . . of Council Meetings. . . . May 6, 1895, AIM New York.
40. Miller, Peter Cameron Scott, Chapter 3-4.
41. Hess Manuscript, op. cit., AIM, New York.
42. Excerpts . . . of Council Meetings. . . op. cit., October 16, 1896: February 16, 1897: March 15, 1898, and October 12, 1898: April 13, 1900, and September 12, 1901; Hess Manuscript, op. cit., AIM, New York.
43. The last two paragraphs are based upon the official AIM history: Kenneth Richardson, Garden of Miracles: A History of African Inland Mission (London: Victory Press, 1968), passim.
44. Hurlburt to All District Councils, England and America, August 2, 1915, AIM, New York.
45. Fletcher to Kirk, September 29, 1929, Kirk File, AIM, New York.
46. Emily Messenger to Hulda Stumpf, April 24, 1924, Stumpf File, AIM, New York.
47. Kirk to Fletcher, September 13, 1922, Kirk File, AIM, New York.
48. Candidate's Papers, 1910-1926, AIM, New York.
49. Minutes of the Chicago District Council of the AIM, 1915-1927, AIM, New York. The United States was divided among several district councils. One of their primary functions was to nominate and to screen prospective missionary candidates before recommending them to the AIM. The Chicago Council handled the entire mid-west area.
50. Kambui Station Files, PCEA Archives; Oral Evidence: Kambui group interview, June 11, 1971.
51. George Rhoad and Gospel Furthering Fellowship Files, 1935-1941, AIM, New York.

52. Hulda Stumpf to H.D. Campbell, Stumpf File, April 6, 1928, AIM New York.
53. Kenya Field Council Minutes, (Confidential) April 4-8, 1949, January 11, 1940, April 10-15, 1950, AIM, New York.
54. John Stauffacher to H.D. Campbell, February 23, 1927, AIM, New York.
55. "Memorandum on Education with its challenge and opportunity as it is related to the Africa Inland Mission. A contribution by the British Home Council for consideration by the International Directorate [of the AIM], n.d. [1952. 1953] AIM, New York.
56. Virginia Blakeslee Candidate Papers, 1910, AIM, New York. Miss Blakeslee never mentions doing medical work in her autobiography. Beyond the Kikuyu Curtain (Chicago: Moody Press, 1956).
57. Inland Africa, (British Edition) November-December, 1926, p. 52, AIM, London.
58. Charles W. Teasdale, "An Examination of the Ecclesiology of the African Inland Mission," unpublished M.A. Thesis, Wheaton College, 1956, p. 41.
59. Report of the Kijabe School for African Girls (Kijabe: African Inland Mission Press, 1928), p. 1, AIM, New York.
60. Blakeslee, Beyond the Kikuyu Curtain, p. 59.
61. Kinyona Prayer Letter, October 8, 1915, AIM, New York.
62. "Suggestions to New Missionaries," Kijabe, British East Africa, August 24, 1915, AIM, New York.
63. McKendrick to Hurlburt, February 3, 1910, McKendrick File, AIM, New York; Oral Evidence: Moses Thuo, March 10, 1971.
64. Inland Africa (British Edition), November, 1934, p. 87, AIM London.
65. "Recommendations re.certain Mission Policies," December, 1938, AIM, New York.
66. David Barrett, Schism and Renewel (Nairobi: Oxford University Press, 1968). Chapter 12.

Chapter 2

Christianity and Colonialism among the Kikuyu to 1920

In 1895 the Imperial British East Africa Company (IBEA) was replaced by the British government and the Kikuyu came under the influence of the Foreign Office and then the Colonial Office after 1905. Though the Kikuyu did not realize it at the time, the arrival of the British government brought permanent occupation of Kikuyuland. This was not immediately noticeable since company personnel were taken on by the government and the tactics of contact with the Kikuyu remained the same. The base of operations around Fort Smith, on the Kikuyu frontier, was slowly enlarged through punitive expeditions to punish those who resisted, and enticement to a growing number of collaborators. Though resistance was by no means over,(1) the government's position on the southern frontier had become reasonably secure. This enabled them to turn their attention from law and order and the provisioning of caravans to a more comprehensive administration in the south and throughout other parts of Kikuyuland too. This led to the establishment of first a military and then an administrative post in central Kikuyu at Mbiri--later named Fort Hall--in 1900 and another further north at Nyeri two years later.(2) But even while this whole process of conquest and collaboration took place, decisions were being made which led to the arrival of European settlers. The impact of these settlers and the resulting situation for the Kikuyu concerning land, labor and taxation will now be examined in some detail, since it provides the backdrop for future reactions toward the missionaries.

Though the bracing climate of the Kikuyu highlands and the fertility of the soil brought some European settlers before the turn of the century, as it had earlier brought trading caravans, it was the completion of the railway to Uganda in 1902 and governmental railway policy that encouraged the first significant numbers to arrive in the same year. The government hoped that the export produce of the European settlers would provide the lifeblood of the railway and therefore repay 5 1/2 million shillings in building costs, made by reluctant British taxpayers.(3)

The first land which these incoming settlers took up was in the vicinity of Nairobi, the new capital of the colony, built on the site of an earlier railway construction depot and on the edge of the Kikuyu frontier near Fort Smith. Partly by neglect and most certainly through careless disregard for the indigenous inhabitants, many settlers took up residence on land not yet surveyed by the government. Once the survey department became engulfed with the work of the first settler arrivals, the practice became common of simply going out into the countryside, laying claim to a site, and then notifying the survey department of the choice. Sometime later, when the department's work schedule permitted, a formal survey was made and

the land was officially turned over to the new owner.   Of   the
102,400 acres Europeans laid claim to in Fort Hall District   by
1915,   a   sizeable number were taken over in this way.(4)   Nor
were all of the large landowners settlers; some were even
missions, as shown below.
     In 1903, the Africa Inland Mission (AIM) took up the
occupation of land approximately thirty miles north and west of
Nairobi in an area known locally as Kijabe.(5) In that year
they obtained a lease from the government for 1,796 acres, and
several years later for 665 additional freehold acres, giving
the mission a total of 2,461 acres. In addition, they occupied
without title or lease an area of adjacent land 200 yards x   2
miles. The land was eventually surveyed and title given to the
mission, but no inquiry was made into indigenous ownership.
Should this have been done, the government would have found
that one Kihehero, a Kikuyu pioneer, had established his Mbari
there long ago and laid claim to the land on which the AIM now
held title from the government.
     This conflict, involving the separation of the rightful
owner from his land, was not speedily settled once Kihehero
made his claim known. Only in the late 1920s was government
notice taken and an investigation begun of a situation that had
festered for more than twenty years.   The investigation
revealed that Kihehero had been evicted from his Mbari at the
turn of the century by railway officials because he sought
forcefully to stop the marauding construction crews who stole
from his gardens and molested his family.   After withdrawing
for a time to Nairobi, he returned to find his land now occupied by the AIM. As his mbari was large, he felt that both his
family and the mission could jointly use the land and he left
it at that, regarding the AIM as squatters on his land.   With
the death of Kihehero shortly afterward, his descendants
continued to occupy their land and to tolerate the mission as
uninvited squatters. After World War I the mission repeatedly
asked Kihehero's descendants to leave, although the mission
was actually only using a small percentage of the land.
Finally, matters came to a head in 1925 with the enactment of
the Resident Native Ordinance which empowered landowners either
to compel trespassers to sign on as official squatters of the
owner or be evicted from it.   Kihehero's descendants, now
numbering 210 people, refused to be labeled as squatters by the
Mission when they had always considered the AIM to be the
trespassers. Finally, two years later, when the government
took up the investigation, the matter was officially brought
to an end, but only to the mission's satisfaction. The settlement gave these Kikuyu 400 acres which was an area only one-
fourth the size to that which they laid claim.   Further, this
acreage was not subtracted from the AIM plot, but taken from
another area to which the Mission falsely laid claim. While in
literally dozens of similar situations the government took no
action, in this case it came late and then put its stamp of
approval on a settlement that gave the rightful owners less

than 2 acres each while the AIM retained more than 2,000 acres, most of which they did not use.

If the settlers and missionaries were lax about protecting Kikuyu land rights, the government itself actually encouraged a disregard for these rights in their legislation concerning land. The 1902 Crown Land Ordinance separated all land into two categories, native and crown; all land clearly occupied was labeled native land, the rest became crown land and only this land was to be alienated for European settlement. However, where a cultivated plot was surrounded by unoccupied crown land (a frequent situation on the Kikuyu frontier), provision was made in the Ordinance for that land to be included in the grant to a European land owner so as not to create a patchwork of both native and crown land in the same area. This provision was an open invitation to push the Kikuyu off their land.(6)

The Crown Land Ordinance of 1915 caused further hardship for some Kikuyu because it enabled the government to disregard ownership even of occupied land. The earlier distinctions between native and crown land were canceled and all Kikuyu now became tenants of the government. In effect, all land became crown land and it could be put to whatever use the government saw fit, including alienation to Europeans.(7) The government, in the orders in council for 1920 and 1921, took the final step in its disregard for indigenous land by stating that ownership existed only in common blocks owned corporately by the entire ethnic group and not among individuals. Individual ownership, common among many Kikuyu, and clearly documented in several contemporary studies,(8) was now ignored.

The reserve system gave no guarantee of Kikuyu land rights either. The idea of "reserving" a defined area for the Kikuyu was put into practice in 1904 but it failed to guarantee a more secure life to the Kikuyu for several reasons. Expansion was now curtailed, and they were forced to live within a specifically defined area. This meant that normal population growth would eventually force larger numbers of people into the same confined area. This natural process was accelerated by the arrival of Pax Britannica and western medicine. In 1919 the density of population in the Kikuyu reserve was approximately 212 per square mile; by 1928 the figure had risen to 235 and in some places up to 400 people per square mile. The average population density in the colony's other reserves was only 78 in the late 1920s.(9) Leakey pointed out in 1934 that the reserve was actually shrinking. He stated that the continued feeding of an increasing number of sheep and goats had caused much reserve land to degenerate and become unusable either for grazing or cultivation.(10)

The Kikuyu reserve was shrinking in another way too. Individual Europeans and the government were continually taking small tracts of this land that was supposedly "protected." Several applications by missions asking for new plots or enlargement of existing plots in the reserve were successfully acted upon by the government; the AIM added ten acres to their holdings at one station, and the Catholic mission in Kiambu received sixty acres to begin new work there. In another case, the forest reserve was enlarged to accommodate a government laboratory and this caused Kikuyu to be displaced.(11) In a number of instances, European farms were found to be encroaching on reserve land. In the most blatant case, the European's house, lawn and several acres of coffee trees were well into the reserve.(12) Finally, twenty acres of reserve land were given to Swift and Rutherford, a large sisal planta- tion, when they wanted to erect a hydro-electric generating plant. In compensation, the people involved were to have the benefit of the electricity.(13) It seems to have been over- looked that these people, now without land, would have had little use for electricity.

The greatest plan to take land from the reserve was the Maragwa-Tana Power Scheme of 1927-30. On the eastern boundary of the reserve, at the confluence of the highland's two largest rivers, the government proposed to build a power plant. Though it was advertised to the Kikuyu as a project for their benefit too, it was chiefly to bring electricity to the nearby European settlers. The dam was projected to flood approxi- mately 2,030 acres and to displace 2,000 Kikuyu who farmed the land. Though this project never actually materialized the Kikuyu suffered the insecurity of not knowing the outcome until the plan was officially terminated twenty years later.(14) The Kikuyu responded to the loss of their land with almost patho- logical suspicion of any new activity in their midst. A 1927 government report noted:

> Every attempt to secure land for the estab-
> lishment of a school--be it mission or Govern-
> ment--for a Native Council Chamber, [or] for
> Hospitals is met by immediate suspicion. Even
> the proposal to commence a system of Registra-
> tion of births and deaths is discussed from the
> point of view that it is a device to find out
> how much land may be taken away. A missionary
> may not plant even fruit trees on school sites
> because the existence of those trees are
> thought to give him a claim to the land.(15)

Inextricably linked to the problems of land, was the threat posed to the Kikuyu by the government's system of labor that evolved following the arrival of settlers. Echoing through Elspeth Huxley's account of Kenya settlers (16), was their firmly held idea that since the government had encouraged them to come to East Africa, it was now responsible for helping make their farming operations a success by solving their labor requirements. To help settlers with their labor needs, the government undertook a massive registration of all males in the colony. The ordinance became law in 1920 and stipulated that

each African adult male above the age of sixteen must register
with his local District Commissioner whether or not he intended
to seek employment outside his Reserve. His fingerprints were
taken and placed on three copies of his registration certificate, one of which he was to wear around his neck in a metal
box. The idea behind this registration was to find out the
labor potential and to control desertion. The certificate had
to be endorsed by the employer before the laborer could lawfully leave his job. The humiliation of such a law was
certainly felt by the Kikuyu who called the registration certificate a Kipande or goat's bell, the implication being that
they were treated like animals.(17)

The other inducement for labor was the levying of taxes.
The Governor of Kenya, Sir Percy Girouard, set this out very
clearly in 1913 when he said, "we consider that taxation is the
only possible method of compelling the native to leave the
reserve for the purpose of seeking work."(18) The Kikuyu had
been paying taxes from a much earlier date, but Girouard's
words brought more comprehensive collection and stiff penalties for non-payment--four shillings and three month's
imprisonment. Taxes were continually raised to apply additional pressure, going from one shilling in 1901 to sixteen
shillings in 1920. Throughout this twenty year period, wages
for unskilled labor remained almost constant, at three to five
shillings a month.(19) Consequently, more time had to be spent
each year to earn enough for one's tax payment.

The colonial chief was the central figure in the conversion of the Kikuyu into the labor system. Before 1919, when
chiefs were ordered to obtain laborers for road building, for
porterage, or for furnishing hospitality when the D.C. toured
the district, they had furnished the recruits. After that date
when the orders were softened to "encourage" Kikuyu to go as
laborers to European areas, they interpreted it as a command,
and people were again brought by force. It was in their own
interests to use force as well, since a 1919 Labor Circular
instructed District Commissioners to "keep a record of those
Chiefs and Headmen who are helpful and those who are not helpful [in recruiting laborers]." The implication was that those
chiefs who did not render assistance would be penalized.(31)
To help evaluate their cooperation, D.C.'s gave chiefs labor
quotas to fill. The chiefs in turn established connections
with labor agents and with specific European farms in their
vicinities. These Europeans were encouraged to come into the
reserve and help coerce Kikuyu into leaving as laborers.
Press-gang tactics resulted, and many Kikuyu were taken into
employment against their will.(20)

Nor was the situation a great deal different when the
laborer arrived at his place of employment. There he attached
his thumb print on a document which he could not read and so
"contracted" to work, usually for a three to six month period
of time. This normally meant:

> . . . six working months of thirty working
> days each--a period of 180 working days, in
> which Sundays, period of illness, casual leave
> and holidays (if any) are not counted and in
> which a half-holiday is unknown. Often it is
> seven or eight months before he can get
> home.(21)

To absent oneself from work, even for emergencies, was not
lawful and the Kipande registration made desertion without
being caught very difficult. The whole situation was filled
with brutalities by Europeans insensitive to Kikuyu needs and
habits. Should he receive his wages (and this did not always
happen with unscrupulous employers), the laborer found that
inflation gave him only declining purchasing power. During the
period from 1910 to 1920, food in the European areas where he
worked rose 600%; such necessities as blankets, American cloth,
salt, beads, wire, and sugar rose 300%, and taxes doubled. Yet
wages remained nearly the same throughout this period, rising
from five or six shillings to only eight shillings per
month.(22)

The squatters, though in a slightly different category,
were no better off than the other laborers, and perhaps worse.
They worked under the same conditions though for a lesser wage,
the balance "being made up in a plot given by their employer on
which they were permitted to build a house, plant a small
garden and keep a few head of livestock." Some were led to
believe that their regular labor at low wages was being credited toward the purchase of this land at the rate of two years'
labor for two acres. Nothing could have been further from the
truth. In fact, the plots became smaller in time and the
restrictions on livestock because such a burden that what
started out as a livable situation for the squatter, became
intolerable. They were also trapped since they had no land to
which they could return in the reserve, having been forced out
by European alienation, confiscation by chiefs or simply an
inheritance too small to farm. By the mid-1930s more than
100,000 Kikuyu were laboring on European farms as squatters.
(23)

Life for those remaining in the Kikuyu reserve was arduous
as well. The La Zoute Conference, meeting in 1921, reached
these conclusions concerning the exodus of laborers from their
homes: "When the demands of labourers for work outside the
Native areas . . . are excessive, tribal life is subjected to
a severe strain."(24) An estimate in 1918 revealed that 70%
were working outside the reserve and nine years later, the
figure had increased to 72.5% in the southern area of the
reserve. The national average for Kenya recorded in the same
year was 38.8% and comparisons with other British colonies (25)
revealed that the Kikuyu were the highest anywhere.

As the demands upon the Kikuyu were developing, so also
was the evangelical machinery of the AIM. By 1910, three of
the four AIM central stations had been built and some of the

first converts began to be made. Those first interested in the mission appear to have been a few uncircumcised boys, whose curiosity had been aroused, together with several cripples and orphans, the least prestigious members of society. Others also came to these stations from time to time, but generally, the Kikuyu did not initially respond to the AIM with great enthusiasm.(26)

But this situation changed as the Kikuyu became aware that there were definite advantages in becoming a Muthomi (pl. Athomi), a reader, or a mission adherent. Some Kikuyu attempted to use Athomi status to be exempted from public-service labor requirements. An early AIM missionary wrote that when the Makanga (chief's assistants) came to her station searching for people to work on the building of a nearby road, the Athomi simply refused to go. The missionary supported this action and, though the local chief and the District Commissioner were upset, they accepted this Athomi exemption.(27) News of this quickly spread and soon one's association with an AIM station carried with it an exemption from public service labor. When the AIM decided to make a road between two of their stations, a distance of thirty miles over very rough terrain, including forests, they called on the local chief to supply the laborers; no Athomi at either of the stations participated in the task. By the time of the Labor Ordinance of 1912, all people associated with missions were exempted from the twenty-four days a year of unpaid labor required of everyone else.(28)

Somewhat the same conditions arose over the recruitment of labor outside the reserve, for the Kikuyu sought to foster the custom that Athomi could not be pressed into this kind of labor either. This was particularly true on the central mission stations. There, under the direct supervision of the missionaries, the idea grew that Athomi were the "missionaries' people," under their protection and out of bounds to the local chief. Occasionally, Makanga would forcibly recruit Athomi attached to one of the satellite or out-schools, usually located at quite a distance from the central station and under more tenuous protection of the missionaries.(29) But, by the end of the First World War, the exemption was largely in force and missionaries were trying to gain official recognition for it. The AIM proposed in a 1918 letter to the District Commissioner at Fort Hall that those who came to their schools should be exempt from the labor force for three years.(30) One year later, the Church Missionary Society took up this idea in response to the 1919 labor circular. In the CMS memorandum of protest against the 1919 labor proposals, they suggested not only that all Athomi should be exempt from labor conscription, but that this exemption should not be terminated if the adherent continued his association with the mission in any other capacity. Soon after, the administrative officers in Fort Hall began to subtract the Athomi of that District from the total number thought available for labor on settler farms.(31)

The Kikuyu also began to look to missions for relief from their shortage of land. With the alienation of their land to settlers and the growing population density in the reserve, the idea was born that since many of the missions were large land-owners, their land could be tapped for use by Athomi. Those who became Athomi on the huge AIM station at Kijabe were given plots of their own to cultivate and similar allotments were made on the Gospel Mission Society (GMS) station at Kambui. Though this station consisted of 100 acres and was therefore only 1/25th the size of Kijabe, plots were parceled out and even a nominal rent was charged to the adherents who took up cultivation.(32) On smaller stations where garden plots could not be large, Athomi practice was to obtain an area near the mission boundary and then slowly extend their cultivation into the reserve. Occasionally uncultivated open-spots still existed in the reserve prior to the First World War. Though they were all claimed by someone under Kikuyu land tenure, the Athomi regarded them as no-man's land and used the mission as a base from which to push out and take up possession of such areas.(33) There is even a case on record where Athomi took over land under cultivation and evicted its owner.(34)

Residence on mission stations also brought tax exemption. Tax officials were off-limits there. If a Muthomi maintained a house elsewhere it was liable for tax and once he moved off the mission station a hut or poll tax had to be paid. But those Athomi who counted no other place but the mission station as their residence paid no tax.(35)

Perhaps what best shows the favored position of the Athomi was the recruitment patterns for the Carrier Corps at the beginning of the First World War.(36) Once it was determined that there was to be an East African theatre to the war, the lack of motorized transport made the recruitment of porters imperative. All Kikuyu males were soon required to report for physical examinations to determine their eligibility.(37) But the government gave automatic exemption to the Athomi. Occasionally, an adherent would be pressed into service like other Kikuyu, but a word from his missionary was enough to secure his release.(38) In 1916, when the anticipated victory over the Germans in Tanganyika had not been realized, and when the results of the physical examinations had shown that over 50% of the 86,715 Kikuyu examined had been declared medically unfit for service, the missions were asked to raise a Carrier Corps contingent under their own leadership. Some Athomi went as personal assistants or servants of the missionaries who led the mission group. The AIM contingent consisted mainly of those who had flocked to the mission in 1915, hoping to gain an Athomi exemption.(39) Even then, conscripts in the mission Carrier Corps were better off than their fellow Kikuyu in regular Corps service. The mission contingent was often called upon for less arduous duties, and the conscripts served under mission personnel; service was probably less dehumanizing than it would have been under military authority. The mission contingent, accompanied by their own mission doctor, had better access to good medical care and probably did not have the same rate of sickness and fatigue experienced by the others.(40) Of the thousands who returned to the Kikuyu reserve and eventually died from smallpox, tuberculosis, and dysentery, contracted during the war, few were mission adherents. The mission corps probably had fewer deserters, too. As a result, the mission corps also experienced fewer fines and penalties, since, according to the martial law in effect throughout the colony during the war, all attached property of deserters would be confiscated.(41)

The mission station also became a refuge for Kikuyu from disagreeable aspects of their own society. Young people who felt that they had been mistreated at home by their parents ran away to the mission. Those who used the mission as a sanctuary to escape from "forced marriages" provoked the greatest controversy. As Mathu notes in his study on Kikuyu marriage, elaborate rituals, prolonged over a period of some weeks, sought to ensure that a prematurely arranged marriage did not take place.

> Each stage and set of rules are meant to fulfill specific purposes and obligations in consolidating the entire marriage relationship. Each stage publicly commits the people of two different families to increasingly binding obligations, such that they must be full participants rather than mere spectators.(42)

Occasionally this ideal pattern of marriage did not take place and the prospective wives sought to terminate pre-marriage ceremonies by fleeing to the mission and reporting that they either had been or were now being forced into a marriage disagreeable to them.(43) It is difficult to say whether "force" was involved, but the availability of the mission now gave people a new alternative for refuge, and some took advantage of it.

The education offered by the missionaries was popular among many Kikuyu too. Regular classes were held during the day, usually in the morning, but there were also sessions in the evening for those who could only come at that time. During such times the missionary gave instruction in the alphabet and vowel sounds; later, some work was done with grammar and sentence structure and a little reading. Many Kikuyu were motivated to become literate because they wanted to become interpreters, tax collectors and other government employees. (44) Though these functionaries were in the most junior administrative positions, they received a desirable wage, they were out of the chief's grasp and they were above local colonial demands. Their position was coveted by many Kikuyu. The missionaries firmly believed that while education was not an end in itself, it could be an effective tool for conversion. These ideas were later to come into conflict with Kikuyu educational aspirations, but for the time being, the Kikuyu were content with the rudimentary instructional offerings and responded in increasingly large numbers, especially when enticed by money and gifts, a practice commonly followed by many early missionaries.(45)

The Athomi, using the mission as a refuge, had successfully challenged the authority of both colonial and traditional society. This challenge was not without its costs, however. It brought tensions and conflicts that were in some ways quite different from those which had existed in pre-colonial society. Struggles within the Mbari existed between generations or between more and less prosperous or powerful sections. But the solution was simple, the Mbari could split along the various Nyumba (house) lines and a new Mbari could be formed. This fission frequently took place and it fueled both the southern and northern advances of the Kikuyu into new frontier areas. (46) With the arrival of the missionaries and the emergence of the Athomi new tensions and conflicts arose from which there was no corporate escape as a family.

In fact, the missionaries' arrival often created problems within families since few who left for the mission went with either the blessing or the permission of their family. This was understandable as the very integrity of the family was at stake. The division of labor prescribed an assignment for everyone and the loss of someone to the mission disrupted local economy. With the simultaneous arrival of colonialism and its labor demands, the drain of human productivity to the mission was especially telling since other members of the family might be absent by law, either doing public service labor or working on a settler's farm. The flight by some women from marital commitment often disrupted the economic or political alliances which established connections outside the kinship group. The ritual component of the family's integrity was threatened too. The departure of one of its members broke the links with the family circle and this disrupted the relationships with the past. The welfare of the family was based upon periodic rituals involving communication through sacrifice with past members of the group. Custom prescribed that these rituals be undertaken only with the entire family in attendance. It was also thought that one's absence diluted the respect of the family for its ancestors. This in turn might arouse their displeasure which could result in harm being done to individual members or to the family as a whole.(47) For the first time people with deviant ideas and practices could escape and Kikuyu society was no longer homogeneous.

The new tensions within Kikuyu society did not remain latent but erupted into overt acts. Though there is no record that these acts went so far as they did in Meru district, where an angry community set fire to a catechist's house, killing the people inside,(48) all AIM stations at one time or another experienced some anti-mission aggression. Sometimes "medicine" was prepared and deposited around the station compound or in the houses or even in the clothes of missionaries and Athomi, with the hope that it would drive them away.(49) When this failed, local people were determined to retrieve their relatives and friends from the mission. But these efforts were often thwarted by the missionaries who refused to release the Athomi and by the fact that local people simply did not know where to start looking. Missionaries often took newly arrived women and minors to a distant station, so that they could not be found easily.(50) This compounded the growing ill-feeling in the community and confirmed the idea that the mission was sabotaging Kikuyu society by stealing its members. The result was often an attempt to strike back at the missionaries' weakest point, their dependence upon the community for such staples as meat, milk, fruit and vegetables. Missionaries were quite simply locked out of the local market. This boycott also extended to the Athomi, especially when they sought to set up residence on a mission station. Then, even the building materials traditionally supplied by friends and neighbors might be denied them.(51) When Athomi attempted to visit in homes off the mission, they often speedily returned with stories of being driven away and warned not to return except under threat of violence. Others found themselves subject to a family curse. Parents or other relatives even committed or attempted suicide (52) to demonstrate the family's rejection and utter contempt for Athomi.

An area of conflict outside the family involved the Athomi and the chiefs, headmen, Athamaki, and elders in the reserve. The Athomi had ambivalent feelings toward this general group. Athomi felt themselves to be under the missionaries' authority and this caused them on occasion to be spiteful and disrespectful to chiefs and headmen.(53)

On the other hand, the Athomi knew they had to depend upon this group once they left the mission. Their counsel and support would be needed when choosing a wife. The acquisition of land in the reserve was totally under their control, whether it was needed for cultivation or the establishment of a mission out-station. Beyond this, it was common sense to cultivate a good relationship with anyone whom the colonial authorities had vested with power.

> It should be borne in mind that it is the first duty of any native to obey and if he considers himself aggrieved he can complain afterwards. If he does not do so he at once places himself in the wrong . . . any native not obeying the order of his headman is liable to a fine of Shs. 150/---or in default, 2 months rigorous imprisonment.(54)

Perhaps the feelings of hostility and the rising tensions of both groups can best be seen in the issue of Athomi representation on the area council or Kiama. The Kiama was instituted by the government in 1909 as both a check on, and an aid to, the chief and headmen. It consisted of the elders in each chief's area and thus was roughly the equivalent of the tradition Kikuyu Kiama. By seeking representation, Athomi hoped to strengthen their weak position in the reserve and at the same time to weaken in general the chiefs and the older generation, with whom they were in conflict. Increasingly after the war, Athomi, now off the mission stations and away from the shelter of the missionary, felt themselves to have been treated unfairly. Since the Kiama acted as the primary court for all misdemeanors and petty civil suits, there was ample opportunity for unfair treatment of Athomi. The Athomi saw that if they gained access to the Kiama, they would be able to give the elders a "taste of their own medicine." As this situation developed during the early 1920s, the campaign of the Athomi became increasingly centered on unseating some of these elders. In some cases, Athomi won Kiama places and elders were successfully ousted. In 1925, one European administrator, commenting on the whole rivalry, said that the Athomi had won too many places on the Kiama.(55) The main outcome, however, was a heightening of the tensions between the two groups.

The Athomi relationship with the general community was little better than that with their families or the chiefs, headmen, and elders. The Athomi felt superior toward the non-Christians. The community, in turn, felt that the Athomi were carrying a disproportionately small share of the burden of the times. Perhaps this was felt most keenly in the areas of settler labor and carrier corps service. The forced participation in the hard work, loneliness, low salary, disease, and abuse inherent in these two experiences carried with it ill-feelings towards those who appeared to continue to let others do their share.

Athomi disregard for rites of passage and social or recreational dances brought them into conflict with the community too. The Athomi went to such gatherings only to proselytize. Often matters got out of hand when Athomi, convinced that the dances were uncivilized, ridiculed the participants. Such confrontation usually provoked a hostile response and the Athomi retreated to the mission station. Eventually the resident missionary would become aware of the situation and if confrontations continued, he would complain to European officials that his adherents were being treated unfairly by the community. Because of this, European officers began to view the dances as disorderly gatherings and often prohibited them.(56)

On a number of occasions, bands of Athomi burned sacred Mugumo trees, and destroyed Miwani, the tools of divination, in the name of Christianity. There was even a case where Athomi dug up the skulls of their own ancestors.(57) These acts were committed in total disregard for the beliefs of local people. The Mugumo tree was held by the community as a sacred contact point with Ngai, the supreme being. Contact with Ngai through prayer and sacrifice under the Mugumo was essential for the continued well being of the community, and critical in times of crisis. Disease, drought, famine and poverty were all possible consequences of these Athomi actions. To destroy a diviner's Miwani and to exhume and desecrate the body of one's ancestor was to tamper with the most serious sort of impurity or Thahu. The Kikuyu had an elaborate repertoire of rituals either to protect from Thahu or to neutralize it, should one have come in contact with it inadvertently. But to contact Thahu purposely was unthinkable and certainly might have severe consequences not only for the person involved and his family, but the entire community. Women and animals could become barren, crops could wither, and disease and eventually death were all thought to be possible consequences.(58)

By 1920 there were many tensions, antagonisms and ill-feelings between Athomi and all other sections of society. Some Kikuyu, in seeking out a sanctuary at the mission station, had managed to avoid the rigors of colonial society and to acquire a new identity as Athomi. They became alienated from their own society but their shared experiences strengthened their identity as Athomi. By the end of the First World War, this new identity had separated and divided them from their own society. This situation was to change rapidly once the first group of Athomi left the mission stations and went back into Kikuyu society for then divisions were to take place among Athomi.

END NOTES

1. Isolated patrols and mail runners were continually attacked by bands of Kikuyu warriors. Meinertzhagen Diaries, I. July 6, 1902, Rhodes House Archives.

2. PC/CP 1/1/1 "Political History of Kenya Province," August 30, 1908. Kenya National Archives (KNA).

3. C.C. Wrigley, "Kenya: Patterns of Economic Life, 1902-45," in Vincent Harlow and E.M. Chilver (eds.), History of East Africa, II (Oxford: Clarendom Press, 1965), 209-22. Ironically, it was African-grown cotton in western Kenya and Uganda that eventually paid for the railroad and not settler agriculture. Bethwell Ogot, "The British Administration in Central Nyanza," Journal of African History, 4, No 2 (1963), 260-66.

4. PC/CP 1/1/1. "Land Alienation," F.H. District, KNA.

5. The following case study is based entirely upon materials found in the Kenya National Archives: PC/CP 9/8/16. "Kijabe Land Dispute."

6. Buell, Native Problem, I, 306; W. McGregor Ross, Kenya From Within (London: Allen and Unwin, 1927), p. 51.

7. Buell, Native Problem, I, 307. Under other provisions of the ordinance, the government could grant 999 year leases on blocks of land up to 5,000 acres where the 1902 ordinance only covered 1,000 acre plots on lease for 99 years.

8. M.W.H. Beech, "Kikuyu System of Land Tenure," Journal of the African Society, (1917), p. 50. In addition to this report by Beech--a government district officer--two pioneer missionaries of long term residence among the Kikuyu presented their findings to the government. Rev. Canon Harry Leakey, M.A., "Memo, re. Kikuyu Land Tenure, etc., 1924, "Presbyterian Archives (PCEA) St. Andrew's Church, Nairobi: A.R. Barlow, "KikuyuLand Tenure and Inheritance," The Journal of the East Africa and Uganda Natural History Society, No. 45-4 (April-July, 1932), pp. 56-66.

9. Report of the Kenya Agricultural Commission, October, 1929, Section 116, quoted in L.S.B. Leakey, "Some Problems Arising From the Part Played by Goats and Sheep in the Social Life of the Kikuyu," Journal of the African Society, 33 (January, 1934), 70; Buell, Native Problem, I, 323.

10. Leakey, "Some Problems. . . .," pp. 70-79.

11. PC/CP 6/5/1, "Native Affairs-Education," P.C. Nyeri to Chief Native Commissioner, September 14, 1918, KNA; PC/CP 1/4/1, Kikuyu District Political Record Book II, KNA.

12. PC/CP 6/6/4, Native Reserve, Fort Hall, D.C.to Commissioner of Lands, September 22, 1922; DC/KBU 4/6, "Land Boundaries 1929-35," DC/KBU to Surveyor General, February 18, 1929, KNA.

13. DC/MKS 25/3/1, Chief Native Commissioner's Circulars 1921-24, KNA.

14. PC/CP 9/19/2, Maragwa Water Power Scheme 1929-30, KNA.

15. PC/CP 4/1/2, Kikuyu Provincial Annual Report, 1927, KNA.

16. Elspeth Huxley, White Man's Country: Lord Delamere and the Making of Kenya (London: Chalto & Windus, 1953).

17. Buell, Native Problem, I, 357; Mugu Gicaru, Land of Sunshine: Scenes of Life in Kenya Before Mau Mau (London: Lawrence & Wishart, 1958), p. 60.

18. East African Standard, February 8, 1913, quoted in Leys, Kenya, p. 186.

19. Ross, Kenya From Within, pp. 145-154; W. Soresby Routledge, With A Prehistoric People (London: Edward Arnold, 1910), p. 332.

20. Leys, Kenya, pp. 172-74, 203 and appendix; PC/CP, 4/1/1, Kenya Province Annual Report 1919-20, KNA.

21. Ross, Kenya From Within, p. 196.

22. PC/CP 6/4/2, "Native Affairs," DC., Fort Hall to P.C. Nyeri, November 12, 1920, KNA.

23. Gicaru, Land of Sunshine, p. 16; Great Britain, Kenya Land Commission Report (Nairobi: Government Printer, 1933), p. 144.

24. E.W. Smith, The Christian Mission in Africa (London: International Missionary Council, 1926), p. 121.

25. Tanganyika--15.5% Southern Rhodesia--27.8%; Quoted in Buell, Native Problem, I, pp. 345-346; PC/CP 4/1/1, Kenya Provincial Annual Report, 1918, KNA.

26. Blakeslee, Behind the Kikuyu Curtain (Chicago: Moody Press, 1956), Chapters 1-12, passim: Oral Evidence: Joseph Kimui, December 9, 1970: Kabui Magu, December 28, 1970.

27. Blakeslee, Beyond the Kikuyu Curtain, p. 117.

28. Oral Evidence: Simon Mwangi, October 31, 1970; PC/CP 1/4/1, Kikuyu District Political Record Book II, 1908-12, KNA.

29. Oral Evidence: Simon Mwangi, October 31, 1970; PC/CP 4/1/1, Kenya Provincial Annual Report, 1912-18 KNA.

30. PC/CP 6/5/1, Native Affairs--Native Education 1918, AIM to DC/FH, n.d. KNA.

31. "The Bishops' Memorandum" seen in Leys, Kenya, appendix; PC/CP 4/1/1, Kenya Provincial Annual Report, 1919, KNA.

32. DC/KMS 10A/4/5, "Kiambu and Mangu Mission Land, 1911," DC/KBU to PC/NBI, December 5, 1911, KNA.

33. DC/MKS 10A/4/5, "KBU and Mangu Mission Land," 1911, PC/NBI to DC/KBU, October 2, 1911; DC/MKS 4/5, "KBU and Mangu Mission Land," 1911, DC/KBU to all missions, October 2, 1911, KNA.

34. PC/CP 1/4/1, Kikuyu District Political Record Book II, 1908-12, KNA.

35. Oral Evidence: Simon Mwangi, October 31, 1970.

36. For a discussion of this topic for the entire Protectorate, see Donald C. Savage and J. Forbes Munro, "Carrier Corps Recruitment in the British East African Protectorate 1914-1918," Journal of African History, 7, No. 2 (1966), 333-342.

37. PC/CP 4/1/1, Kenya Provincial Annual Report, 1916-17, KNA.

38. Oral Evidence: Jeremiah Kimone, December 9, 1970.

39. PC/CP 4/1/1, Kenya Provincial Annual Report, 1916-17, KNA; Oral Evidence: Isaac Karanja, December 8, 1970; Johanna Mutaro, December, 1966, KIM File, NCCK-Limuru Archives.

40. Kenneth Richardson, Garden of Miracles: A History of the Africa Inland Mission (London: Victory Press, 1968), p. 73.

41. In 1917 there were more than 100 fatal cases of smallpox reported in the Province brought in by returning carrier corps and in one of the Kikuyu districts 2000 returning carrier corps died of dysentery brought with them from the field. PC/CP 4/1/1 Kenya Provincial Annual Report 1911/17. KNA.

42. George W. Mathu, "Kikuyu Marriage: Beliefs and Practices," Institute of African Studies Discussion Paper No. 17, mimeo (Nairobi: University of Nairobi, March, 1971), p. 3.

43. Oral Evidence: Johana Nyenjeri, August 25, 1970, read at NCCK-Limuru Archives: PC/CP 1/4/1; Kikuyu District Political Record Book II, 1908-12, July 27, 1912, KNA.

44. Oral Evidence: Ngenda Church Elders, March 12, 1971; Oral Evidence: Jeremiah Kimoni, December 9, 1970.

45. Rachel Stuart Watt, In the Heart of Savagedom (Glasgow: Pickings & Inglis, 3rd edition, n.d.), p. 27.

46. Godrey Muriuki, A History of the Kikuyu 1500-1900 (Nairobi: Oxford University Press, 1974).

47. Oral Evidence: Ndebe Kambogo, December 7, 1970.

48. Oral Evidence: Samuel Mutiga, n.d. Meru File, No. 4, read at NCCK-Limuru Archives.

49. Oral Evidence: Kabui Magu, December 28, 1966, KIK File, read at NCCK-Limuru Archives.

50. Oral Evidence: Simon Mwangi, October 31, 1970. This practice continued for some time and caused much irritation among the Kikuyu. Hartsock to Campbell, September 8, 1931, Hartsock File, AIM, New York.

51. "Christian Native Converts," Minute Paper 64/252/1, District Commissioner, Nairobi, 5/1/1912, KNA.

52. Oral Evidence: Jeremiah Waita Kihori, KIN File, NCCK-Limuru Archives; Routledge, With a Prehistoric People, pp. 241, 248; Blakeslee, Beyond the Kikuyu Curtain, p. 118.

53. Inland Africa (British Edition), March-April 1926, p. 14, AIM, London; C.W. Hobley, Kenya From Chartered Company to Crown Colony (London: H.F. & G. Witherby, 1929), p. 229.

54. Secretariat: Native Affairs, D.C. to all Missionaries, April 28, 1925, KNA.

55. CP/PC 1/1/1, Kenya Province Political Record Book; PC/CP 1/7/1, Fort Hall Political Record Book, <u>KNA</u>; DC/FH 2/1/(b), Fort Hall Handing Over Reports, <u>KNA</u>.

56. PC/CP 1/4/1, Kikuyu District Political Record Book II, 1912 and PC/CP 1/4/3, Kikuyu District Political Book III, 1915, <u>KNA</u>.

57. Christian Native Converts, Minute Paper 64/252/A. "Kiambu meeting between Government, Converts and Elders." April 25-26, 1912, <u>KNA</u>.

58. Two articles by M.W.H. Beech have been helpful in assessing the burning of Mugumu trees: "The Sacred Fig-tree of the A-Kikuyu of East Africa," <u>Man</u> 13, No. 3 (1913), 4-6; "A Ceremony at a <u>Mugumu</u> or Sacred Fig-tree of East Africa," <u>Man</u> 13, No. 51 (1913), 86-89.

Chapter 3

Mission Control and Out-Station Autonomy

Immediately following the First World War, many Athomi
began to leave the central mission stations. They had received
the rudiments of Christianity, together with some literacy in
their own language and occasionally, some instruction in
English. The missionaries did ask a few Athomi to remain as
pupil teachers, but the others they encouraged to leave to make
room for new inquirers. The exodus which ensued produced the
out-stations of the 1920s.

Except for those who went to Nairobi or other places to
find work, most Athomi went back to the countryside. Some were
attracted to areas in which they had preached, but it was not
unusual for them to return to their own home communities. Here
is where they had ties to the land and if they were to return
to rural life, the land was vital for their livelihood. In
some areas local feeling against Athomi was so strong that they
were prevented from going home. Occasionally, they would find
someone else who was sympathetic to their situation such as the
parent of a fellow Muthomi, or a relative and would be given
land by them.

In this way, many Athomi took up their life in a Kikuyu
community again. Such was the case of both Johana Mitaro and
Njuguna Njoroge.(1) Each had been a Muthomi for some time in a
GMS or AIM community. They now returned to their home areas
after an absence of nearly five years, and began to farm the
plots given them. Mitaro took over the land of his deceased
father; the uncle of Njuguna Njoroge gave him some land to
avoid a family quarrel upon his return. These men had not
returned home as they had left it, for now they were both
Christians and both literate. This combination drew others to
them and it was not long before they began to minister to a
small group of young men and women, preaching to them on
Sundays and teaching them on weekdays. Neither of these men
had been commissioned by the missionaries to begin schools or
churches, but Kikuyu curiosity about Christianity and the
rising demand for education prompted both men to take up this
work.

Other Athomi had similar experiences and it was not long
before a number of schools and churches dotted the countryside
around central mission stations. Missionaries were delighted
with this turn of events. Sometimes these lay teacher/
evangelists received small salaries from the central stations
or financial support through the mission from abroad but for
the most part the spontaneous and autonomous churches and
schools initially went their own way with mission blessing.
The missionaries might refer to them as their out-stations, but
the question of mission control over these churches and
schools had not yet arisen.

As part of this same process, the earlier antagonism between the Athomi and the community began to soften and a general repairing of relations took place between them. The community saw that the Athomi really had something to offer-- education. Throughout the 1920s, the Kikuyu increasingly began to see education as a route toward limited modernization. The teaching staff and facilities of the central station were limited; the only other available education was through the Athomi, and the community began to see them making increasingly important contributions.

The Athomi also began to revise their attitude toward the community. Life at the mission had bred separation and isolation. The Athomi had taken on a new identity that was reinforced by daily contact with each other and the missionary, as well as by separation from other Kikuyu. Use of the mission as a sanctuary implied a wish to separate from the community. This was changed by the departure from central station life. Now their corporate identity as Athomi was diluted by their return to the community. Similarly, the control and influence of the missionary was now limited by the distance from the central station. As Athomi contact with mission station life weakened, their relationship with the community was daily being strengthened. They began to ease themselves back into their ritual life of the community, sharing in the festivities of the rites of passage, and the joys of a good harvest or experiencing the hardship of drought and disease. The Athomi and the community were drawn closer together in the work of establishing a school too. Even though the end result was a small thatched building, perhaps just large enough for a dozen pupils, its completion was based upon the joint effort of the teacher, his students, their families, and an ever-widening circle of other people in the community. Community participation was clearly evident in subsequent efforts to build larger schools. Plots of land, building materials and labor were all donated; the erection of the building was very much a community activity. Aid and local interest continued once the school was built. Instructional materials, the teacher's salary, and even his house were often provided. The teacher often found older members of the community in his classes. Sometimes a special period of instruction was held in the evening for such people. Occasionally, the building itself became a community center with dances being held in the surrounding yard and the local Kiama using it for deliberations. By the mid-twenties, what had begun in a mood of uneasiness with a few inquirers receiving instruction in the teacher's house, had developed into the focal point of community interest.(2)

As schools began to grow, it became apparent to the Athomi that they needed the good will of the community, especially the leaders. A friendly relationship with the local headman or chief would be an asset when seeking to have students excused from communal work projects. Local leaders might grant the school a larger plot if they were on friendly terms with the teacher.(3) Unfortunately, many chiefs continued to feel that _Athomi_ were a threat to their authority.

With the sanctuary of the mission station behind them, the _Athomi_ were confronted like everyone else with the harsh realities of reserve life. Now they had to face the very things that had driven them to the mission: high taxes, low wages, and particularly land shortage. Those rigors of reserve life not only enabled _Athomi_ to identify with the community of which they were now a part, but their separation from the mission also enabled them to view the missionaries with some detachment. In fact, as the 1920s unfolded, _Athomi_ became increasingly critical of missionary insensitivity to local needs, some examples of which will now be examined.

Missions in general were recognized as large land holders. The White Sisters' Mission, near the AIM in Kiambu, had sold 300 acres of unneeded land to a settler. This particularly irritated the Kikuyu as the land was adjacent to the reserve and many felt that its location demanded that it be given back to the Kikuyu.(4) Much to the distress of the surrounding Kikuyu, the AIM applied about the same time for an expansion of land on its Githumu station. The mission could not escape the accusation that they were land owners, especially as they had the land registered in the name of the missionary. Of the 100 acres on the GMS station at Kambui, 30 acres were held freehold by Reverend Knapp.(5) Mission farms were cultivated in much the same way as settler farms. At the 2,400 acre AIM station at Kijabe, all afternoons were reserved for working in the large garden. This enterprise was built upon unpaid _Athomi_ labor and became so large that the mission began to supply vegetables to hotels in the vicinity, the proceeds of which went, not to the _Athomi_ or even for instructional materials or facilities for the school, but to the missionaries for the purchase of a new automobile.(6)

If the missionaries in their use of land took on the appearance of the settlers, the Kikuyu could also find evidence that would associate the missionaries with the ideas and policies of the settlers and the government. For instance, the Alliance of Protestant Missions, of which the AIM and GMS were members, supported (7) the stand taken by the Church Missionary Society on the infamous 1919 labor circular. However, this public statement gave little comfort to the Kikuyu for it did not condemn forced labor, but merely attacked the subtle and morally questionable methods by which the government and the settlers sought to recruit such labor. In fact, missions defended it and called for its legalization so long as it was ". . . _confined to able-bodied men_ . . . _done under proper conditions_ . . . _clearly defined and_ . . . _directed primarily to state work._ . . ." (italics in the original)(8). The missionaries did not ask for the abolition of forced labor, only its reform.

Further insensitivity toward the Kikuyu was demonstrated by the mission's determination, often with government help, to limit the practice of local customs. At Githumu, the missionaries succeeded in having a government ban placed upon all sacrifices to Ngai, the Kikuyu creator god and the spiritual entity to whom one turned in times of crisis. At the time that this prohibition was given, the Kikuyu were experiencing a drought and the beginnings of serious famine conditions. When a number of Athamaki leaders appealed to Ngai, through a sacrifice, to send rain, they were detained by the government.(9)

This direct attack upon some Kikuyu customs was also paralleled by more subtle mission maneuvers against the Kikuyu. A government marriage law enacted in 1902 stated that:

> under the ordinance only one marriage is allowed and any person who has contracted a marriage by native law or customs with one person cannot contract another marriage under the ordinance with a different person and further no person married under the ordinance can contract a marriage with another person by Native law or custom. In both of the above cases the culprit is liable to five years hard labor.(10)

Missionaries sought to pressure Athomi into marriages recognized by Ordinance (marriage by licensed minister or government official) and thereby to trap them into monogamy. In addition to the various forms of church discipline which missionaries could invoke, they could now use the threat of prison toward any adherents who considered polygamy. They also gave poor references to prospective employers of those Athomi who sidestepped the whole issue by continuing to marry under Kikuyu custom, and thereby lawfully being able to have multiple wives in the future. When missions were asked to help in the optional registration of births, marriages, and deaths, AIM missionaries encouraged local people to think that registration was mandatory and urged people to fulfill the law by becoming Christians.(11)

The missionaries also hoped that the government would ban customs offensive to Christian morality. Kikuyu custom called for property to be divided among the sons upon the death of their father. Provision was made for a son's wife in the event of his death too; one of his brothers would take her into his home and care for her. She would not inherit her husband's property for that would pass to his sons. The missionaries felt that it was immoral for a Christian woman to live with her deceased husband's brother. They further held that she should receive part of her husband's estate; the passing of all the land to sons cheated the wife of her rightful inheritance. In these as in the attempt to get a decrease in dowry for poorer Athomi, the missionaries sought to have the government change

Kikuyu custom. Though the government was reluctant to tamper with these customs, the general community, and even some Athomi, were enraged by the mission attempts at forced change.(12)

Another area of friction was education. In Kenya, the missions took up the task of education largely by default. The government came to expect that some service would be given to local people in return for mission plots in the reserve. By the 1920s, a pledge of either a medical or an educational facility was necessary to establish a mission station.(13) But the emphasis of both the AIM and the GMS had always been on evangelism, and while there was occasionally some conflict between the American and British missionaries as to how important a place education should have, the basic policy carried into the 1920s was to give evangelism top priority in the mission's program.(14) Some kind of school was required of the AIM by the government, but no standards were established or inspections carried out until the mission began to receive government grants in the late 1930s.(15)

Though education, after the First World War, continued to hold a position subordinate to evangelism, its availability underwent change. Following the war, the AIM sought to use the schools as a means for evangelism, to snare people for Christianity, as one teacher remarked.(16) In the missionary mind, the out-schools were to become merely an extension of the evangelical arm of the central station. Writing of the 1920s, one long-term AIM missionary said:

> in this period Church and School still were largely synonymous terms, for the many little bush schools had as their main motive teaching people to read the word of God. . . . They were evangelizing centers rather than schools in the true sense of the word.(17)

This ran directly counter to Kikuyu interests. As Anderson has noted, Christian evangelism was born out of a need in European and American societies and not among Africans.(18)

The AIM was ill-equipped to satisfy Kikuyu needs for education. There was never a single AIM missionary who worked among the Kikuyu as a trained teacher. In fact, few AIM missionaries had finished normal school.(19) In addition, the missionaries had language problems, certainly a liability in the classroom. One informant, who had known all the AIM missionaries among the Kikuyu, said that not one of them really knew the Kikuyu language well.(20) The Kikuyu also found that AIM stations offered only three years of instruction and often considerably less. Classes were largely unimaginative, with rote learning the instructional medium. The first African teachers were those who had learned to read a Gospel in Kikuyu. Later, graduates from the third grade were automatically placed into teaching positions. The assumption was that those who had learned could automatically become teachers; no formal teacher training was begun until the late 1930s. Those Kikuyu who did become out-station teachers found that conditions were poor, salaries were low and even went unpaid for many months by the mission. The lack of concern for legitimate grievances led many AIM teachers to seek employment elsewhere at the first opportunity.(21)

The criticism of all these educational inadequacies was coupled with an indictment against what seemed to be a double standard employed by the missions. For education, the case in point was the Rift Valley Academy (RVA), a school for missionary children which the mission operated at Kijabe starting in 1903.(22) It may have seemed natural that the missionaries would provide education for their children, but by the 1920s this education seemed to be at the expense of the Kikuyu. The Kikuyu observed that while "shortage of funds" was often the reply given for the low salaries and poor instructional materials available to them, funds always seemed to be available for RVA. A large stone building was erected in 1909 (the corner stone laid by Teddy Roosevelt); trained teachers were brought out from the United States, and the materials and equipment were far superior to anything made available to the Kikuyu schools, even to the one next to RVA on the Kijabe station itself.(23) The Kikuyu felt that the educational affluence at RVA was in direct contradiction to the AIM philosophy of encouraging evangelism over education. The Kikuyu were even prohibited from attending RVA, a situation that continued until the 1960s.

The Kikuyu came to believe that the missionaries looked upon them solely as material for evangelism and not as people with their own needs for fulfillment and desires for respect. When a missionary at Kijabe shot and killed a Kikuyu man on a hunting trip, he excused himself by saying that he had mistaken the man for a baboon.(24) Virginia Blakeslee, a long term missionary doctor at Githumu, repeatedly referred to the church elders there as "my boys" even though they were all middle-aged men, about her own age.(25) Some Kikuyu saw the low standard of education as evidence of a mission attempt to keep the Kikuyu in subordinate positions. The fact that the missionaries were against even the building of a Bible school seemed to reinforce the idea that they did not want to share leadership in the church or the school.(26)

Finally, missionary insensitivity to local people was exhibited in church discipline. In seeking to translate the complexities of Christianity from one culture to another, the AIM succeeded only in reducing Christianity to a set of rules. Christianity was cast from the outset in negative tones; Christians were those people who did not do certain things. In addition to the ten commandments there were prohibitions concerning social and religious practices: polygamy, traditional marriage, sacrificing, consulting diviners, and female circumcision. While a number of Kikuyu Christians began to question the supposed incompatibility of their customs and Christianity, a great number objected to the fact that the missionaries treated the breach of these prohibitions as crimes, to be punished severely. Hearsay evidence was enough to bring an alleged offender before the missionary. He acted as both judge and jury, and only full confession was deemed sufficient to prevent immediate and sometimes permanent dismissal from the church. During each Sunday service the crime(s) of those who did confess would be read out to the congregation. The offender would then be placed upon a black stool and would be required to sit there for a specified number of Sunday services according to the sentence given by the missionary. In the late 1920s, a public confession was added to this ordeal.(27)

Many Kikuyu felt that the missionaries were continually scrutinizing the quality of their faith as though not believing the Kikuyu had the capacity to be mature Christians. Some Kikuyu felt that the missionaries actually enjoyed finding and punishing people who had broken the church rules. The mission-aries seemed ready to believe the flimsiest evidence and to disregard the strongest denials. The accused were almost assumed to be guilty unless they could produce evidence showing their innocence.(28)

Intertwined with and even fostering criticism of the AIM was a growing Athomi political awareness among the Kikuyu. Rosberg and Nottingham have provided a valuable account of Kikuyu political history. They have left the impression, how-ever, that organized discussion of grievances came only with experience in urban areas. Only later, so their argument goes, did people in the countryside organize themselves, and this came mainly through contact with people who had been to the cities.(29) In particular, these authors and others (30) focus on Harry Thuku and his East African Association which developed in Nairobi during the early 1920s. They date a rural political awakening only with the following he attracted on a number of rural visits just prior to his detention in March of 1922. Thuku's followers are depicted as an enthusiastic group, fascinated with his oratory and sympathetic to his criticism of both mission and government. They are seen as leaderless after his detention and horrified with the riot outside his cell in which more than fifty people were killed by government forces and European settlers. The followers are thought to have melted away in the immediate aftermath. Historians have con-fined all other political awareness to the Kikuyu Association, a rural group initially begun by and under the direction of missionaries. It was mainly composed of chiefs, their assis-tants, and a few of the older Athomi from the CMS and CSM stations at Kabete and Thogoto respectively. As government employees, they accepted its plan for political change and took little part in the Thuku activities.

While there is no denying the importance of Thuku's pioneering effort, and to a lesser extent, the contributions of

the Kikuyu Association, they did not hold a monopoly on political awareness.(31) A similar kind of awareness, though more
nebulous and less dramatic, had been developing outside the
cities. Since many of the Kikuyu grievances were based on
rural problems--conscripted labor, taxes, land alienation and
the excesses practiced by chiefs and their assistants--it is
not surprising to find political awareness developing in the
countryside.

Such was the case at Gakarara in Southern Fort Hall
(Murang'a) district. For sometime before Thuku's public
meeting there in 1922, a number of local people had been
meeting informally in each other's houses to discuss their
problems. The meetings appear to be linked with the establishment of AIM schools and churches in the surrounding area, out-
stations of Githumu. Initially, the membership consisted of
AIM preachers and teachers and their new adherents. They met
together to compare notes on confrontations with chiefs and
other administrative officials and to discuss the latest
demands made upon them and their adherents. Later, as
relationships with the surrounding communities improved, non-
Christians began to attend these meetings too. A third group
which attended included people who had been adherents but who
had left the mission. The "drop-outs" also felt the lack of
mission protection.

Meetings were not held on a regular schedule and the
membership was fluid. The return of a local resident from work
in Nairobi or from one of the settler farms might prompt a
meeting at his house at which time he would share his experiences and bring the news from other local people, also away
from home, whom he had met. A confrontation with an administrative official, a recent baraza or an indignity suffered at
the hands of the local chief might be the basis for another
meeting. Such matters as the conscription of labor for local
work projects, or the discussion of a missionary's recent visit
to neighboring out-stations might prompt other meetings.

Though leadership was diffuse, the non-Christians and
mission drop-outs seemed to be taking a much larger part. This
was evident at an emergency meeting called at the beginning of
1922 to discuss an apparent breach in secrecy. Though the
activities of this group and others like it seems to have been
limited to discussion, it was often very critical of the
government and the need to be secret about these meetings was
imperative.(32) This had become a source of concern for some
of the non-mission members, for several had recently been
harassed by chiefs and their assistants. In particular, the
non-Christians felt that the Athomi members had inadvertently
revealed their meetings in conversation with other Athomi and
perhaps even to AIM missionaries who in turn told local
authorities. As a result, all Athomi were told that they would
not be welcome at future meetings unless they were prepared to
take an oath to maintain total secrecy about their discussions
together, which they did. But it was now clear that what had

begun as a simple coming together of <u>Athomi</u> to share common problems had developed into a larger and more heterogeneous gathering in which mission adherents were no longer in sole control.(33)

Similar kinds of meetings took place in other parts of the district. At Mununǧa, near the Aberdare forest and close to the AIM station at Kinyona, a group had formed to discuss grievances against both the mission and the government. Membership centered around Gideon Kamanja, who had quit teaching at Kinyona in 1920, and included others who had stopped attending the school and church with him, as well as non-mission members of the community. In a "prayer house" erected on Kamanja's land, they held their meetings and weekly church services for those who had left the mission. By 1921, contacts had been established with Thuku in Nairobi and Kamanja had attended some of the East African Association meetings.(34) In the Githumu area, ten miles south of Mununǧa, other meetings of a similar nature took place about the same time. There, membership was more homogeneous since all participants were <u>Athomi</u> and still attending Githumu as pupils or teachers.(35) In each case, local conditions were the subject of early meetings, but the format soon changed to allow broad political discussion.

It was this kind of political activity which Harry Thuku found several months later when he visited southern Muranǧa. When news came that he was to address a public meeting nearby at Thika, a number of people from Muranǧa district attended. Some time later, in March 1922, he came into the district itself, to Keragoya, near Gakarara, most probably through an invitation extended to him at the Thika meeting. Word of his coming was spread by those in the Gakarara discussion group and several hundred people turned out to hear him. Though he really spoke of nothing new, he became an articulate focus for all their frustrations and grievances. He appealed to everyone: he had spent considerable time as an adherent and teacher at the GMS station at Kambui and could identify with the <u>Athomi</u>, whom he now asked to pray for him in his struggles to help the Kikuyu. He had left the mission, however, and could therefore offer words of encouragement from his own experience to those who had "dropped out." Lastly, he spoke fervently of the colonial occupation and the resulting land alienation, taxation, and the obnoxious practices of some chiefs, things with which everyone could identify, particularly the non-Christians.(36)

It was within this rising tide of political awareness, inspired now by Thuku to a new boldness, that criticism of the AIM turned to an outright challenge of mission authority. Those churches and schools which had developed so spontaneously during the post-war era, often with the mission's blessing, had become an increasing source of mission concern. So popular had out-schools become that attendance had dropped off alarmingly at some central stations.

The convenience of attending a neighborhood school also helped to offset the former attractiveness of the central mission station sanctuary. The local community felt more secure with the social change taking place at a school in their midst, rather than at some distant place under the control of foreigners. The newer groups of Athomi coming from out-stations as preachers and teachers, also helped to project the attractiveness of out-station school experience.

The AIM at Githumu central station were particularly anxious to bring the twenty churches and schools in their vicinity into closer orbit with the mission. Not only had they successfully grown as Githumu seemed to decline in attendance, but the local communities and their Athomi leaders seemed to relish their increasingly strong position and Githumu's weakness. This could not be tolerated; a new education director was posted to Githumu and immediately took steps to bring these out-stations firmly under mission control. The first exercise of control was attempted in the early 1920s at Kamunyaka, an out-station eight miles from Githumu.(37) Kamunyaka was, in fact, Githumu's first out-station. It was begun in 1918, when several Athomi, on a preaching tour from Githumu, found that the people were interested in both Christianity and education. Subsequent visits revealed that a number of people were anxious to attend school but considered Githumu too far away. Two lay evangelists from Githumu began to spend long weekends at Kamunyaka and were soon attracting prospective students to their preaching and teaching sessions. One of these students offered a plot on which to build a school and the Githumu evangelists secured some aid from the missionary there who was receptive to the idea that these men should preach and teach at Kamunyaka. The teachers encountered opposition from the local chief and his headmen, mainly in the form of threats to draft them as laborers for work on European farms. But the lay evangelists stayed and slowly settled into the community. The actions of these evangelists were scrutinized; when local people saw that these men did not match the stereotype of the over-zealous Athomi, the Kamunyaka community did not obstruct their teaching and preaching. The evangelists felt that their probationary period was over when their classes began to expand. By 1920, there were several dozen coming to the school during the week and even more attending the services on Sunday.

Githumu's education director now proposed to upset Kamunyaka's autonomy by insisting that the two lay evangelists be rotated to other out-stations and that the congregation turn over their Sunday collection money to the mission.

The teachers, though they had not come from the area, had been almost completely accepted, and felt that this had earned them continued residence. They had come to identify closely with the local community. The people of Kamunyaka had built and maintained the church with little help from the mission and now felt that they should continue to control it. This included disbursing church collections as they saw fit. Money had repeatedly been used for improvements to the school and the church building, and as a supplement to the teachers' salaries, which were supposed to be supplied by the mission but in fact were often left unpaid. To turn collections over to the mission would have been like paying a tribute. The Kamunyaka Christians felt that they owed the mission nothing; their investment was in their own community.

Debate within the community and pressure from Githumu continued until several Kamunyaka residents heard Harry Thuku speak in the early months of 1922. He publicly stated all of the privately held criticisms concerning missionary arrogance, practice of the color bar, and their attack on Kikuyu customs. When he pointed out how the missionaries and the government collaborated to the disadvantage of the Kikuyu, even to the point that some AIM missionaries said criticism of colonialism was sinful because government was the work of God,(38) he was not telling them anything that they had not experienced. The people from Kamunyaka felt that Thuku, in his description of missionaries, had fairly characterized the AIM at Githumu.

When Thuku was detained on March 21st, in Nairobi, at least one Muthomi from Kamunyaka went to investigate. Several days later, when the Kamunyaka people learned that the government had fired upon the demonstrators and had wounded the Muthomi, they decided to defy the mission. Accordingly, a decision was made permanently to withhold Sunday collections, and to encourage the teachers to stay indefinitely.

The challenge to mission authority was not limited at this time to Kamunyaka. A dispute over marriage rites took place in the early 1920s at the AIM station at Kinyona. Relationships between the Kikuyu and the missionaries had never been good on this station and the dispute over marriage was the last in a long series of conflicts.

When Njiri wa Karanja, the Muthamaki of Kinyona, invited the AIM to come and live in his area, he was seeking to tap the power and prestige that surrounded the white man in the same way as Karuri, his colleague to the north, had invited Mcgregor of the Church Missionary Society some years earlier.(39) The AIM established a small station at Kinyona in 1911, and Njiri came to regret his decision. As the government-appointed chief for the area, he felt his authority being undercut when the missionaries would not allow their adherents to be recruited for labor or conscripted for the carrier corps. He also objected to the missionaries' lack of respect for the Kikuyu way of life. In particular, both Njiri and the community objected to the abrasive and insensitive mission doctor at Kinyona. Her outspoken criticism of the community's customs upset everyone, especially Njiri, a confirmed polygamist.(40)

A group of Kikuyu were attracted to the mission, but their relations with the rest of the community were so severely strained that Athomi were forcibly taken away from school by their parents, and the missionaries had to retreat to Kijabe on more than one occasion.(41) When the Githumu mission was

opened seven miles away, in 1914, Athomi went there to escape
the tension and conflict that surrounded their existence at
Kinyona.

Much of this conflict centered on the idea advanced by the
missions that each decision to become a Muthomi was also a
decision to reject the community. Once the Kinyona Athomi took
up residence at Githumu, they sought to correct this idea by
siding with the community against the missionaries in a dispute
over mission attempts to enlarge Githumu station. The original
mission site of ten acres was taken without community approval,
and when the mission sought to enlarge this site by purchasing
some of the surrounding land, the community resisted. The
mission then slowly encroached on the surrounding land. When
this was detected, the community proposed that the trench
around the station, used earlier for defense, now be redug.
The Kinyona Athomi participated in this excavation project,
much against the will of the missionaries.(42) Though the
"Kinyona Crowd," as they were now called, were not dismissed
from Githumu, their relations were strained with both the
missionaries and the Githumu Athomi who had supported the
missionaries over the land issue. New adherents from Kinyona
were not encouraged at Githumu and by the early 1920s all those
from Kinyona had returned home. At the same time, the AIM
decided to withdraw missionaries from the Kinyona station and
place it under the official control of Githumu.(43) At least
for a time, this meant that Kinyona adherents could go their
own way. And while Githumu was directing its energies toward
establishing out-stations elsewhere, the Kinyona Christians
were training a second generation of Athomi; the original
adherents were sending their children to school and church
under the direction of local evangelists and teachers.

This process of growth in church and school was the basis
for continual friction with the Githumu mission. The Christians at Kinyona, drawing on their experience at Githumu and
following the same pattern as Kamunyaka, found that good relations with the local non-Christian community were vital to
their welfare. This became particularly apparent when Athomi
made plans to marry. The mission insisted that Athomi have
church weddings.(44) Most Athomi were reluctant when they
learned that they would be ineligible unless both bride and
groom were Christians. As few Christian young women were
available, the rule meant that brides would first have to take
instruction in Christianity and then be baptized before being
permitted to marry Athomi. This process could take two years
or even longer.

Of equal importance to the Athomi was the attitude of the
community toward the marriage rule. The community knew that
at best, marriage to a Muthomi was considered risky and many in
the community opposed it outright. If forced conversion of
one's daughter was now one of the conditions of marriage the
already difficult position of Athomi bachelors would become
impossible. For these reasons, as well as Athomi doubts about

the superiority of the Christian ritual, most Athomi were married according to Kikuyu custom. The few marriages of this sort that had taken place before the missionary departure from Kinyona had been declared invalid by the missionaries and the participants had been excommunicated. Once the missionaries left, the excommunicants came back to the church and other customary marriages took place, some even in church. When missionaries of Githumu heard of this in 1924, they declared all the marriages invalid and sought to excommunicate everyone involved. Kinyona ignored the directive, and since the AIM was not able or willing to place a resident missionary at Kinyona, there was little that the mission could do. Though Kinyona did not officially secede from the AIM, its Christians were definitely making their own decisions, as Kamunyaka had done earlier.

Throughout 1924 and into 1925, the missionaries at Githumu were clearly troubled. By that time, the call by teachers and their communities for better salaries and more education had reached a crescendo and the resistance at Kamunyaka and Kinyona was considered outright insubordination. But it was the Githumu water scheme that sparked the missionary counter-offensive.

Githumu's sole water supply was the river that ran below the hill on which the station was located. The girls and young women staying at the Icii or hostel, were given, as their daily task, the collection of water from the river. The girls often had to make several trips a day down to the river and then back up the hill with their ten gallon barrels. Many of the girls considered this work forced labor and a number left the mission rather than endure it further.(45) When local Athomi suggested a pump as a substitute for the girls' labor, they were told that such an expenditure was unwarranted when able-bodied people were available to do it. When several of the churchmen and evangelists offered to invest their own money in the project, the suggestion was interpreted by the missionaries as another challenge to their authority. In response, the doctrine of the "New Church" was promulgated.(46)

This doctrine was the mission's attempt to gain maximum authority over Githumu and its surrounding outstations. It held that since the missionaries were God's servants, their authority came from God and, therefore, their word must be obeyed. To disobey or even doubt a mission directive was tantamount to disobeying God. In general, this meant that whatever the issue, the mission decision was final. Specifically, the doctrine meant that the line would be held on more and better education and higher teacher's salaries. Also, local autonomy would be ended and the attack on Kikuyu customs would continue.

The growing political awareness of the Kikuyu was singled out for special attention too. The missionaries wanted to separate their adherents from "politics."(47) It was their

belief that Athomi should not be concerned about their condition in this life; their efforts should be spent preparing
themselves spiritually for the life to come. Some missionaries
even held to the millenarian idea that the end of the world was
at hand and all effort should be spent preparing for it. Such
people considered political protest a waste of valuable time.
Other missionaries simply associated political consciousness
with religious autonomy, and they felt their authority threatened.

Now to institute the doctrine of the "New Church," a
document was drawn up stating the points mentioned including an
abstention of all future involvement in "politics." All evangelists, teachers, and other church and school leaders were
told to come forward and sign it.   Those who did would be
considered members of the "New Church;" those who did not would
be cut off completely from the mission's schools and churches.

When a significant number of out-station leaders failed to
come forward at a mass meeting late in 1925, the mission began
to employ threats and intimidation. Word was sent out that all
who would not sign might be detained by the government. Several
out-school leaders claimed that chiefs and headmen harassed
them. The mission also announced that all churches and schools
would be closed on the out-stations where the leaders did not
sign.

In response, some left the mission, like Joseph Kang'ethe,
Kikuyu Central Association (KCA) president,(48) totally unwilling to compromise his political beliefs even at the cost of
being unable to finish his education.   But most adherents
remained. Some were thoroughly cowed, at least for the moment,
by the mission attack upon them.   They heartily denounced
politics and accepted the sanctity of mission authority.
Others, like Ezekiel Kamau, at the Githumu out-station of
Gaitegi, were not prepared to sever their connections with the
mission. He, and others, only partially compromised their
principles, for while they publicly denounced Thuku and promised to refrain from all future political involvement, they did
so only to keep their employment with the mission; there had
been no inner change of mind.   Kamau kept discreetly in touch
with the politicians in his area, particularly Kang'ethe, and
more than once helped to collect money for political
causes.(49)

At Kinyona, the mission threat to close the church and
school did not force compliance.   When one of their teachers
gave assent to the "New Church," the local community dismissed
him from his position.(50) Kinyona did not actually sever its
AIM connection, but the Christian community continued to maintain the autonomy it had acquired after the missionary departure in 1924.   All future attempts to place a missionary or a
Githumu evangelist or teacher at Kinyona were rejected.

At Kamunyaka, part of the out-station community became so
disgusted with AIM attempts to tamper with local autonomy that

they severed their connection with the mission church altogether in 1926. Each Sunday thereafter, this group met under
the trees in an area adjacent to the out-station. Many of
these people would have liked to continue their education, but
this was now denied them by the AIM and their education was
reduced to what they could learn while listening outside the
school house windows.(51) The AIM was not prepared to allow
people into schools who were not obedient to the tenets of the
"New Church." Education was clearly reserved for those who
were at least in outward agreement with the mission.

The drama at Kinyona and Kamunyaka was repeated throughout
much of the area under Githumu's auspices. In the day-to-day
existence of most out-stations, the mission had been in the
background and its attempts to gain control were resisted
almost everywhere. At three out-stations, the "New Church"
teachers sent by the mission were boycotted by the communities.
All children were kept out of the school and provisions and
housing were denied the men who were quickly forced to leave.
The original teachers, who were critical of the mission, took
up their posts once again. A directive requiring all teachers
and evangelists to report to Githumu each Friday afternoon for
in-service training did not meet with success either. Once the
teachers saw that the meetings were simply being used for the
propagation of "New Church" doctrines, attendance fell off
rapidly. Throughout much of 1926, Githumu hospital was boycotted as a protest against the mission. Attendance dropped
off so much that news of it even reached the District Commissioner at Fort Hall.(52) The battle over autonomy even
affected Kihumbuini, the GMS out-station that was located in
AIM territory. The desire to establish autonomy from the GMS
central station at Ngenda resulted in the dismissal of the
evangelist, who was identified too closely with the mission. A
year later, he returned, but only with the prior approval of
the community.(53)

The quest for out-station autonomy even affected the Rift
Valley where Kikuyu laborers and squatters brought their demand
for education and their interest in Christianity. According to
the Labor Department Ordinances, estate owners were to provide
for both the secular and religious education of any juveniles
they employed.(54) In actual fact, employers had for a long
time established schools and churches at their own expense.
Athomi employed on these estates, were often persuaded to teach
the fundamentals of education for any interested laborer after
working hours. When the AIM began to expand into the Rift
Valley during the 1920s, the itinerant schools and churches
provided a ready-made field of operation. The AIM was able to
take control of many of the farm schools and churches and knit
them together with others which they initiated, into a network
of out-stations similar to those around Githumu. In return
for some direction, financial assistance, and an occasional
teacher, the AIM sought to establish its authority and control

throughout the Rift Valley. Though the AIM did not here
attempt to impose the "New Church" doctrine, the mission's
tightened control and its campaign against Kikuyu customs were
deeply resented. Many of the out-stations sought to regain
independence in the middle 1920s.(55)

As a final rebuke to the autonomy movement and a demonstration of its power and authority, the AIM callously withdrew
financial support and teachers from some newly acquired and
struggling out-stations. Most of these had been acquired in
1919 (56) and they were quite far from Githumu, some more
than twenty miles away. The mission's inability to maintain
effective control over such a distance was certainly an important element in this decision. The missionaries also feared
that the new stations would eventually seek their own autonomy
anyway. Although some new stations were attempting to do this,
others offered no resistance. Nevertheless, the missionaries
punished the vulnerable new stations, in response to the indi-
gnities suffered at the hands of mature and stable stations
like Kamunyaka and Kinyona.

A number of these former out-stations managed to struggle
along, either on their own or with one another's' help. At a
half dozen places, several adjacent areas banded together to
support one joint school and church. These consolidated centers employed their own teachers/evangelists and continued to
be viable until the government insisted that they affiliate
with some mission. Several were able to do this: Kandani
church and school became affiliated with the CMS. Two other
stations, Muthithi and Githumu (not the AIM central station),
managed to enlist the help of the CMS.(57) Three other abandoned out-stations badgered the government into giving them
aid.(58) Their move was patterned on the success of Gakarara,
an AIM outstation which had struck out on its own in 1922 and
had successfully enlisted government aid by 1926.(59) Gakarara
and the three other areas must have been very cleverly persua-
sive to have obtained government assistance. The government
did not offer education subsidies to independent schools for
another decade.

The public fight for autonomy masked a less viable, though
equally important phenomenon which had taken place. By 1928,
it was apparent that a great division had developed within the
AIM community, between the early adherents, who remained
devoted to the mission, and the younger Athomi who were
increasingly critical. The early adherents had often shared a
common religious and educational experience on the central
stations and their struggles against their parents and against
the surrounding communities had forced them to come to know and
depend upon each other. Similar mutual dependence and friendship had developed between these first Athomi and the missionaries. They had often been the first Kikuyu the missionaries
had known. It was from the early adherents that the missionaries had learned the language and a smattering of Kikuyu
culture.

Out of this double dependence had grown a solid mutual loyalty. These Athomi did not seek outside employment but remained close to the mission after their educational and religious training had been completed. Many were employed on central stations as evangelists and teachers, or even as household servants of the missionaries. Others became out-station supervisors. When Harry Thuku began to criticize missions, and local critics began to focus specifically on the AIM, these Athomi remained loyal to the mission. They publicly disassociated themselves from the critics, and became mission apologists. Even the arrogance of the "New Church" doctrine of missionary infallibility did not shake many from their defense of the AIM. They remained steadfast in their belief that an attack upon the mission was an attack upon Christianity. Their formative years on the central mission stations had convinced them of the rightness of Christianity, and while some of them did not like missionary arrogance or subscribe to the AIM idea that all Kikuyu customs were incompatible with Christianity, they did not want anything to slow down or halt the growth of the Christian church among the Kikuyu. Their plan was to weather the storm of criticism and dissent, while privately trying to bring some slow change from within.

The second group consisted of those who had become estranged from the AIM, mainly younger Athomi in the second wave of adherents. While the central mission compounds were the sanctuaries of the first group, the out-stations were the geographical focal point for this second group. They had been drawn there, largely after World War I, by a desire for education and a curiosity about Christianity. It is difficult to characterize these Athomi as a group, for while each out-station produced a handful of these people, there never existed the camaraderie among them that was found among the earlier adherents. The cohesiveness of each out-station group was weakened by the occasional transfer or departure from mission work of the teacher/evangelist. But many of these people did share an increasingly critical attitude toward the AIM. The poor salaries held only a few of them as teacher/evangelists. Travel and work in other areas proved how inferior AIM education was to that of other missions. The CMS schools at Kabete and Mombasa and the Thogoto school of the CSM were all found to be superior to AIM schools. Competition with Athomi from other missions often put the AIM school leavers at a disadvantage for jobs.(60)

The close ties of the later Athomi with the community increased their estrangement from the mission. They identified very strongly with the desire of the community for local church and school autonomy. They had no personal friendships with missionaries, and they rejected the "New Church" doctrine. Their perspective also afforded them the ability to separate the missionaries from Christianity.

The division among generations of Athomi was not just an example of infighting among the Christian elite; the out-

station _Athomi_ identified more and more with the community in
which they lived.   The community, in turn, shared its concerns
about educational excellence and missionary arrogance with
their local _Athomi_.

END NOTES

1. The following section is based upon interviews with both of these men: Johana Mitaro, June 30, 1971, and Njuguna Njoroge, February 8, 1971, February 13, 1971.
2. Oral Evidence: Njuguna Njoroge, February 8, 1971; Oral Evidence: Rev. Johana Gitau, May 22, 1971; Oral Evidence: Simon Mwangi, October 31, 1970.
3. DC/FH to all Missionaries, April 28, 1925, Secretariat File, Native Affairs, KNA.
4. Welbourn, East Africa Rebels, p. 236.
5. Oral Evidence: Kambui Church Interviews, Ex-chief Magugu, May 20, 1971; Oral Evidence: Moses Murugu, February 14, 1971
6. Inland Africa (British Edition), April, 1925, AIM, London.
7. Welbourn, East Africa Rebels, p. 128.
8. Norman Leys, Kenya (London: Hogarth Press, 1925), Appendix.
9. Oral Evidence: Wambui, December 7, 1970.
10. Marriage Memo, Commissioner of Mombasa to Scott, Kikuyu, October 12, 1903, Marriage Questions File, Presbyterian Church of East Africa (PCEA) Archives, Nairobi.
11. PC/CP 1/41/1, Kikuyu District Political Record Book I, KNA; Oral Evidence: Emma Mathys, November 19, 1970.
12. PC/CP 6/4/5, Native Affairs, General Policies 1925-57, KNA.
13. Native Affairs Dept. Circular No. 30, September 1, 1925, PC/CP 9/1/1, Land Grants to Missions 1921-28, KNA.
14. Moody to Campbell, January 13, 1929, Moody File, AIM, New York. For a discussion of the conflict between evangelism and education among missions in East Africa, particularly Kenya, see John Anderson, The Struggle For the School (Nairobi: Longmans, 1970) Chapter Two.
15. D.C. Nyeri to Director of Education, August 6, 1938, DC/FH 6/2, Inspection of Schools 1934-50, KNA.
16. Oral Evidence: Johanna Nyenjeri, n.d., Kik File, NCCK-Limuru Archives.
17. Virginia Blakeslee, Behind the Kikuyu Curtain (Chicago: Moody Press, 1956), p. 179.
18. Anderson, Struggle for the School, p. 10.
19. Report of Education Commission, Nairobi 1919, evidence given by L.H. Downing, AIM Field Director, KNA.
20. Oral Evidence: Johanna Nyenjeri, NCCK-Limuru Archives. While conducting field work, I met an AIM missionary who had worked nearly forty years among the Kikuyu but still made major grammatical errors when speaking Kikuyu.
21. AIM Kijabe Teachers to Director of Education, August 12, 1928, AIM Kijabe, Education 1/1064, AIM, New York.
22. Henry O. Weller, Kenya Without Prejudice (London: East African Newspaper, 1931), p. 126.

68

23. Edith Holman and Ruth Truesdale Files, AIM, New York.
24. PC/CP 1/4/1, Kikuyu District Political Record Book II, KNA.
25. Oral Evidence: Emma Mathys, November 19, 1970.
26. Oral Evidence: Johanna Nyenjeri, n.d., Kik File, NCCK-Limuru Archives.
27. Oral Evidence: John Mwirigi, February 18, 1971.
28. Oral Evidence: Johanna Nyenjeri, n.d., Kik File, NCCK-Limuru Archives.
29. Carl G. Rosberg, Jr. and John Nottingham, The Myth of "Mau Mau": Nationalism in Kenya (New York: Praeger, 1966), especially Chapters 2-3.
30. Jack R. Roelker in The Genesis of African Protest: Harry Thuku and the British Administration in Kenya, 1920-22, Syracuse University Program in East African Studies occasional paper No. 41, has put together a detailed account of Thuku and political activities based on all the written primary and secondary sources available. He perpetuates the idea that these political activities in Nairobi pre-date all others among the Kikuyu, as do two other accounts: George Bennet, Kenya, A Political History (London: Oxford University Press, 1963); John Middleton, "Kenya: Changes in African Life, 1912-1945" in Vincent Harlow and E.M. Chilvers History of East Africa II (Oxford: Clarendon Press, 1965), 333-392.
31. Thuku, in an autobiography completed shortly before his death in 1970, gives the historian unparalleled insight into the Nairobi political world of the early 1920s, but unfortunately he has little to say of political consciousness in the countryside. Harry Thuku, An Autobiography, with the assistance of Kenneth King, (Nairobi: Oxford University Press, 1970).
32. By 1922, if not before, the Kikuyu called a discussion of grievances and a general attitude critical of the missions and government "politics." Those who participated in such discussions called themselves politicians. At first the English words were used; later politics became Uteti and politicians--Ateti (sing. Muteti). From Guteta, to grumble.
33. The reconstruction of this activity in the Gakarara area is based upon a manuscript, "The Origin of Independence" prepared by Ezekiel Kamau, for my first interview with him on January 4, 1971.
34. Oral Evidence: Gideon Kamanja, April 27, 1971.
35. Oral Evidence: Jeremiah Kimone, December 9, 1970.
36. Oral Evidence: Ezekiel Kamau, January 4, 1971.
37. The following case is based upon Oral Evidence: Joseph Kimui Thong'o, December 7, 1970: Jairus Maiteni, December 8, 1970.
38. Oral Evidence: Samuel Wanjihia, March 10, 1971.

39. Kinyona Prayer Letter, October 8, 1915. Early History File, AIM, For Karuri see: Robert W. Strayer, The Making of Mission Communities in East Africa (London: Heinemann, 1978), p. 43-46. I wish to thank Professor Strayer for kindly allowing me to read and discuss with him his study while it was still in manuscript form.

40. Njiri was a legend in his own time, a man who claimed to have had fifty-seven wives. Oral Evidence: Njiri wa Karanja, March 24 & 30, 1971.

41. Unless otherwise noted, this case is based upon Oral Evidence: Joseph Muthungu, February 24, March 5, and April 6, 1971.

42. Oral Evidence: Ndebe Kambongo, December 7, 1970; Oral Evidence: Moses Murugu, February 14, 1971.

43. Laura Collins Prayer Letter, October 8, 1924, AIM, New York.

44. An alternative acceptable to the AIM was to have a civil ceremony performed by an administration official, but this had little appeal to the Kikuyu. L.H.Downing to D.C. Kiambu, November 16, 1923, AIM, New York.

45. Oral Evidence: Samuel Wanjihia, April 23, 1971. The use of women's labor by the government was the very thing that Harry Thuku lobbied against and which earned him the nick-name among Kikuyu women of "Munene wa Nyaching'a"--chief of women. Harry Thuku an Autobiography, p. 47. Its parallel application now by the AIM at Githumu was certainly apparent to the Kikuyu.

46. The section which follows on the "New Church" is based upon Oral Evidence: Samuel Wanjihia, April 23, 1971. Simon Mwangi, October 31, 1970, and Paul Githagoge, December 28, 1970, and January 8, 1971; and a PC/CP 6/4/5, D.C. Fort Hall to Chief Native Commissioner, Nairobi, No. 22/c/26, KNA.

47. "Politics," was a semantic catch-all used by the missionaries to mean anything from membership in or support of a political organization to criticism of individual missionaries. The missionaries attributed the water scheme, suggested by the Githumu church leaders, to "politics."

48. By 1925, Harry Thuku's Young Kikuyu Association, which disintegrated following his arrest and detention, had been reorganized by and was under the leadership of Joseph Kang'ethe under a new name, the Kikuyu Central Association. Many politically aware Kikuyu were now members of the KCA. For details, see Rosberg and Nottingham, Myth of Mau Mau, Chapter Three.

49. Oral Evidence: Joseph Kang'ethe, June 16, 1971; Oral Evidence: Ezekiel Kamau and Ndegwa Metho, February 16, 1971.

50. D.C. Fort Hall to Acting Director of Education, Nairobi, May 14, 1928, Dep. 1/4, Village Schools in Fort Hall District, KNA.

51. Oral Evidence: Simon Mwangi, October 13, 1970.
52. PC/CP, 4/1/2, Central Provincial Annual Reports, 1926, 1927, KNA.
53. Oral Evidence: Johanna Mitaro n.d., KIM File, NCCK-Limuru Archives. It is worth noting that twenty years earlier, Kihumbuini was the site of strong government resistance and eventually a massacre in which the military killed many Kikuyu in the area. Richard Meinertzhagen, Kenya Diary, 1902-1906, (London: Oliver and Boyd, 1957), pp. 51-52.
54. DC/MKS, 15/3/1, Labor Commission Report, 1927, KNA.
55. Oral Evidence: Rev. Johanna Gitau, May 22, 1971.
56. Government records reveal that ten out-station applications were filed by the AIM in that year. PC/CP 1/7/1, Fort Hall District Political Record Book, KNA.
57. Oral Evidence: Morris Gitiri Ng'ang'a, January 9, 1971.
58. Education Department Inspection Report, June 21, 1928, Education 1/4, Village Schools, Fort Hall, KNA.
59. Memorandum on Schools of Fort Hall District to Director of Education, Nairobi, July 28, 1928. Department of Education 1/4, KNA.
60. Oral Evidence: Ezekiel Kamau and Ndegwa Metho, Gakarara interviews, February 16, 1971.

Chapter 4

The Female Circumcision Crisis

The growing tensions of the 1920s reached their climax and resolution in the Female Circumcision Crisis at the end of the decade. The divisions created at that time, between the AIM and some of its adherents, and among the adherents themselves, have continued to the present. This chapter will discuss the events leading up to the circumcision crisis by examining the positions of the various participants, while the next chapter will present the details of the separation and its outcome.

Circumcision was the central focus of Kikuyu initiation. There were equivalent rites for both men and women. The operation was only the outward sign of an inner transformation to adulthood. This transformation was fostered by the whole of traditional education where Kikuyu boys and girls learned from an early age about pastoral and agricultural skills by copying adults; they also learned codes of behavior, tradition, folklore, and religion through customary instruction often following the evening meal.

With the approach of puberty, instruction intensified and finally culminated in the half year of events that surrounded circumcision.(1) Though there were a great variety of rites during this period, each one called attention to the transition that was taking place within the participants. First, emphasis was placed on the fact that initiation made one a recognized individual and an adult. Though children were considered persons after infancy, and had specific duties to perform, it was initiation that stamped one as a full member of society. With initiation came the removal of the prohibitions against sexual intercourse, and the opening doorway to marriage and parenthood. The link between initiation and adulthood was so strong that uninitiated women were commonly believed to be unable to bear children. It was not thought possible that a girl would jeopardize her future as a woman by foregoing initiation or that a man would marry such a person even if she could be found.

Initiation also forged a closer relationship with the supernatural. Three or four days before circumcision, the initiates and their friends and relatives held an evening of singing and dancing. They also took part in the ceremony of Koraria Morungu, or brewing beer for the ancestral god Morungu. It was a time of particularly close communion between the initiates and Morungu. They asked for his guidance and protection and for the wisdom of their forefathers.(2) Several days later, at the time of the Great Dance, a short ceremony took place where the initiates' relationships with the ancestors of their clans were established.

Far from being an isolated custom, standing alone and easily separated from other Kikuyu beliefs, initiation,

72

finalized by circumcision, was at the very heart of Kikuyu
society. It was considered the point of graduation from adolescent education it was held to be the only entrance thought
possible to adulthood; and it was the specific time when the
individual was formally brought into close fellowship with both
the living and the living-dead of the community. It was a time,
as one scholar has remarked, when an antological change took
place, a change in one's very nature and state of being.(3)
       To be sure, the AIM had but the sketchiest understanding
of initiation and its significance to Kikuyu society. Problems
with language prevented complete understanding of a topic as
embedded in the fabric of society as initiation. Also the
teachers of the missionaries had little information. The
Athomi, while being taught by the missionaries, also became the
only regular teachers of these missionaries. As some of them
were uninitiated adolescents, their knowledge was very incom-
plete. The divisions that had developed between the missionaries and the larger community cut off information that might
have come from that source.
       Missionaries had no training in the understanding of cul-
tures different from their own. Most had only a secondary
school education with one or two additional years of Bible
school.(4) Candidates received a thorough examination in the
interpretation of the scriptures and little else. Often, a
missionary's acceptance and his arrival in the field were
separated only by the three to four weeks required for the
journey from the USA to Kenya. In addition, throughout the AIM
there ran an anti-intellectualism and a suspicion of learning
that has remained to this day. The missionaries believed they
had come to teach and convert, not to learn or be taught.(5)
It was not only circumstance, then, that prevented the missionaries from acquiring knowledge of the Kikuyu but also active
design.
       Since the AIM did not want to learn about the Kikuyu, it
is not surprising that the missionaries knew little of initiation beyond the physical operation. It was this aspect of
initiation that came to their attention because it was the
dramatic climax of a long process. The male operation was
familiar to the missionaries, as it had long been practiced in
the West. The female operation or clitoridectomy increasingly
came to their notice. By 1915, a number of Kikuyu had felt
secure enough to attend the AIM hospitals at Kijabe and
Githumu, and it was in these places that the physiology of
clitoridectomy became known. Mission doctors became convinced
that the operation was unnatural because they felt it
obstructed child-birth. The scar tissue left by the operation
was said to reduce the elasticity of the pelvic muscles. This
often caused a difficult childbirth and sometimes the death of
the newborn child or the mother.
       These revelations fed the already gathering doubts other
missionaries had about the lack of scriptural support for the
Kikuyu rituals associated with circumcision, as well as the

practice of clitoridectomy itself. During the second decade of the twentieth-century the missionaries began to focus on both the male and female operations, having ignorantly separated them out from the rest of the initiation process. Consequently, initiation was narrowed, in the missionary mind, to circumcision, and the AIM began to feel that both the male and female operations were pagan and evil, comparable to witchcraft, polygamy, beer drinking, and so on. The last step came when missionaries declared circumcision to be incompatible with Christianity and labeled it as an area in which Athomi were expected to bring their ideas and beliefs in line with missionary thinking.(6)

Early mission ideas on circumcision did not go unchallenged. In fact, what took place was different only in scale from the circumcision crisis that shook the Church a little more than a decade later, in 1929. Since almost all of the first AIM Athomi were men, many of whom were uninitiated but approaching puberty, the prohibition of circumcision (and the implied prohibition of initiation) was of more immediate concern than the church laws against polygamy and witchcraft. Athomi realized that their very identity as Kikuyu was involved in this issue and they were, therefore, willing to contest mission ideas. After it was found that many westerners practiced male circumcision, the Athomi felt that they had a good argument for keeping their rite too. The fact that circumcision was not prohibited in the New Testament,(7) but that instead many New Testament Christians actually had practiced it, confirmed Athomi suspicions that the rite was anything but pagan and clinched their argument for keeping it. Community opinion had been very much against the mission stand, but it was essentially the Athomi who forced the AIM to back down. The mission finally said that male circumcision could be practiced if the operation was undertaken by a mission doctor. Later, this was modified to the extent that Kikuyu medical assistants were trained at the AIM hospitals at Kijabe and Githumu to perform the operation.(8)

The strong AIM feeling against female circumcision continued unabated, however. Mission teaching continued to claim that the operation was not compatible with Christianity. In this the AIM was in agreement with other mission societies in Kenya. At a conference held in Mombasa in 1918, all the Protestant missions which attended signed a statement saying:

> . . . the native custom of circumcision of girls practiced among certain tribes in the Protectorate is in all instances purposeless and useless while in some Districts it is highly dangerous and barbarous and that the custom ought to be abolished.(9)

One year later, the Alliance of Protestant Missions issued a similar statement condemning female circumcision, and by the

time the AIM had officially denounced it in 1921, similar moves
had been made by the CMS and the GMS.(9)

This did not close the issue for either the Kikuyu or the
AIM. Indeed, the 1920s saw the development of a great muddle
over the female circumcision issue. As Leakey clearly pointed
out, part of this muddle was linguistic and of the missionaries' own making. He related, for example, that the word
virgin, even in reference to the Virgin Mary, was translated
into Kikuyu and found in the Bible as Muiritu. This word had
one very clear meaning--an unmarried but initiated woman.(10)
If the Mother of Jesus was by definition initiated, then why
were the missionaries teaching against it?

Further confusion was caused by the missionary translation
of Irua, or circumcision. To the English reader this word has
only male connotations but to the Kikuyu, Irua is the word used
to describe the whole initiation process including circumcision
for both male and female. Unfortunately, this was the very
word the missionaries used to translate the word circumcision
in the New Testament. Why, Athomi began to ask, were the
missionaries saying that female circumcision was wicked when
Paul said that Irua was a symbol of the Christian elect and
that one profited by it (Colossians 2:11-13). Added to this
linguistic confusion was the missionary decision at Kijabe, its
headquarters station, to employ a circumcisor to come period-
ically and circumcise all the girls at the mission Icci, or
hostel, who wished to under go circumcision without the accom-
panying rites.(11) The practice at least implied indirect
approval and diluted their argument that the custom was evil.

The Kikuyu also considered it significant that the government did not support the missionary prohibition of female
circumcision. As repugnant as it might have been to the European officials,they "considered that the decision to abolish it
should come from within and not through the intervention of the
government." They reasoned that to abolish it would merely
drive the custom underground; to make its performance illegal
and therefore a punishable offence, would set the Kikuyu
against the government even more.(12) The government did not
manage to remain in the background for long but for the time
being, they took no action even when a forced circumcision came
to their notice in 1926.(13) By the mid-1920s then, the AIM,
together with the other Protestant missions, had taken a hard
line on the practice of female circumcision, but this position
had been undercut by inaccurate scriptural translation, incon-
sistent mission practice, and government silence.

Some Athomi supported the missions' ideas, and after the
First World War there were a few girls who remained uninitiated. Though several of them were AIM Athomi and an AIM
teacher even married an uninitiated girl in the late 1920s,(14)
the prevailing pattern for AIM Athomi was to ignore the ban,
quietly continue the custom and wait and see what further
developed.

This impasse changed after 1926 when all Protestant missions among the Kikuyu took the initiative. As they were to describe in their memorandum issued several years later,(15) missionary doctors became increasingly convinced that the operation had become more severe and brutal and that something needed to be done to put a stop to it. Several years before the end of the decade, a group of medical missionaries, including a representative from the AIM, prepared a comprehensive clinical definition of the operation, emphasizing its physical severity. The missionaries using this memorandum for support, introduced the term mutilation to describe the operation and by 1929, the phrase, "the sexual mutilation of women" was officially adopted by the Kenya Missionary Council as a substitute for female circumcision or clitoridectomy. Further, the government was induced to maintain some control over the operation and this found expression in a number of Local Native Council (LNC) resolutions. Efforts were also made to intensify the teaching against the custom and some coordination of ideas among the missions was attempted as the custom became an increasingly frequent topic of discussion among the representatives of the Kenya Mission Council.

The flash point of the crisis came when the missions introduced a loyalty oath. It was first used at a meeting held at Nyeri in 1928 and attended by the leading Kikuyu chiefs and European administrative officers. There, a number of Athomi members of the Kikuyu Central Association (KCA) who were also present, forcefully stated that Kikuyu customs including female circumcision, could not be discontinued without undermining the very unity of the Kikuyu themselves.(16)

Although Athomi were present from all missions, and the president and several other leaders of the KCA were members of the AIM,(17) the majority were from the CSM mission at Tumutumu. This mission felt that the loyalty of their Athomi was brought into question by the support they gave to the KCA statement. In particular, the CSM stated that the Athomi were in violation of the rule adopted nine years earlier banning circumcision among CSM adherents. The missionaries now demanded that these Athomi recant their statement and take an oath of loyalty; all who would not were to be suspended from the mission. Shortly after that, on a tour of CSM work in Meru district, Dr. Arthur, of the CSM, pressed Chogoria mission station to hold its Athomi to the firm position CSM had taken on the circumcision issue. As in the case of the Tumutumu mission, Chogoria then asked its members to take an oath of loyalty or risk suspension. Similar actions were taken by the CSM at Thogoto and the GMS stations at Kambui, Ngenda and Kihumbuini. The AIM had been watching all of these activities. They expressed complete sympathy with the stand taken by the CSM and at their annual mission conference in March of 1930, they passed a strong resolution which stated that both female circumcision and the KCA must be repudiated by all adherents. All AIM Athomi now had to affix their signature or thumbprint to a statement of loyalty as an act of formal acceptance of this mission ruling. Those unwilling to do so were suspended.(18)

The official mission accounts portray the circumcision controversy in the most simplistic terms: the Protestant missions are represented as trying only to safeguard the Kikuyu from a custom incompatible with Christianity, while the Athomi are pictured as being unable to let go of their savage past. The issue of out-station autonomy is neglected, as are the divisions between Athomi; reference to the non-Christian community is omitted altogether. These are grievous omissions because all three areas were closely involved in the circumcision issue. The remaining part of this chapter will seek to rectify these issues by carefully examining all of the positions in the controversy.

Mission determination to bring all out-stations back under firm control contributed to the circumcision crisis. The missionaries came to believe that victory on the circumcision issue would mark a good beginning for the restoration of authority over out-stations. The attempt to link the KCA with the proposed ban on circumcision was an indication of this. The missionaries believed that a few dissident leaders, the Kinyona crowd, for instance, had caused the protests and boycotts of the earlier 1920s, while the majority of the people had blindly followed. The missionaries rightfully thought that the dissidents must be members of the KCA, even though the missionaries had little knowledge of that organization.(19) If some way could be found to cut these people off from the mission, then the leaderless majority which remained would be amenable to the pressures which the mission hoped to bring to bear. The clause in the loyalty oath repudiating the KCA was aimed at out-station leaders who had challenged mission authority. It was the AIM's hope that these leaders would refuse to make such repudiation, and therefore could be forced out of the church, leaving it "purified" of their activity.(20)

Other pressures were brought to bear upon rank and file church members. If they should continue to believe in the correctness of female circumcision, they would be shunned by the missionaries, closed out of church and thereby refused access to Holy Communion. By being so cast out of the mission fold, missionaries led Athomi to believe they would be separated from God Himself. The mission hoped also to reinforce spiritual warfare with government action. The AIM strongly supported the Local Native Council restrictions on circumcision and even felt that stronger government action should be taken.

Added to both spiritual and government pressure was the clear threat of losing one's education. In a reaffirmation of the dual evangelistic components of church and school, the mission stated that as one could be barred from church membership for not supporting the ban on circumcision, so also could one be evicted from the mission school. In practice, this rule came to be enforced among non-Christians as well; should

parents, whether _Athomi_ or not, ignore the mission prohibition
and circumcise their girls, their children would not be re-
admitted into the mission school. In addition, all paid
mission agents such as teachers and evangelists would be
relieved of their jobs unless they pledged their loyalty to the
mission on this issue.

Lastly, the AIM hoped to shame adherents into repudiating
clitoridectomy. Missionaries argued that the custom was brutal
and primitive. People who practiced it or were in sympathy
with its retention were un-enlightened and bound to the past.
They had been shown a better mode of behavior and had rejected
it. Those who supported the ban, however, were honored for
accepting mission sponsored change, discerning that it was the
way to a modern Christian life. Missionaries also said that
such people, being clear-minded, would not be "taken in" by the
KCA propaganda.(21)

The oath of loyalty to the AIM caught all _Athomi_ off
balance. Up to 1929 all but a few adherents had safely been
able to ignore mission statements against the custom as they
had been recognized as unenforceable mission opinion rather
than law. Now, every _Muthomi_ was forced for the first time to
declare his or her loyalties. The elimination of the middle
ground made tension between groups of _Athomi_ as serious as the
tension between the _Athomi_ and the AIM. The second generation
of adherents, those that had been critical of the mission, knew
they could not take the oath of loyalty and support the ban on
circumcision. They could find no Biblical justification for
the ban. In fact, they felt that the missionary campaign to
tamper with their ethnicity was a perversion of Christianity.

The second generation _Athomi_ were also determined not to
let the circumcision issue contribute to their separation from
local Kikuyu communities. The cooperative building of out-
schools and churches had helped to eliminate local resentment
and _Athomi_ now wanted this pattern of mending to continue.
They recognized that their relationship with the communities
was the key to local politics and influence, the acquisition
of land (in short supply by the 1920s) and satisfactory marriage arrangements. The communities could not be easily
ignored, yet this was exactly what the mission asked their
adherents to do. By refusing to become circumcised, girls
would lose their main opportunity to be formally introduced,
accepted and recognized as adult Kikuyu women. The local
communities were bound to become angered against individuals
or families who allowed this to happen.

The _Athomi_ also realized that if they defeated the ban,
they would have succeeded in throwing off mission control and
authority. In their eyes, the ban was not simply a mission
attack upon Kikuyu culture but part of the ongoing struggle to
maintain local autonomy from the AIM. This was particularly
true at Kinyona, Kamunyaka, and Gakarara, the areas that had
successfully challenged AIM authority in the middle 1920s. In
the divisions between first generation and second generation

Athomi, each group took the ban as an opportunity to advance
its case for mission authority or autonomy. Dissident groups,
at the out-stations where they had not been in the majority,
hoped to use the circumcision ban as a means for expanding
their numbers.

There still were a number of Athomi who remained loyal to
the AIM. Geographically, their stronghold was on and around
the AIM central stations at Mataara, Kijabe and Githumu, where
they had been among the first adherents. Others were scattered
throughout the entire AIM area where they had gone as the first
teachers and evangelists.

These loyalists, like the missionaries, had become isolated from the majority of the AIM's adherents. Through the
early 1920s, they had suffered ridicule at the out-stations,
leading them to withdraw from the younger adherents and the
community and to coalesce into small tightly knit groups.
Where possible, older friendships among like-minded Athomi were
renewed, even among people who lived at some distance. In some
cases, if an AIM central station was near, loyalists
sought out more agreeable relationships there, as they abandoned contacts in their own communities. Loyalists allowed
their memberships in local out-station churches to lapse if
they were able to attend central station churches. Some even
left out-stations to take up residence on or near a central
mission station.

When the circumcision crisis came, the loyalists were
often too isolated to fully understand the situation. Though
some had already been subjected to the intensity of adverse
community feelings, they did not understand either the depth of
this feeling or the breadth of its spread. They viewed the
circumcision crisis, or at least the beginning stages, as a
momentary challenge to the mission, something they would have
to live through with a little discomfort, but which could be
weathered. As the earlier challenges to the mission had left
the church intact, so now they thought there was little reason
to believe that the church was to be split apart.(22)

The loyalists did not doubt their position. They rejected
female circumcision because they had accepted a new pattern of
education and a new belief system; they were content in their
identity as mission people and they feared loss of educational
privileges. Missionaries told the students at the Kijabe Bible
School, all of them from this early group of adherents, that
the continuation of education and graduation as AIM pastors and
evangelists was contingent upon supporting the mission on the
circumcision issue.

A decision against circumcision also meant an end to
friendly relations with missionaries. One man reported that
after the missionary at Githumu, a life-long friend, learned
that he had refused to sign the loyalty oath, the missionary
never spoke to him again and even began to circulate slanderous
rumors about him. Those who worked for the mission in any
capacity could expect their employment terminated. Caretakers,

handymen and household servants of missionaries found that
their jobs were threatened if a relative or friend, prominent
in the mission church, refused to accept the circumcision ban.
With the threat of such economic sanctions, some Athomi continued to remain loyal to the mission.(23)

Strangely, the chiefs also tended to be loyal to the
mission and support the ban on circumcision.(24) This was
largely because of the rivalry that existed between chiefs and
Athomi.(25)

The untouchable position of Athomi had always made the
chief's duties difficult to perform and even struck at their
very authority to rule. The Athomi were exempt from public-
service labor and they could not easily be recruited as
laborers for settler farms. The chiefs also viewed with
increasing alarm the rapprochement developing between out-
station Athomi and the local community. The chiefs did not
like the idea of their constituency being influenced by the
Athomi who were often their opponents on all matters.

It was in their eagerness to oppose the Athomi that a
number of chiefs decided to support the ban on female circumcision. This was a curious position to take since they had, in
their initial encounters with Athomi, characterized themselves
as the guardians of Kikuyu tradition, protecting it from the
iconoclastic Athomi.

Not only did the missionaries, the two groups of Athomi
and the chiefs take a position on the circumcision issue, but
non-Christian Kikuyu became involved in the controversy as
well. Though they were uneasy over the mission presence and
sometimes angry with the zealousness of Athomi and their
immunity from the rigors of colonial life, it had been the
demands of the colonial government rather than Christianity
that had occupied the attention of the community until now.

In the early 1920s, many members of the non-Christian
community had agreed with the criticisms leveled by Harry Thuku
against the missions but this had not materialized into any
action against the AIM by them. Later, in the mid-1920s when
some Athomi had openly challenged AIM authority, the community
had remained unmoved. The circumcision controversy changed
this attitude, for the non-Christians were almost universally
enraged by the mission ban.

Several reasons can be offered for the reaction. First,
governmental laws increasingly restricted circumcision. The
chief governmental concern was that ceremonies could lead to
disorder and to a disruption in the flow of laborers to the
settler farms. To prevent this, an ordinance restricted the
ceremonies to one or two weeks out of the year in 1920.(26)
Later this was modified to a two month period with the proviso
that administrative officers do all in their power to pressure
local people to circumcise both men and women at an earlier age
so that the convalescent period would be shorter and workers
could return to settler employment sooner.(27)

In the mid-1920s government restrictions were placed upon
the operation itself. These restrictions came largely through
the continued emphasis on the alleged physical damage done to
the reproductive organs and birth canal. Their argument
stressed that such injury prevented normal child-birth and
actually threatened the life of both mother and child.
Recently the operation may have become more brutal too. Julian
Huxley noted that:

> . . . the presence of white civilization has
> made the operation more cruel and more
> dangerous. What with squatters living outside
> the reserves, girls going with their parents to
> live in the towns . . . it is no longer
> practical for candidates to be initiated at a
> few central places. This means that instead of
> the operation being performed only by a select
> band of skilled old women, it is often carried
> out by bungling unpracticed hands, with
> disastrous results.(28)

Whether due to "unpracticed hands" or not, both missionaries
and the government came to hold that the operation was in
excess of what had traditionally taken place and must be controlled. Consequently, in 1926, the government instructed all
Provincial Commissioners to initiate legislation in their Local
Native Councils (LNCs) that would place further restrictions
upon female circumcision. In May of the following year, the
Fort Hall LNC (and shortly afterwards the Kiambu LNC) passed an
ordinance which stated that: (1) only people licensed by them
could perform the operation, (2) only the "minor" operation
(simple clitoridectomy) could be performed and (3) no one was
to undergo the operation against her will.(29)
    The government assumed with these restrictions now on the
books and in the absence of any convictions, that they were
being obeyed. In fact, they were not; the Kikuyu were ignoring
them altogether, and when a mission/governmental investigation
took place in the early months of 1929 the total disregard for
the restrictions was revealed. Much correspondence followed
among senior members of the administration and a number of
proposals were made. All were aimed either at even greater
restriction of circumcision, such as requiring initiates to
obtain a permit before a legal operation could take place, or
providing harsher penalties for those convicted of breaking any
of the restrictions. One Provincial Commissioner advocated
penalties from a 1,000 shillings ($150.00) fine and one year
imprisonment for the first conviction, to a 5,000 shilling fine
and not less than four years imprisonment for a third conviction.(30) The government stopped short of implementing
any of these plans and settled for a new spate of LNC resolutions backed up with the threat of criminal prosecution. At
this point, the government decided to "avoid all appearance of

enforcing Christian doctrine by fines and imprisonment,"(31) and a policy of "masterly inactivity" was adopted toward circumcision. This was defined as "propaganda on the evil effects female circumcision [has] on childbirth by administrative and medical officers. . . ."(32)

But the governmental policy of non-interference did not come soon enough. The non-Christian community felt that both the government and the missions had overstepped themselves. A measure of the community's anger and power can be seen in the fact that the Kiambu LNC repudiated its circumcision resolution in response to the sharp community reaction against it.(33) While it might be legitimate for the government to control the actions of Athomi, non-Christians reasoned that it had no business in their traditional affairs. They considered the restrictions to be another example of the governmental meddling, akin to its earlier ban of sacrifices in some areas and the condoning of Athomi excesses at other times.

As deeply as the non-Christians resented government actions, they held the missions to greater account. They felt that the missionaries were behind the governmental laws. The circumcision issue was only the most recent example of the missionaries using the government against the Kikuyu.(34) With uncharacteristic insight, an AIM missionary said that the Kikuyu had come to think of the AIM and other missions as the real law-makers in Kenya who should ultimately be held responsible for the convictions against breaking LNC resolutions.(35)

More potentially dangerous to non-Christians than governmental restrictions and the meddling of the missionaries was the fear that these two groups had set in motion currents which would eventually lead to the abolition of circumcision for everyone and not just mission adherents. If circumcision was banned, initiation would certainly come to an end as well, and with it Kikuyu traditional education. Kikuyu society was already under severe strain, with large numbers having to live away from home while laboring for Europeans. To sweep away the system used for teaching traditional values and morality would completely undermine society.

Frederick Welbourn,(36) and Robert Macpherson, have argued that if there had been no circumcision crisis, the precipitant for Kikuyu action would have come sooner or later over another issue. Macpherson writes, "the determining factor in the crisis was the refusal by all Kikuyu to accept the idea that they could be perpetually 'pushed around' by anyone. . . ."(37) Clearly, there is abundant evidence that the Kikuyu had been "pushed around" from the beginning of the century by both government and missionaries. However, the circumcision crisis was more than an outburst caused by an accumulation of restraints pent up for a period of three decades. It was also a complex, multi-faceted conflict in which emerging divisions in Kikuyu society sparred with missionaries, government and increasingly with each other, all hoping to use the circumcision crisis to maximize their own position. Just how and to what extent this was realized will be examined in the next chapter.

END NOTES

1. The fullest descriptions of these events are to be found in: W. Soresby Routledge, With a Prehistoric People (London: Edward Arnold, 1910), 154ff; Charles W. Hobley, Bantu Beliefs and Magic (London: H.F.&G. Witherby Ltd., 1938), 77ff; Father C. Cagnolo, The Kikuyu (Neri: Mathari Press, 1933), 81ff; and Jomo Kenyatta, Facing Mt. Kenya (London: 1938 rpt., Vintage, 1962), Chapter Six. As Kenyatta is the best authority for the AIM area of central Kikuyu, I have depended heavily on his account.
2. Kenyatta, Facing Mt. Kenya, p. 3.
3. Frederick Welbourn, "Keyo Initiation," Journal of Religion in Africa, I, No. 3(1968) 212, 232.
4. Candidates papers, 1915-26, AIM, New York.
5. Oral Evidence: Kenneth Downing, November 22, 1970.
6. This idea is implied throughout much of the AIM correspondence of the time. For example, see Stumpf to Palmer, May 11, 1916, Stumpf File, Aim, New York.
7. Portions of the Kikuyu New Testament were available in the first decade of the twentieth-century, though it was not until 1926 that the New Testament was entirely translated and appeared in one volume.
8. Virginia Blakeslee, Beyond the Kikuyu Curtain (Chicago: Moody Press, 1956), p. 113; Oral Evidence: Johanna Nyenjeri, KIM, NCCK-Limuru Archives.
9. Coast Province, PC/DC 52/128, Conference of Missionary Societies, September 13, 1918, Circular File of Native Girls, KNA. Feelers had been put out two years earlier at a similar mission conference and since the Kikuyu delegates had not strongly objected at that time, the missions were confident that a strong anti-mission statement was in order at the 1918 meeting. File G/2, Conference of the Native Church in Southern Kikuyuland, PCEA Archives.
10. L.S.B. Leakey, "The Problem of the Initiation of Girls," Journal of the Royal Anthropological Institute, 61 (1931), 277-285; a separate complication was that the word Muiritu implied the practice of a form of sexual intercourse sanctioned for unmarried people under the Kikuyu custom. See Kenyatta, Facing Mt. Kenya, Chapter Seven. As the AIM taught against any sexual activity outside of marriage, the use of Muiritu created a second problem for the mission.
11. Oral Evidence: Johanna Nyenjeri, August 25, 1970, KIK File, NCCK-Limuru Archives.
12. PC/CP Coast 52/1280, P.C. Mombasa to acting Chief Secretary, Nairobi, October 22, 1918, File on Native Girls, KNA.
13. CP/PC 4/1/2, Central Province Annual Report, 1926, KNA.
14. Oral Evidence: Ezekiel Kamau and Ndegwa Metho, March 4, 1971.

84

15. Church of Scotland, Female Circumcision: Memorandum
Prepared by the Mission Council of the Church of Scotland,
Kikuyu 19131, Confidential (Mimeo), seen as DC/FH 3/2,
KNA. Although the CSM actually wrote this lengthy
memorandum much collaboration with the AIM and the other
protestant missions went into its preparation and they all
gave their assent when it was completed. Unless otherwise
noted, material for this part of the chapter was drawn
from Sections 2, 4, and 5 of the CSM Memorandum.

16. For a detailed account of the meeting see the KCA
Publication Kuigwithania, I no. 9 (February, 1929), 8-16,
translated by the CID, Nairobi and seen as AC/MKS
10B/13/1, Confidential, KNA.

17. Oral Evidence: Joseph Kang'ethe, June 16, 1971.

18. Stauffacher to Campbell, September 17, 1930. Stauffacher
File, AIM, New York.

19. Though most AIM missionaries linked the origin of the KCA
with the events surrounding the Thuku riot of 1922, in the
years since that time they had not acquired any specific
knowledge about it. Some thought that it was an Indian
inspired political group while others called it the
"bolshevik element." See Hartsock to Campbell, October
10, 1928, Hartsock File, AIM, New York.

20. Blakeslee, Beyond the Kikuyu Curtain, p. 8.

21. This is implied throughout Section IV of the CSM
Memorandum.

22. Several of these Athomi revealed their isolation by
insisting that the circumcision crisis came quickly and
without warning. Oral Evidence: Interviews with Ngenda
church elders, April 2, 1971. Similar claims were made
by the missionaries in the CSM Memorandum, pp. 8-9.

23. Oral Evidence: Moses Thuo wa Chege, August 4, 1970, read
at NCCK-Limuru Archives; Oral Evidence: Johanna Nyenjeri,
August 15, 1970, seen in KIK File, NCCK-Limuru Archives;
Oral Evidence: Joel Mwithiga, n.d. NCCK-Limuru Archives;
Oral Evidence: Emma Mathys, November 19, 1970. Oral
Evidence: Ezekiel Kamau, January 4, 1971; Oral Evidence:
Ezekiel Kamau and Ndegwa Metho, March 4, 1971; Oral
Evidence: Rev. Johanna Gitau, May 22, 1971; Oral Evidence:
Simon Mwangi, October 31, 1971.

24. Both the Kikuyu Association and the Progressive Kikuyu
Party were largely composed of chiefs and headmen and they
publicly came out against the Athomi stand on the
circumcision ban. See their statements recorded in the
CSM Memorandum, Appendix IV, No. 2,3.

25. Njiri s/o Karanja, government Chief in the area around the
Githumu and Kinyora missions stations, repeatedly resisted
AIM attempts to interest him in Christianity and held
firmly to Kikuyu culture, believing that he had inherited
the traditional position of Murathi (prophet or seer) from
his father. Yet he supported the AIM ban on female
circumcision because it provided him with an opportunity

to harass his opponents the <u>Athomi</u>. <u>Oral Evidence</u>: Njiri s/o Karanja, March 30, 1971.

26. PC/CP 6/4/2, to DC/FH, May 28, 1920, Native Affairs, General Policies, <u>KNA</u>.

27. PC/CP 7/1/2, DC/FH to PC/CP, September 18, 1920, Native Customs and Laws, Circumcision, 1920, <u>KNA</u>.

28. Julian Huxley, <u>African View</u> (New York: Harper & Row, 1931), pp. 203-4.

29. Fort Hall LNC Circumcision Resolution. The LNC there steadfastly maintained that it was improper to discuss such a personal subject. At the same time and perhaps revealing their true feelings, they said that such a resolution would be widely unpopular and it would upset the people. PC/CP 6/4/5, P.C. Nyeri to D.C. Fort Hall, May 25, 1927, Native Affairs, General Policies, 1925-27, <u>KNA</u>.

30. PC/RVP/6B 1/5/1, P.C. Kericho to CNC Nairobi, September 25, 1929 and D.C. Nyeri to Chief Native Commissioner, Nairobi, November 28, 1929, Female Circumcision, RVP, <u>KNA</u>.

31. RVP/6B 1/5/1, D.C. Nyeri to CNC Nairobi, November 28, 1929, Female Circumcision, <u>KNA</u>.

32. CP/PC 8/1/1, PC Kikuyu to Colonial Sec., Nairobi, October 12, 1929, Female Circumcision, <u>KNA</u>.

33. DC/KBU 7/3, LNC/KBU resolution, February 21, 1929, Female Circumcision, <u>KNA</u>.

34. One official openly acknowledged this by saying that he had received mission pressure to limit circumcision to a short period of time each year. Such action would make it easier for the mission to keep close watch over their girls so they would neither escape nor be taken away by parents to circumcised. DC/KBU 7/3, DC/KBU to PC Nyeri, June 4, 1929, Female Circumcision, <u>KNA</u>.

35. John Stauffacher to H.D. Campbell, Brooklyn, N.Y., November 19, 1929, Stauffacher File, <u>AIM</u>, New York.

36. Frederick Welbourn, <u>East African Rebels</u> (London: SCM Press, 1961), p. 142.

37. Robert Macpherson, <u>The Presbyterian Church in Kenya</u> (Nairobi: PCEA Press, 1970), p. 120.

Chapter 5

The _Aregi_ Exodus

Whether the AIM, together with the other missions, totally misjudged the depth of feeling with which the Kikuyu regarded circumcision, or whether they were prepared to sacrifice much of their membership, as one missionary said, "to purify and strengthen the church"(1) is open to question. Most AIM missionaries felt that their monopoly on education gave them sufficient leverage to force the mission's will upon the Kikuyu, for they reasoned that few Kikuyu would sacrifice their education and their future for a custom from the past. The missionaries felt there was little risk in continuing to confront the Kikuyu with the circumcision issue, but they were also in a position where any risk would have been worth taking if it bent the Kikuyu to the mission will. Others, perhaps in closer touch with their students and parishioners, were not so sure. They did not make their misgivings known then, but years later confided that they had feared the mission had pushed the Kikuyu too far.(2) Quite apart from this maze of mission intentions, risks and knowledge, two matters are quite clear: the Kikuyu left the AIM in massive numbers and this ushered in a period of even greater tension and conflict, and reinforced the divisions among _Athomi_.

Throughout the second half of 1929, amid the incessant mission attack and the tightening of governmental regulations against circumcision, some Kikuyu began to pull their children out of school or to stop attending church themselves as a limited protest. Isolated incidents of this sort were found at all the central AIM stations and even at a few out-stations. Many Kikuyu had decided that they could no longer tolerate the preaching and teaching against circumcision, and their boycott was aimed at demonstrating this to both the AIM and the government. Later in the year, when the government had adopted its non-involvement policy, the issue was limited to a battle of wills between the _Athomi_ and the mission. The AIM's insistence on a formal pledge of loyalty took place in two stages. During the first stage, only teachers, preachers and other agents were required to sign. Even this limited pledge increased the number of boycotts greatly.(3) By the end of 1929 it had become apparent to many Kikuyu that the mission was not going to back down, so that even before the AIM decided in March, 1930 to require a loyalty pledge from all adherents, the exodus from the mission had become a flood.(4)

Throughout the AIM area, the exodus was remarkably complete. Not a station escaped the drop in both church and school attendance; in most places only a handful of loyalists were left. Kijabe and Githumu, the only central stations that the AIM now held among the Kikuyu, were reduced to two or three loyal families each. Pupils from such families remember that

only a few others came to school with them and it was not
unusual for Sunday services to be reduced to a dozen or so in
attendance. Most out-stations were even harder hit; they
remained empty more often than not.(5) It would not be inaccurate wrong to estimate that the AIM in the early months of 1930
had only several dozen loyal supporters who broke the boycott
and continued to be active attenders of mission churches and
schools. In 1931, at a combined AIM and GMS meeting held at
Alliance High School for loyal adherents, only fourteen
attended. The paucity of AIM supporters is also reflected by
the sharp decline in church marriages at Githumu: three in
1930 compared to twelve in 1929.(6) An estimate of those who
left is harder to make as one often suspects mission figures
were inflated, but since the AIM claimed more than 500 Kikuyu
supporters in 1926 (7) and a steady increase after that, a
reasonable estimate would be that at least 500 Kikuyu left the
AIM and quite probably many more.

     All informants remember the closing days of 1929 and most
of 1930 as one of the most trying times of their life. The two
sides in the conflict were labeled Kirore, meaning thumbprint
for those who signed the loyalty pledge, and Aregi, for those
who refused, from Kurega, to refuse. Abuse and insults were
exchanged daily between Kirore and Aregi. Aregi used intimidation in some areas to make the boycott more successful. In
some instances schools which did not observe the boycott were
forced to close, and church services were brought to an end by
force. The normal flow of life was completely disrupted as the
circumcision issue took over central importance in all social
relationships.(8) Actions taken in this period forever
estranged members of the same family, age group, or out-
station.

     In the next stage of the conflict, Kirore in some areas
attempted to continue their church activities. They did this
in order to carry on normal religious life and to taunt the
Aregi. They rang the church bells long and hard before the
scheduled services and the most public area of a stream was
chosen for a baptismal service. Such services increasingly
became the scenes of heated discussion and name calling. One
missionary recalled a service at which catechumens were taken
from the church down to a river whose banks were lined with the
Aregi members of the same congregation. As the catechumens
were led into the water to repeat their vows, one of which was
a denunciation of female circumcision, shouts of disgust broke
out and jeers rebuked them.(9)

     With this attempt by the Kirore to resume religious activ-
ities at both the central missions and out-stations, the Aregi
sought to reclaim the use of buildings to which they felt they
had an equal right. In some cases, when the buildings had
been put up as a result of their money and labor, or if one of
their members had given the land upon which the buildings
stood, the Aregi felt that they should have the sole use of
them. The Kirore, in turn, felt themselves the sole custodians

of local church and school property because most of them were local Christian leaders. The issue was one of religious legitimacy. Many _Aregi_ wanted to continue attending religious services. Neither _Kirore_ hostility, nor the AIM stand on female circumcision, had driven all the _Aregi_ from Christianity. Most still considered themselves Christians, and Christian worship remained important to them. The conflicting claims over church property were evidence of the sincere desire among some _Aregi_ to use the buildings for continued worship, albeit on their own terms and under their own leadership.(10)

With each group seeking to use the church, one of the first arrangements in some places was a joint or shared service. This lasted a very short time as innumerable disagreements took place over the choice of hymns and prayers and what part each group would have in the service.(11) Another and more widespread arrangement was two separate services, back to back, with first one group and then the other officiating, but both groups attending each service. In most places this arrangement did not become permanent either for each group began to disrupt the other's service with uncomplimentary remarks. Johanna Mitaro, the _Kirore_ pastor at Kihumbuini, kept an account of such disruptions in his notebook.(12) Several dozen notations were made in 1930, ranging from an occasional comment during the course of a service to the outbreak of more vocal hostilities which prevented a service from continuing. This seems to have become increasingly the pattern in many places for, as these joint services became unworkable, they came to an end, and one or the other of the groups sought to secure the church solely for itself.

In some areas the worshipers would gather earlier than usual by pre-arrangement, and bar members of the other group from entering the church. The following Sunday, the group which had been previously barred, might succeed in locking out the others. Frequently, the group left out would hold an outdoor service considerably louder than usual to disrupt those inside. In several cases one group, having been locked out repeatedly on Sundays, took the furniture from the church during the week, hid it and then produced it on Sunday for its own outdoor service, leaving those inside holding their service standing or sitting on the floor.(13)

Repeated actions of this sort eventually led to violence. On a number of out-stations, it became a common sight to see _Kirore_ and _Aregi_ carrying clubs or _pangas_ (machetes which are all-purpose household and agricultural instruments). Mission correspondence of the time reveals that the AIM felt the _Kirore_ loyalists were being systematically attacked, and were in fear of their lives.(14) One _Kirore_ elder felt that it was only his last minute decision to take another route home that enabled him to escape being murdered. Upon reaching home he was told that _Aregi_ from his own congregation, having been deeply angered by his repeated denunciations, were lying in wait for

him.(15)   As the Kirore were definitely a minority in most
places, they probably did receive more than a little verbal
abuse and an occasional roughing up. Consequently the missionaries, feeling that the few who remained loyal to them were
being persecuted, intervened in a number of cases, sometimes
with the help of the government.   Mitaro records two instances
in his Notebook where alleged actions against Kirore brought
government fines and imprisonment for Aregi at Kihumbuini.(16)
By mid-1930, the government had fined or imprisoned several
dozen circumcisors, parents or guardians in circumcision cases
and many more Aregi and Kirore for assault.(17)

Kikuyu did not only do violence against one another, even
missionaries were the object of violent attacks during the
circumcision controversy.   One woman, Hulda Stumpf, a sixty-
four year old AIM missionary at Kijabe, was the object of great
hostility because of her arrogant and sharp attitude, which had
been resented even before the boycott.(18)   In February, 1930,
L.H. Downing, the superintendent of Kijabe and the AIM field
director for Kenya, intervened in an out-station dispute, forbidding Aregi from using a church building for their separate
services.   Shortly afterwards, Hulda Stumpf's body was found.
She had been forceably circumcised and suffocated.(19)

It was during this time of conflict and violence that
Muthirigu, a song of protest, first appeared. Most Kikuyu say
that Muthirigu originated at the Government Native Industrial
Training Depot at Kabete. This trade school in Kiambu had a
reputation for protest. An earlier protest song had originated
there. It is possible the the Muthirigu evolved from work songs
at the school.   Some Kikuyu even say that Muthirigu originated
with Ngai.   They say that Ngai sent Muthirigu through a dream
to a student at the Kabete school who immediately learned it
and taught it to his fellow students. Regardless of the exact
origin and evolution of the song, it soon spread throughout the
Kikuyu area, carried by students.   It was not long before the
song's reputation even went before it so that a student, upon
his return home, might find the community already assembled and
eager to learn Muthirigu.   In other cases, people who knew the
song were invited to come and teach it. Later, there were even
teams which toured the districts and taught all who had not yet
learned. In many cases, the teachers would assemble those who
wanted to learn on a piece of flat ground, usually the local
school's playing field and by demonstration and practice, teach
the entire community including any Athomi who were interested.
Repeated practice insured a familiarity with the words, movements and bell and drum accompaniment so that a certain rhythm
could be achieved and maintained.(20)

Muthirigu had no fixed or orthodox version; if there was a
Kabete original, it soon became covered over with layers of
local variations.   But certain themes, important to the Aregi,
and also to the non-Christian community, kept repeating themselves. The text of Muthirigu is, therefore, worth examination
as well as the use to which it was put.

The dominant and most explicit theme woven throughout
Muthirigu was abhorrence for Irigu or uncircumcised girls.
Irigu were held to be worthless, an unnatural social division.
They were labeled as sterile or otherwise unable to produce
children; they were immature and were said even to continue to
"wet their beds."

> Girls of Kihumbu-ini,
> you're good in front of the eyes
> But you are measured
> in pounds like meat
> Be beaten or even cut but Muthirigu
> continue.
>
> And to know that it is really bad,
> it (Kirigu) will urinate in the bed and say
> that the bed has become cold.
>
> You will marry but your mother is circumcised,
> therefore where will you build for it (Kirigu).
>
> Irigu are not costly;
> only seven dogs and you marry in the Church.
>
> We want Githomo (education or religion)
> but where can we be schooling because of
> the bad smell of Irigu.

A related idea in Muthirigu is that government officials have
used the sexual services of Irigu. The implication is that
Kikuyu morals are in the process of decay, for no true Kikuyu
woman would ever have permitted herself to be used in this way
by the Europeans. It was only the Irigu that would have
consented to this and their moral lapse has brought loss and
contamination on all Kikuyu.

> The D.C. -------------
> Is bribed with uncircumcised girls,
> So that the land may go.

Accumulated ill-feeling toward the missionaries and the
Kirore was vented in the words of Muthirigu too. The missionaries, left with only a remnant of their former membership and
little prospect for new members, were ridiculed now as having
reduced to baptizing monkeys in the forest. The Kirore church
elders were castigated for their hypocrisy; they married
circumcised wives and then agreed to the ban on circumcision,
thus preventing younger Athomi from access to circumcised
wives.

> The church you are clever
> The church you are clever

"You ate a peeled potato
now you give it unpeeled"
Rather let me be arrested but let

Muthirigu continue.

He who signs
Shall be crucified.

You elders of the Church.
You are fools.
Would you sell your lives for money?

Scattered throughout the stanzas is the idea that the coming of
foreigners and the resulting westernization were disasters for
the Kikuyu. Occasional references were made to the loss of
Kikuyu land to Europeans. But the lament on westernization ran
deeper. Westernization had brought a passing of the old ways.
A frequently used image is that of the matchbox and the fire
stick.

Kikuyu you are foolish
Kikuyu you are foolish
You left "Githegethi" for match boxes
Arara, arara, arara, for match boxes.

The convenience of the matchbox had terminated the passage from
generation to generation of the technique and skill of building
a fire with a fire stick. Ancient skills which made the Kikuyu
self sufficient had been sacrificed to convenience.
    The realization that the Kikuyu had lost part of their
past, was dwelt upon further; it was the subtlest and most
sober of the themes contained in Muthirigu. The traditional
rhythm of daily life, interrupted previously by land alienation
and labor conscription, had now further been upset. The ban on
circumcision had destroyed family, clan and age-group harmony
by setting Aregi against Kirore. In drawing attention to this
disharmony, the singing of Muthirigu directed the participants
to remember a past time when things were better.

If I were to say, Koinange and Waruhiu
    (colonial chiefs)
Would be buried alive.
Land, Land, This Land
Was left to us by Iregi (our ancestors).

But Muthirigu did not leave things with this backward
glance. Contained throughout the song was a determination to
persevere. Many stanzas contained a refrain which emphasized
this: "even if I go to jail or am beaten or cut, let Muthirigu
go on." Other stanzas spoke of the desire not to change, but
to spurn the mission and even Christianity.

> Kurinu I will never be a Christian
> Kurinu I will never be a Christian
> I became a Christian a long time ago
> and I experienced loss rather than gain.

Emphasis was also placed upon the fact that though the Kikuyu were foolish to have allowed foreign intrusion, knowledge of the loss made it a condition of the past.

Coupled with this was hope for the future, for the condition of the Kikuyu would change for the better upon Kenyatta's return from England. He would set things right as Harry Thuku had once done and in this he would have great support; even now money was being collected for his use.

> Ten thousand shillings
> Were given for Harry;
> Now the same amount
> Is Offered for John.

> When Johnstone shall return
> With the King of the Kikuyu
> Philip and Koinange
> Will don woman's robes.

Optimism was also expressed by the idea that the Christian god supported the community. The sanctions of the Divine would befall those who retaliated against the community: "If you want to kill me--do it, but you will be struck down by the sword of Jehovah." Certainly embodied here too was the idea that it was right and proper to challenge mission and government actions for they were unjust and thus in divine disfavor.

All Kikuyu, whether Christian or not, sang _Muthirigu_ except the _Kirore_. Many times the song was sung at _Kirore_ as a challenge and a denunciation of their loyalty to the AIM. The presence of a _Kirore_ anywhere might provoke those nearby to strike up the song, which was frequently used to disrupt church services.(21)

The CMS _Memorandum_ labeled the song as seditious. The government agreed and banned it. From mid-1931 people sang _Muthirigu_ at the risk of imprisonment. In fact, AIM correspondence of the time reveals that both the mission and the government expected _Muthirigu_ to develop into a general Kikuyu uprising. The missionaries at Kijabe felt particularly vulnerable in light of the Stumpf murder and a more recent one in which the husband of a local _Kirore_ woman killed her while she was undergoing medical treatment at Kijabe hospital. Many Kijabe missionaries felt that being surrounded on three sides by the Kikuyu reserve and isolated on the edge of the Rift Valley put their lives in danger. When the government began to distribute arms and ammunition, the missionaries eagerly stocked up, (22) and apparently saw no irony in the fact that they were arming themselves against their own converts.

Up to the time of Muthirigu, the departure of Kikuyu from the AIM was a boycott rather than an irreparable separation. By the end of 1930, however, many missionaries were aware that they had misjudged the Kikuyu reaction on female circumcision. About 95% of all AIM adherents had boycotted the mission now for more than a year. At the annual mission conference in March 1931, some missionaries expressed the opinion that something must be done, even if it meant reversing earlier decisions.(23) At the same time, the government was distressed over the sustained absence from school of so many Kikuyu children. Though many administrative officials were sympathetic with the mission stand on the circumcision issue, they did not feel that children should be barred from school for failing to comply with the mission ruling, especially since the government did not want to provide alternative education.(24) In this light, the government entered into negotiation with the AIM, the result of which was an agreement that both parties thought would attract the Kikuyu back to the mission and particularly to the schools. The AIM was still able to maintain that circumcision was sinful and unChristian, but people who did not share this opinion would still be allowed into school. Further, teachers would reserve instruction about initiation for baptismal classes held after school hours on a voluntary basis.(25)

Also included in this "gentlemen's agreement," as Kenyatta described it, was a relaxation of the loyalty oath. Now, only mission teachers had to denounce female circumcision publicly; others could now remain members of the church without taking the oath.(26)

Such concessions enabled the AIM to save face over a miscalculation and supposedly ensured the return of their flock without having to compromise any of the mission's principles concerning Kikuyu custom. Few Kikuyu responded to the concessions, however. To be sure, a few more were added to the handful of Kirore, but the numbers were not large.(27) The people who returned often were unofficial Kirore, people who were in sympathy with the mission but had not signed the oath and had remained away from the AIM because of intimidation. The missionaries knew that the return of these people did not signal a change of heart among the Aregi in general. They thought the Kikuyu were holding out for more concessions.

In their eagerness to patch over ruptured relations, the AIM began to compromise its very principles concerning Kikuyu customs and out-station autonomy. In a complete about-face, the AIM amended church law and accepted female circumcision so long as the "minor" operation was practiced.(28) As this was the essence of the Local Native Councils' unenforceable resolutions concerning initiation some years before, the mission had actually given its approval for the Kikuyu to practice their custom just as they had in the past. Following this, a mission committee was set the task of formulating ways in which female initiation could be "Christianized." Though many within mission

ranks disapproved of such a venture, the success of the Univer-
sities Mission to Central Africa (UMCA) in a similar project
with male initiation (29) was known to the AIM.(30)   Finally,
in an effort to woo those Aregi interested in local autonomy,
the mission gave recognition of the valuable work done by out-
school leaders and stated that economic stringency dictated
even less missionary supervision than before.   The implication
was that out-stations would be largely autonomous if Aregi
returned to the mission.(31) These concessions were no more
productive in bringing back the Aregi than were the earlier
ones.   The Aregi were not holding out for concessions, but had
decided that they did not ever want to return to the AIM.   The
boycott of the mission and the singing of Muthirigu had been
accompanied by humiliation, hardship, intimidation, fines,
imprisonment, beatings, and even death. The AIM was naive to
think that only the right combination of concessions was
needed to bring the Kikuyu back.   In addition, the concessions
offered were strictly mission creations; the loyal Kirore had
not been consulted, and at least some of them did not particularly want the Aregi back.(32) By late 1931, most of the Aregi
came to realize that no inducement made the prospect of going
back to the AIM look attractive.
     The boycott of 'the mission had given the Aregi a long
period of freedom from AIM control.   They realized that the
freedom and excitement of being "independent" could never be
duplicated under mission authority.   Having come to this con-
clusion, various Kikuyu church and school groups, previously
under AIM control, now set about to create a religious and
educational system permanently independent of the mission.

END NOTES

1. Virginia Blakeslee, _Beyond the Kikuyu Curtain_ (Chicago: Moody Press, 1956), p. 8.
2. _Oral Evidence:_ Emma Mathys, November 19, 1970.
3. _Oral Evidence:_ Rev. Johanna Gitau, May 22, 1971.
4. Stauffacher to Campbell, September 17, 1930, Stauffacher File, _AIM_, New York.
5. _Oral Evidence:_ Samuel Wanjihia, March 17, 1971; _Oral Evidence:_ Ezekiel Kamau and Ndegwa Metho, March 4, 1971.
6. _Johanna Mitaro's Notebook; AIM Marriage Register_, copies of both in my possession.
7. _Inland Africa_ (British Edition), March-April 1926, p. 14, _AIM_, London. This is a reasonable figure as approximately one-third that number had already been married in the church. _AIM Marriage Register_.
8. Hartsock to Campbell, March 2, 1920, Hartsock File, _AIM_, New York; one participant in such activities has characterized the whole period of time as "mouth war," _Oral Evidence:_ Johanna Nyenjeri, August 14, 1970, _NCCK-Limuru Archives_.
9. McKenrick Prayer Letter, November 6, 1930, McKenrick File. For an example of a baptismal vow, see _Hearing and Doing_ (American Edition), No. 15 (1910), p. 10, _AIM_, New York. Gicaru also comments on baptismal vows and gives another version in _Land of Sunshine, Scenes of Life in Kenya Before Mau Mau_ (London: Lawrence and Wishost, 1958), p. 77.
10. One informant said that since many dissidents continued to read their Bibles, they continued to be practicing Christians. _Oral Evidence:_ Samuel Wanjihia, April 23, 1971.
11. Statement of Josiah Kangithe Kitiange, December 20, 1929, _PCEA Archives_.
12. _Mitaro's Notebook_.
13. PC/CP 9/291, "Tenure of Churches and Schools in the Native Reserve." April 30, 1930, and DC/FH 1/1, "Unauthorized songs and dances 1930-50," Knapp (Kambui) to DC/FH, June 7, 1930, _KNA_.
14. McKendrick to Campbell, March 13, 1930, McKendrick File, _AIM_, New York.
15. _Oral Evidence:_ Samuel Wanjihia, April 22, 1971.
16. _Mitaro's Notebook_.
17. PC/CP 4/1/2, Kikuyu Provincial Annual Report, 1931, _KNA_.
18. _East African Standard_, February 15, 1930.
19. PC/CP 8/1 "Female Circumcision 1928-30," GMS Knapp to D.C. F.H. March 5, 1930; PC/CP 9/29/1 "Tenure of Church and School in Local Native Reserves," April 13, 1930, _KNA_; McKendrick to Campbell, March 30, 1930, _AIM_, New York.

20. L.S.B. Leakey, Kenya Contrasts and Problems (London: Hodder and Stoughton, 1936), p. 143; CSM Memorandum, p. 34 and Appendix V; Oral Evidence: Simon Mwangi, October 31, 1970, Mugo Mwangi, September 12, 1965, NCCK-Limuru Archives. Several versions of Muthirigu appear in Appendix III.

21. Some Kirore retaliated by composing their own songs about the Aregi, but they were as popular as Muthirigu; Oral Evidence: Reah Wambui, December 22, 1970.

22. Elsie Clark to Campbell, December 3, 1929, Clark File, AIM, New York.

23. Oral Evidence: Emma Mathys, November 19, 1970.

24. To their distress, as will be shown below, field officers had begun to receive requests from Kikuyu to establish government schools on the out-stations they were now boycotting.

25. PC/CP 8/2/1, Female Circumcision, 1930-032, District Commissioner, Kiambu to Provincial Commissioner, Nyeri, January 27, 1932, KNA.

26. Jomo Kenyatta, Facing Mt. Kenya, (London: 1938, Vintage, 1962), p. 126.

27. The special church services planned as festive occasions to welcome back the Aregi, became hollow affairs, attended mainly by Kirore and a few missionaries.

28. My reconstruction of the motivation leading up to this decision is based solely upon what I think probable. Though my research has uncovered nothing to the contrary, both missionary and African informants were unable to provide the reasoning behind the decision. The AIM received no money from the government so the threat of the government withdrawing its financing was not present. The document cited below states only that the decision was made and does not speak about the motivation. "Female Circumcision," Elwood L. Davis, Kenya Field Director to A.D. Campbell, General Secretary, September 4, 1931, AIM, New York.

29. For a description and interpretation of this UMCA project, see T.O. Ranger, "Missionary Adaptation of African Religious Institutions," in T.O. Ranger and I.N. Kimanbo (eds.), The Historical Study of African Religion (Berkeley: UCLA Press, 1972), pp. 221-251.

30. Female Circumcision, Davis to Campbell, September 4, 1931, AIM, New York. This letter contains, among other things, a summary of the minutes of the first meeting of an AIM committee looking into the "christianizing" of female initiation. Though the tone of these minutes reflect a sincere effort to consider the matter, no further documents have come to light on the topic and since the desired result did not take place, the investigation was apparently dropped.

98

31. Inland Africa (British Edition), September-October, 1931, pp. 58-59, AIM, London.

32. Oral Evidence: Samuel Wanjihia, April 23, 1971; Blakeslee also expressed this opinion, saying that the Aregi exit purified the church and thereby she implied that at least some considered this good riddance. Beyond the Kikuyu Curtain, p. 8.

Chapter 6

Independent Churches and Schools

Once _Aregi_ made the decision to leave the AIM permanently, they began arrangements for independent churches and schools of their own. The initial and most pressing need was a place to meet.

In the last few months of 1930 most _Aregi_ had left their out-stations under increasing pressure from _Kirore_ and government chiefs. The move did not come easily, and many were bitter about giving up the churches and schools which they had built. _Aregi_ at Kihumbuini wanted to take with them the corrugated iron sheets from the church roof when they left; they were only prevented from doing so by the local chief and his armed retainers. At a GMS out-station of Kambui, the _Aregi_ were so angry at having to leave the _Kirore_, what they considered their property, that they burned down the church and school building. In similar cases, the _Kirore_ retaliated by disrupting independents' meetings and destroying their buildings.(1)

By 1931, many groups of _Aregi_ were meeting regularly each Sunday. The worship service of hymn singing and prayer followed by a discussion of their problems was held in one of their homes, out-of-doors or in a temporary structure made of banana leaves. One immediate problem was permission from the government to meet each week. On Saturday a representative from each of these independent groups had to request permission from the D.C. at Fort Hall to hold the following Sunday's meeting. It was always granted, but the inconvenience of making a fifty-mile journey or more on foot was to test the independents' determination to continue meeting together.(2)

Then there was the lack of ordained clergy. The AIM had not ordained any Kikuyu clergy before the _Aregi_ severed their connection with the mission. Among the GMS, there were two Kikuyu pastors, but both were _Kirore_. The subsequent discussion reveals that the independents felt that their clergy needed to be trained and ordained by an agency with appropriate credentials for such activity. They were not prepared to simply ordain their own clergy (at least not in the first instance) and risk the criticism that by so doing, their clergy were not legitimate.

Trained clergy were needed then to give legitimacy to the church but also to administer the sacraments. At the independent church at Gakarara the sacrament of baptism was their immediate concern and they tried to persuade the Githumu missionaries to baptize several of its members. Prior to the circumcision crisis, some Gakarara members had been receiving baptismal instruction at Githumu but had left the AIM at the point of being baptized. The missionaries at Githumu refused to baptize any of these people now that they were independents.

The Gakarara church turned next to Johana Mitaro, the GMS pastor at Kihumbuini. Though a <u>Kirore</u>, he agreed to baptize these independents since they had already received three years of AIM instruction. Throughout the rest of 1930, Mitaro also baptized a number of other independents at Gakarara Church. All of them were from the surrounding area and had completed their instruction at Githumu prior to the circumcision crisis. The arrangement did not last for more than a few months, however. Many Gakarara independents resented Mitaro as a <u>Kirore</u> and felt that he should have no influence at Gakarara. So great was their resentment toward <u>Kirore</u> and all associated with them, that Mitaro's services as a baptizer were terminated in early 1931 and James Kairu, who originally made the arrangement with Mitaro, was temporarily dismissed from church membership at Gakarara.(3)

For the next two years the independents at Gakarara, together with five other neighboring groups, met many times to discuss their need for an organized church with ordained clergy; the two elements could not be separated. Daudi Maina Kiragu, the lay evangelist at Gakarara, stressed the importance of church and clergy for the independents.

> All these years of hardship taught us that we should have a religious body for we reckoned that nothing could run smoothly without offering praise and supplication to God. Therefore, there should be churches where we could worship our Creator for we are His children and we should always be praising Him.

> We thought of where our people could get training to become ministers and be ordained to serve the Kikuyu in a way that showed them the way to God and His son Jesus Christ.(4)

So great was the independents' desire for ordained clergy, that they even considered affiliating with a mission society. At Gakarara in June 1933, seventeen leaders from independent groups throughout southern Fort Hall District delegated Daudi Maina Kiragu to write to the Church Missionary Society (CMS) Bishop. He was to ask that Stephano Wachira, Elija Kibacia and he be accepted for theological training at the CMS Divinity School at Limuru. The CMS was also asked to send pastors to minister to the independents while the three men were being trained.(5)

In response, the Bishop invited the independents to the Annual CMS Conference. Daudi Maina Kiragu, Justus Kangethe (the teacher at Gakarara) and several other representatives went to negotiate for theological training. They said that independents were prepared to give "ecclesiastical allegiance" to the CMS in return for the training of their initial independent pastors. When pressed by the missionaries as to whether this meant the independents wanted to join the Church of England or establish their own, Kiragu replied that as a CMS trained pastor he would take instructions from the Bishop on Biblical teaching but not on church government. Kiragu stated further that he and the other two men would consider themselves pastors for the independents and not for the CMS. Their affil- iation with the CMS would only be temporary--until the indepen- dents had their first ordained clergy. The CMS refused to accept the independent theological candidates under these con- ditions. Kiragu, Kang'ethe and the other representatives were dismissed with the advice that it was wrong for the Kikuyu to have churches independent from mission societies.(6)

Another alternative for solving the problem of ordained clergy came through the visit of Daniel William Alexander, Archbishop of the African Orthodox Church of South Africa. Alexander met two Kikuyu KCA members, living in Mombasa as he passed through that city on his return from Uganda to South Africa.(7) These men, James Beauttah and Parmenas Githendu Mukeri, recommended Alexander to the independents. The independents at Gakarara and the group nearby at Gituamba, wrote to Alexander for help in 1934 after the CMS had refused to train their pastors.(8) In his reply, Alexander stated that in 1921 in New York City he had been properly ordained by George Alexander McGuire. Alexander gave a detailed account of how McGuire, and therefore he himself, were in direct apostolic succession to the apostle Peter, the first Bishop of Rome, in the first century A.D. Alexander also related that he was consecrated Archbishop of the African Orthodox Church of South Africa in 1927, at the Church of St. Michael's and All Angels in Boston, Massachusetts. His full title was then:

> Daniel William Alexander; by Divine Providence,
> Doctor of Divinity, Archbishop in the one Holy
> Catholic and Apostalic Church of the Orthodox
> Faith; Chevalier Prelate, Commander of the
> Crown of Thomas, Doctor of Christianity,
> Primate of the Province of South and Central
> Africa and Rhodesia.(9)

The independents were impressed with Alexander's creden- tials. Here was a man who could train their pastors and give prestige to their church. When he agreed to come to Kenya, the independents quickly raised 1000 shillings (approx. $175.00) for his fare.

The Archbishop arrived in Mombasa on November 8, 1935 and he was met by a group of independents. He was honored with a reception lasting several days; during this time he conducted a worship service and baptized Kimani wa Kibero from Kiambu. The whole group took the train to Nairobi and then traveled to Fort Hall District.(10) The independents from the GMS out-station at Kihumbuini had made arrangements for Alexander to stay nearby at Gituamba, their new meeting place. He established

himself in the stone house which was built for him there and he
set about to organize his new seminary.(11)

Alexander began to teach five theological students on
November 15, 1935. During the next six months three more came
and finally in March, 1937 the last was added. All were
young ex-mission Athomi; most had been school teachers and were
literate in Kikuyu. Alexander insisted that each also be
married, according to general Christian practice.

Some disagreement arose over the length of the course.
Initially, Alexander proposed a period of preparation that
would take up to fourteen years. But when told very directly
by the independents that their candidates must be ordained in
less than two years, the Archbishop accepted the decision.

After this, matters moved along quickly and smoothly.
Alexander had to teach entirely by interpreter since he knew
very little Kikuyu. But apparently this was not a great problem and instruction was facilitated by the fact that most of
the instructional materials were already in Kikuyu. Alexander
drew heavily from the Anglican Prayer Book and from Catholic
materials he borrowed from the nearby Catholic mission at
Gatanga.(12) The Archbishop also used The Divine Liturgy, the
official Order-of-Service in the African Orthodox Church. It
was a blend of the Catholic and Anglican ritual originally
composed in New York in September, 1921. Alexander had it
reprinted in Nairobi in 1936 in order that it be available to
his soon-to-be ordained students.(13)

On Sundays, the seminary students preached and conducted
worship services among the various groups of independents in
Fort Hall District. Alexander attended these services too, and
his critiques became the subject of instruction during the
following week at the seminary. At times, Alexander himself
conducted services in the district to give practical examples
to his students and also to provide opportunities for them to
assist him under his direct supervision. Many independents
were baptized by Alexander at these services. He carefully
examined them and for those in need of preparatory instruction,
he established his own catechumen class at Gituamba. One
independent whom he baptized described him as having a
"spell-binding, wise. . . dynamic personality. . . [and a]
larger following in the country than any local preacher."(14)
Alexander also conducted Christian marriages throughout his
stay at Gituamba.(15)

Alexander ordained three students on June 27, 1937,
after more than eighteen months instruction: Daudi Maina
Kiragu, Harrison Gacokia and Philip Kiande. All the others had
dropped out before finishing the course except Arthur Gatungu,
who was dismissed by the independent leaders of the Gakarara/
Gituamba area and by his fellow seminary students.(16)

> [He had been] found guilty of doing the
> following (which are prohibited of Law No. 8 of
> the Church).

1. Being imprisoned because of a serious misdoing.
2. Being drunk and interested in other worldly pleasures.
3. Being unpopular with other independents.

Independents throughout Kikuyuland came to the ordination together with others from greater distances such as Meru, the Rift Valley and even Mombasa. On the previous day and through-out the night, the candidates had been secluded in prayer and fasting. According to Ndungu's account, "Their eyes were shielded so that they could not be distracted and the sign of the cross was made on their heads by the cutting of their hair." The ordination itself was an elaborate ceremony con-ducted by Archbishop Alexander. One extensive part was devoted to the candidates washing each other's feet, an act taken from the New Testament (17) and now used to symbolize service to each other and to the people of the independent church.(18) At the very end of the ceremony, Alexander placed his hands on the head of each candidate and proclaimed him an officially ordained priest of the African Orthodox Church.

During the last months prior to the ordination service, a split had developed between Alexander and the independent leaders. They accused him of pocketing the money which he collected for baptisms instead of leaving it with the local congregation as the independents had wanted. They also did not approve of his friendship with Arthur Gatungu. Alexander, on his own authority, had asked Gatungu to join the seminary in March, 1936, more than six months after the other students had begun their training. The independents felt that Gatungu was of questionable moral character, and they finally expelled him because of his continued misdeeds. Nor could the independent leaders accept Alexander's future plans for their church. Alexander wanted a large church to be built at Gituamba and named after him, and he expected that all priests which he ordained would come under his authority. This was totally unacceptable to the independents and they told him to finish the seminary course quickly, ordain the men, and then leave. This Alexander did, staying a few days with Gatungu in Kiambu, during which time he ordained him, and then left Kenya for his home in South Africa on July 6, 1937. A year later, ill-will toward Alexander had subsided; in the official account of both their church and their school system, the independents expressed "a deep debt of gratitude" toward Alexander and regarded him as their "spiritual father."(19)

In September 1937, the independent religious leaders met at Ngangariithi in Nyeri district to discuss church organiza-tion. Arthur Gatungu of Kiambu and Philip Kiande of Nyeri both wanted to follow Archbishop Alexander's example and call their organization the African Orthodox Church (AOC). The Fort Hall independents, under the leadership of Daudi Maina Kiragu and Harrison Cacokia, suggested the African Independent Pentecostal

Church (AIPC) as the title instead. They were against any link
with Alexander, even if only in name, and they wanted to stress
this independence and their legitimacy as a church with the
word pentecost.   According to Kiragu, just as the Holy Spirit
had descended upon the early Christian Church after Christ's
ascension,   so now the Holy Spirit had descended upon the
Kikuyu independent church.   Since neither group would compromise, each went its own way and two independent church bodies
developed.(20)

Soon the cooperation between Gatungu and Kiande disintegrated too.   Though both continued to use the African Orthodox
Church as their name, Kiande's AOC organization of both
churches and schools at Nyeri later split over leadership
rivalry with Gatungu.(21) Gatungu established his AOC headquarters at Waithaka in Kiambu, and he soon developed a network
of schools under the title of the Kikuyu Karing'a Education
Association.   Gatungu continued to develop his church and
school system throughout the 1930s, and at the outbreak of the
Mau Mau rebellion in 1952, a network stretched west into the
Rift Valley and Nyanza Provinces and south to Arusha,
Tanganyika.(22)

Kiragu and Gacokia also set about organizing their
independent churches: Kiragu in Fort Hall among the Kikuyu
who had separated from the AIM and Gacokia in Northern Kiambu
among independents who were former GMS adherents.   Each toured
his respective area, rallying the independents and consecrating
their banana leaf structures as official churches of the
AIPC.(23) From this heartland, the AIPC spread throughout
Kikuyuland, the Rift Valley, Embu and Meru. By his own count,
Kiragu was able to record the names of 111 AIPC Congregations.(24)

Throughout the 1930s and 1940s, Kiragu was the unelected,
though widely recognized, leader of the AIPC. Largely through
his efforts, the independents now had an ordained clergy.   He
helped initially to bring many local independent groups in Fort
Hall and Kiambu under AIPC auspices, and later his missionary
tours throughout Kikuyuland and beyond expanded the church even
more.   Throughout this time he baptized hundreds of people and
gave instruction at Gakarara to men he asked to become AIPC
clergymen.   By mid-1948, he had ordained sixteen more priests
to serve the expanding church.(25)

Kiragu wrote to the colonial government frequently on
behalf of the AIPC.   Initially the letters concerned Kirore
damage to independent churches.   The government was reluctant
even to recognize the independents, but in 1942 they grudgingly told Kiragu that so long as independents' churches were
located on their own land, "they should not be bothered by
anyone."(26)   Later, Kiragu repeatedly asked that AIPC priests
be licensed by the government like other clergy so that they
could legally marry people.   Other letters concerned requests
for township plots to build churches in Nairobi and Mombasa

(27) and the need for burial grounds at Mombasa, Nakuru, Nanyuki and Rumuruti.(28)

The AIPC organization was loosely structured even with Kiragu's de facto leadership. It was basically a collection of autonomous congregations, each with its own committee of elders. They looked after the church building and scheduled and led the services. Kiragu's ordained clergy had little part in the life of most congregations; there were simply too few priests. At first such rituals as holy communion, baptism and marriage only took place in Fort Hall district at Kiragu's Gakarara Church. Later, when other clergy had been ordained, such special services became more widespread.(29)

On Sunday morning and sometimes during the week, each congregation would meet together for a simple worship service. Much of the ritual was the same as it had been before under the AIM or GMS. Hymn singing, praying, Bible reading and preaching constituted the normal order of these services. Occasionally, the more formal liturgy of the Anglican Church was used, particularly when an AIPC priest took the service. By the 1940s some independents had their own copies of the Anglican Prayer Book, and the Anglican service began to be used more frequently. In 1954 when the Anglican Church Missionary Society took control of the independent church at Giachuki, following the church's closure by the government at the out-break of the Mau Mau rebellion, the congregation had long used the Anglican liturgy so that little needed to be changed.

Public confession, an important part in the AIM and GMS services, was omitted by the independents. The missionaries had used such occasions to accuse and humiliate, and the independents now felt that it had no part in a church service. The baptismal ritual was modified too. Sprinkling the catechumens was substituted for the earlier AIM practice of total immersion. Sprinkling was the Anglican practice and was also the procedure which Alexander used. Some independents felt that the change came to pacify catechumens' fear of the river and to stop rumors among non-Christians that one was held under water all night when baptised.

Most independents were serious in their Christian beliefs. In the AIPC's Constitution, the following was set out:

> The church has laid down its own method of
> procedure in observing and preserving the
> principles of Christianity and the followers
> and members of this Church shall regard the
> BIBLE (both the Old and the New Testaments) as
> the only material to study the ways of God and
> His Son Jesus Christ.(30)

The rituals learned at the mission continued to be prac-ticed. Baptism still marked full church membership, though the period of instruction was reduced from three years to several months. Baptism was only one of seven sacraments which the

independents observed. The others were: confirmation, holy
communion, confession, annoinment, ordination and holy matri-
mony. For new members who had been married according to Kikuyu
custom, a special church service was held in which their
marriage was renewed by Christian ritual.(31)
     The AIPC also thought that it had struck the right balance
between Kikuyu customs and Christianity. The constitution
stated:

> This Church does not wish to disturb old
> customs of Kikuyus such as circumcision of
> women but will leave it entirely to every
> individual concerned to do in the matter [sic]
> as he or she may think fit.(32)

Polygamy was not a bar to church membership but rather was an
individual decision. Other customs were revived, too, such as
the exchange of beer between the groups involved in marriage
negotiations. The AIM and GMS had said that beer drinking was
sinful and had demanded that sugar be substituted for this
exchange.
     Independents did not consider the revival of these customs
a departure from Christian practice as did the Kirore, the
missionaries and most other Europeans.(33) Rather, by stripping
mission Christianity of its ethnocentric and repressive nature,
the independents felt they had returned Christianity to its
rightful state.
     The independents were intensely interested in education
free from mission control. Education had been sporadic or had
ceased altogether for most independents during the turmoil of
the circumcision crisis and the period of reorganization that
followed. But the link between Christianity and education was
very strong, and as the independents began to meet together and
build their "prayer houses," the use of these buildings as
schools followed quite naturally.
     The government initially directed that all the "bush
schools" close, at least in some areas, because they did not
want to encourage an independent educational system. Most
independents also found that their temporary schools were too
small to handle the large numbers of pupils coming to them. By
late 1931 many independent groups lost their schools and were
secretly having to conduct school lessons out of doors.
     At the ex-AIM out-station at Gakarara, independent educa-
tion had developed differently. When Gakarara separated from
Githumu in 1926, it successfully negotiated government assistance. From 1927-29, two teachers paid for by the education
department kept the school open. To the government, this was a
temporary measure until the out-station controversy could be
resolved and Gakarara reunited with the AIM.(34) However,
when the circumcision crisis prevented all reconciliation, the
government withdrew the assistance, since it did not want to
support the beginning of a permanent independent school system.

But the school at Gakarara continued on its own. A twelve-
member committee composed of independent church members and led
by Daudi Maina Kiragu was formed to direct school financing and
staffing. The government permitted the school to continue,
hoping that it would die "a natural death."(35) By late 1930
when Gakarara showed no sign of dying, the government gave its
official sanction for the school to continue operation, hoping
now that it would provide sufficient educational facilities to
the independents in the District.(36)

At the beginning of 1932, when Justus Kang'ethe came as
headmaster, Gakarara had grown a great deal. Students were
coming from the secret "banana leaf" schools in the vicinity,
from farther away in the district and even from Nyeri.
Kang'ethe hastily built more classrooms and began to run both
morning and afternoon shifts to accommodate everyone. It was
not long before there were 200 students at the school and more
coming all the time. Kang'ethe, his teachers and the school
committee struggled on, but the numbers of students were an
increasing problem.(37)

In an effort to reduce the school to a more manageable
size, Kang'ethe and the school committee began to encourage
other independents to begin their own schools, using Gakarara
as the model. After a couple of terms at Gakarara, mature
students were sent back to their home areas with ideas of
starting a school of their own. Kang'ethe also brought pupils'
parents to Gakarara to discuss with them the details of establishing their own school.(38)

The origins of the Kikuyu Independent Schools Association
(KISA) lay in the action at Gakarara to organize and expand the
number of Kikuyu independent schools. As the meetings there
and at the nearby independent center at Gituamba continued, the
idea developed to form an educational association for all
Kikuyu independents. Finally in 1934 at Mahiga in Nyeri District, representatives from independent groups throughout
Kikuyuland and Embu elected four KISA officers and a central
committee of fourteen. In time KISA was to provide centralized
leadership and guidance for independents and was to represent
them to the government when educational problems arose. But
for the time being, the formation of KISA had two immediate
effects: the government relaxed its ban on independent schools
and local independent groups were given the impetus to build
and manage their own schools.(39)

The formation of KISA together with the lifting of the
government ban brought independent school activity out into the
open and accelerated it after 1934. At first in the Gakarara/
Gituamba area and then throughout the Fort Hall District and
Northern Kiambu, local groups began to make plans for building
and managing their own schools. The first schools were quite
modest structures. They usually consisted of a single building
with two or three adjoining rooms. The main idea was to provide immediate shelter for the pupils. Most of these early
schools were self-help projects; all pupils and their parents

contributed materials and labor. As the buildings were made from local materials--thatched roofs, mud and wattle walls and dung floors--professional builders were not required, and the schools were erected quickly, usually on the site where the prayer house had stood.

Occasionally, two neighboring groups decided to build a joint school. This was the case for Kamunyaka and Thare, both ex-AIM out-stations. Each had tried to maintain a small secret school for several years. In 1933 Paul Githagoge, the independent leader at Kamunyaka, suggested that a bigger and better school might be available to both groups if they shared the cost and built it together. Each group at first wanted the school located in its own area, but both compromised in 1934 and built on a site between the two at Gatieguru.(40)

Throughout the late 1930s and 1940s a great deal of building activity took place as independent groups enlarged their schools. Kiangari, Mariira, Gakarara, Gituamba and many others begun to replace their mud and wattle buildings with permanent stone structures.

One of the most ambitious independent school building projects took place at Kaiiri, in northern Kiambu. When the independents separated from the GSM out-station at Kanjeria in 1930, they built a one room school nearby at Kaiiri. As the number of pupils increased over the next decade, several more mud classrooms were built. By the early 1940s the parents, teachers and pupils planned to upgrade the school with a stone building. Several abortive attempts were made before 1945 when the school committee finally hired Eli Ngugi, a returned war veteran and former pupil at Kaiiri, as teacher, and treasurer, and put him in charge of the organization for building the new school. Several interviews with Ngugi and others on the school committee, and close scrutiny of his account books reveal an amazingly complex and successful project, masterfully coordinated by him and fully participated in by a community enthusiastic to have its own showpiece school.(41)

The first matter of business was financing the construction project. Some building materials had been bought in 1942 during an earlier attempt to start construction, but the money collected then had not been enough and the school committee was 400 shillings ($60.00) in debt. Ngugi's plan was to collect enough money to cancel this debt--owed to a member of the school committee who had loaned the balance to pay for the materials--and begin construction. Throughout 1946, he collected subscriptions to the building fund or obtained pledges for future payment from everyone who was sending children to Kaiiri or who hoped to in the future. Husbands and wives made individual contributions as did adult sons and daughters who were still living at home. Some people at first refused to make pledges, but then the school committee threatened to confiscate property, and in some places forcibly seized livestock. By the end of 1946, Ngugi had subscriptions or promises of future payment from 348 people. The total amount pledged was 24,059.38 shillings ($3500.00). The debt was paid and construction of the school began in February, 1947.

Personal contributions, though significant, were not sufficient to pay for the new school. The school committee organized fund-raising activities including sports contests and bazaars. Sports days were occasionally used by independents throughout Kikuyuland (42) to raise money, but Kaiiri refined the technique. The first was held shortly after the building began. Several hundred people from the surrounding area paid admission to see Kaiiri athletes compete in track and field events. The school committee and Eli Ngugi realized that such events had great revenue potential and planning immediately began for the future. Over the next two years four other sports days were held at Kaiiri and a total of 3230.75 shillings (approximately $500.00) was raised. A full-time secretary was hired to develop and coordinate the various activities. The athletic competition was broadened to include several schools as well as individual contestants. Sometimes a soccer match between rival schools or communities was included in the program. Cooked food, garden produce, and local handicrafts were sold throughout the day. At the end of the day, prizes were given to the winners, and the school committee gave a progress report and conducted a tour of the school. Occasionally government officials or other invited guests spoke to the crowd. The official guest speakers at one Kaiiri sports day in 1949 were Jomo Kenyatta, then the President of the Kenya African Union and Eliud Mathu, the first African member of the Legislative Council. The promise of hearing these nationalists and discussing political issues with them drew the largest sports day attendance at Kaiiri.

Each month the school committee held a bazaar on the school grounds to sell all the items that had been donated to the building fund. Garden produce, livestock, handmade clothing, charcoal, firewood and building materials were sold to the surrounding community. Goods purchased in Nairobi at wholesale prices were also brought to Kaiiri to be sold. These sales provided a service to the area because such items as used clothing and other dry goods were not always locally available. There would normally have been little market for garden produce, charcoal and firewood since they usually duplicated what was available at home. The people who continued to purchase these items were obviously making a further contribution to the school.

In addition, each year local circumcision candidates paid a fee that went to the building fund. Tickets were sold for an annual Christmas tea party. Kaiiri students grew maize on the school plot to sell. The students also stripped off and sold the bark on a neighboring stand of wattle trees that had been given to the school. One recently formed age-set, Riika ria kununge ya Kaiiri, made their own donation each year.

Kaiiri Independent Church provided revenue to the school. Each Sunday's offering was turned over to the school treasurer. The customary contribution made to the church for baptisms and weddings went to the building fund as did a new donation for receiving holy communion.

Throughout all of these money-raising ventures, the women at Kaiiri provided valuable assistance. Nearly 100 of the 248 people who made individual contributions were women, both single and married. In 1947, ten women, most of them married to church or school elders, formed an association. They encouraged families to send their girls to school and to contribute to the building fund. The association helped with the monthly bazaars, the Christmas tea parties and the sports days. A year later a non-Christian woman's association was also formed to help with the same activities and the two groups jointly held two womens' sports days in 1949.

On January 26, 1950, the new Kaiiri Independent School was officially opened. Actually, parts of the school had been used for some time because as soon as a classroom or an office had been finished, it was put to use. Delegations came from many independent communities in Fort Hall and Kiambu, some bringing gifts (43) for the school. Representatives were also present from the government and the education department. A number of speeches were made and the school committee made its report in which it stated that the money raised had been sufficient to pay all debts (44) and to leave a balance in the treasury. Part of the balance had already been spent on timber and carpentry tools for the school's industrial arts program. The committee hoped that with the money left and with what could be raised in the near future, a dormitory could be built to accommodate the increasing number of students coming to Kaiiri from some distance.(45) The celebration ended with a tea party and a tour of the school.

KISA played little part in the actual building of independent schools, though there was some central funding. Financing and school management were in the hands of autonomous school committees like Kaiiri. KISA did help with the two problems experienced by all independent schools once they began to operate: gaining government approval and finding teachers.

The Kenya government had tried to ignore the independent movement in the hope that it would disappear. When both the churches and schools grew and prospered, the government attempted to control them. The education department wanted the schools to follow the government syllabus, particularly for English language instruction, which was not to begin until after the fourth year. The independents were very interested in English instruction, which the AIM had only grudgingly given on occasion at Githumu. Several independent schools secretly began teaching English in the second year. Some even substituted it for Swahili, the language required by the government syllabus. The Kikuyu felt Swahili to be a language of servitude because of its use, often in a bastard form, by the white

settlers.(46)   Even though the school log was often falsified
to cover up the teaching of English and a sharp watch was kept
in case a school inspector made a surprise visit, the government did find out and took action: all educational grants to
such schools were forbidden and the pupils were not permitted
to take the standard primary school leaving examinations.(47)

KISA appealed to the government to halt this discrimina-
tion and on August 11, 1936, a meeting was held at which representatives from the government, the education department and
the KISA executive committee were present.(48) The KISA officials impressed upon the government that "a good opportunity"
had arisen for the independents "to help" the government with
Kikuyu education. But KISA must be allowed to help in its own
way, without governmental controls.(49)   A compromise was
reached in which the government allowed English to be taught in
the third year with Swahili an optional subject.   KISA agreed
to cooperate with the education department, to follow the
government syllabus,(50) and to accept a "special inspector
with the sole function of inspecting and coordinating the work
of these [independent] schools."(51)

The 1936 meeting marked the beginning of a more sympathetic relationship between KISA and the education department.
KISA had communicated the deep Kikuyu desire for an independent
educational system, and the education department felt that this
should not be discouraged.   By 1940 a number of governmental
grants had been given to independent schools, and the director
of education said, ". . . Government has come around to the
view that much good education is being accomplished in these
independent schools and much cooperation has taken place."(52)

The favorable inspection reports that began to circulate
in the education department reinforced the sympathetic
relationship.   The 1936 agreement provided for an inspector to
visit each independent school annually beginning in 1938.   He
was surprised at the rapport that he had with the independents
and with the quality of education that he found in the
schools.(53) School committees were "noticeably keen and ready
to cooperate." Many independent schools had "reached a very
fair standard of efficiency" and teachers were "trying hard"
and were "very enthusiastic" about their work.(54) This was in
contrast to the AIM schools, which the government felt were
just getting with the least possible effort.(55)   The
inspector was also very impressed with independents' school
buildings.   He made this statement about Giachuki in 1941:
"This community has recently erected what is undoubtedly the
best school building in any Reserve in the whole of Central
Province."(56)

But even then independent school students found it difficult to gain admission for more advanced work in the government
school system.   Eli Ngugi, the treasurer at Kaiiri, said the
only way he could gain admittance to Kagumo, the government
advanced school at Nyeri, was to have a sympathetic headmaster
at a mission school claim that he had attended there rather

than at Kaiiri. Another informant said that only with great difficulty was he accepted at the government teacher training school at Kabete. While there he was discriminated against, as were other independents, by both staff and mission students, even though they did very well in their studies.(57) Corfield quite obviously ignored the favorable inspection reports and fed only on the negative opinion in order to have so boldly written, "From the purely education viewpoint, the standards in all independent schools were deplorable. . . ." (58)

KISA established a Fort Hall District Committee to improve cooperation between independents and the government. The Fort Hall executive secretary, the only full-time committee member, worked closely with the government school inspector and generally tried to help with school problems. In 1938 his investigation helped to quash the rumor circulating among many independents, that the government was going to fail all KISA students taking exams that year. The Fort Hall Executive Secretary also helped to arbitrate local independent disputes such as the case of Kihumbuini where the president of the school committee was accused of using school funds for his own purpose.(59) When E.M. Wambico, the Fort Hall Executive Secretary, also became the General Secretary, he had direct charge of the KISA annual general meeting and the quarterly teachers conferences. He was also supposed to help with the awarding of scholarships, the establishment of medical dispensaries at various independent centers, and the coordination of monthly hygiene meetings for Kikuyu mothers.(60) Unfortunately, few of these duties were ever executed, because Wambico and his successors spent most of their time in trying to solve KISA's biggest problem; the recruitment of teachers.(61)

By the late 1930s most KISA schools in Fort Hall District had 200 to 300 students, and the demand for qualified teachers was high.(62) Such teachers were not to be found among the former AIM and GMS adherents because these missions had had no teacher training program. Wambico regularly went to Nyeri and Kiambu to look for teachers among former CMS and CSM adherents.(63) Gakarara was able to staff its school almost completely with teachers who had gone to CSM Thogoto, and the Kaiiri school committee financed a number of trips to Nairobi in search of similar teachers.(64)

To offset the shortage, KISA first contracted with CMS to have independent teachers trained at Kahuhia--a scheme that proved too expensive--and later planned to enlarge Githunguri independent school into a teacher training college. Peter Mbiyu Koinange, recently returned from study in Britain and the United States, became Githunguri's first principal. In his book *The People of Kenya Speak for Themselves*, he described the enthusiasm and dedication with which the Kikuyu built Githunguri.(65) It was a joint venture between KISA and the Kikuyu Karing'a Education Association (KKEA), the small Kiambu-based independent group led by Arthur Gatungu.(66) Large amounts of money were raised throughout Kikuyuland and

particularly at Githunguri.(67) The school, including primary
and secondary sections, was co-educational and multi-ethnic.
On January 7, 1939, the first class of future teachers began
its two-year course but the college never became the reservoir
of teachers for independent schools it was intended to be. The
teacher trainers were not qualified, and Koinange, hoping to
offer a non-western educational experience for his students did
not use the governmental syllabus. Consequently, the government refused to certify those who graduated as licensed
teachers.   Independent schools wanted nothing less than fully
qualified teachers, and throughout the 1940s they continued to
search for and to employ mission-trained teachers.(68)
     From the very beginning of the movement, independent
churches and schools were inextricably linked.   The same
building was often used for both institutions;   week-day
teachers were Sunday preachers, and church and school leadership involved many of the same people. Perhaps Daudi Maina
Kiragu is the best example here, for he was active in the
origins of both KISA and the Kikuyu Independent Pentecostal
Church.   The Kikuyu had never considered one without the other;
as one parent stated, ". . . what is the use of my son learning
to read and write if he cannot be baptized?"(69)
     The selection of teachers also points up the close asso-
ciation between independent church and school.   Kiragu
believed that ". . . independent schools were to be directed by
people who were religiously commendable."(70) It was partly
Arthur Gatungu's poor moral reputation as a teacher at
Gituamba that led to his dismissal at Alexander's seminary.(71) Church and school committees met together to discuss
the Christian influence of teachers.   The church elders often
insisted on being able to veto all candidates they felt morally
undesirable.(72)
     The financing of schools through church contributions was
not limited to Kaiiri but was a widespread practice. Not only
were Sunday church collections turned over to the school treasurer, but a portion of the gifts given to clergy at baptisms,
weddings and funerals were considered school property too.
Indeed, it was Alexander's failure to honor this practice that
caused much antagonism between he and the independents.
Following his departure, it became a specific duty of KISA's
General Secretary to keep track of baptisms and to claim KISA's
portion.
     Independent churches and schools were also linked to the
Kikuyu political movement of the 1930s and 1940s. Many informants have testified that indeed the Kikuyu Central Association
(KCA) and the independent church and school movement were
identical: "All independent people were members of the KCA."
Others claimed that, "The politically-minded people after
Muthirigu were the independents." Still others saw the relationship in financial terms.   ". . . because independents were
all politicians and critical of the government, they contributed to the KCA." While it would be difficult to support all

of these understandable but overstated claims, specific linkages can be found between the independents and the KCA, and
later the Kikuyu Provincial Association (KPA), a group which
separated from the KCA in 1935.

In 1932, when the <u>Mubea</u> (Catholic priest) of Ruchu mission
threatened to halt construction of the new independent church
at Gakarara, the fledgling congregation asked the KCA for help.

> The church committee met and decided to send
> James Kairu to the KCA in Nairobi and the KCA
> sent a letter to the director of education who
> in turn took up the matter with the D.C. of
> Fort Hall, telling him that construction should
> continue. Construction then did resume and the
> stone church was completed.(73)

About the same time, the Kiangare independents asked the
Nairobi KCA for advice on establishing an independent church in
their area. Joseph Kang'ethe, the KCA president, drafted sam-
ple letters to the Fort Hall District Commissioner and sent
them to Kiangare where they were used to secure government
permission to open an independent church. This KCA service to
independents was not uncommon; Gideon Kamanja, who frequently
attended Nairobi KCA meetings, has said that a good part of
each session was spent listening to or reading appeals for help
from outlying areas. Occasionally, the KCA even helped to
finance an independent church or school themselves.

KCA members outside Nairobi also gave aid to the independency movement. After the Ngorongo congregation had separated
itself from the GMS, it was the KCA, active nearby in the
Kaiiri area, that led the Ngorongo <u>Aregi</u> to establish their
independent church and school in the early 1930s.

Other independents were members of the KCA or at least
strong supporters of the Kikuyu political movement. Money from
the Kaiiri school account was used to send local people to
political meetings in Nairobi and elsewhere.(74) Mwangi
Wambico, Headmaster of Gakarara and KISA General Secretary,
regularly paid subscriptions to the KCA from school funds.
Indeed, so close was the identification between the KCA and the
independent schools and churches that some Kikuyu contributed
to the independency movement as a political protest while
others considered their donations to be synonymous with KCA
membership.

Prior to <u>Muthirigu</u> and the separation from missions, KCA
members had met secretly in private homes or in such improbable
places as the public latrines in Nairobi to conduct their
business. Now independent churches and schools became natural
meeting places for KCA members and they began to boldly meet on
a regular basis in many independent centers in the 1930s and
1940s. The independent church and school became a forum for
political discussion. The church and school committee often
turned its attention to political topics during their meetings.

Representatives sent to Nairobi KCA meetings returned to report to these committees and sometimes to the entire congregation.

In 1935 Harry Thuku seceded from the KCA and organized the Kikuyu Provincial Association (KPA).(75) Among others, Gideon Kamanja of Mununga and Jeremiah Kimone of Githumu moved with Thuku into the new organization. In the next few years independent churches and schools became the arena for competition between the KCA and the KPA. Each tried to increase its membership and influence among the Kikuyu by helping to build local independent churches and schools. At Mununga, the KPA group led by Gideon Kamanja, enlarged its membership and increased its local prestige when they successfully built and staffed an independent church and school there. Kamanja and his KPA group hoped to counter KCA influence by helping other areas with independent churches and schools too.(76) Jeremiah Kimone convinced a number of his friends to join the KPA under his leadership at Githumu. He offered assistance to the independents at Kangare who wanted to build their own church and school. He was particularly motivated to offer KPA help when he heard that Kangare had asked the KCA for assistance. Kimone successfully persuaded Kangare to accept the KPA and the school and church was built in 1942.(77)

Even when the government banned the KCA in 1940 as a subversive group, and detained the Nairobi leadership, rural independents continued their political meetings and discussions. (78) Some Kikuyu may have shifted to the KPA, which remained a lawful organization,(79) but many independents continued to consider themselves KCA members. Ndegwa Metho considered his job of Fort Hall district secretary for KISA, 1948-52, as work for the KCA. As KISA secretary, he toured the district helping to solve educational problems. He also rallied KCA members and administered oaths of unity.(80)

The Aregi exodus of 1929-30, begun in conflict and frustration, and sometimes with no more direction or motivation than to be free of mission control, had developed into an enormous independency venture. Several hundred churches and schools had been planned, financed and built in the Kikuyu highlands and even farther afield; spiritual and educational support had been provided to thousands in an atmosphere compatible with both Christianity and Kikuyu culture. Church and school independency also worked concomitantly with the Kikuyu political movement. Indeed, the same leaders and followers were shared by each group to such an extent that some people did not distinguish between religious and political profiles. By the early 1950s, the independents, to the surprise and consternation of the government, the AIM and the Kirore had become very successful in the church and school enterprises.

116

END NOTES

1. D.M. Kiragu, *Kiria Giatumire Independent Igie* (Independent Church Origins), n.d. (Nairobi: Regal Press Ltd.) Gakarara, Thika Kenya, p. 3; *Oral Evidence*: Jeremiah Gichuru, January 7, 1971 and Kambui group interview, June 4, 1971.
2. *Oral Evidence*: Eli Ngugi, February 8, 1971.
3. *Oral Evidence*: Ezekiel Kamau and Ndegwa Metho, February 16, 1971 and April 14, 1971.
4. Kiragu, *Kiria Giatumire Independent Igie*, p. 6.
5. David Maina to the Rev. Bishop of Mombasa, July 5, 1953, Fort Hall and Naaro I File, *PCEA Archives*; Kiragu, *Kiria Giatumire Independent Igie*, p. 6.
6. Minutes of the Church Missionary Society Conference, Kahuhia, October 13-16, 1933, Fort Hall and Naaro I File, *PCEA Archives*.
7. Alexander had just ordained Reuben Spartus and his brother Obadia as priests of the African Orthodox Church of Uganda. For a full description see Frederick Welbourn, *East African Rebels*, (London: SCM Press, 1961), pp. 77-110.
8. *Report and Constitution, Kikuyu Independent Schools Association, connected with the African Independent Pentecostal Church*, 1938, seen as DC/EBU 4/5, *KNA*.
9. "Apostolic Succession in the African Orthodox Church," seen as DC/NYI 2/82, *KNA*.
10. Manuscript prepared by Ezekiel Kamau for an interview on January 4, 1971; *Report and Constitution . . . African Independent Pentecostal Church*, p. 2.
11. Unless otherwise cited, the following section on the Gituamba seminary comes from Frederick Welbourn, *East African Rebels* (London: SCM Press, 1961), Chapter 8 and Joseph B. Ndungu, "Gituamba and Kikuyu Independency in Church and School," in *Ngano*, edited by Brian G. McIntosh (Nairobi: East African Publishing House, 1969), pp. 130-50. Ndungu interviewed the elders of Gituamba Church and Welbourn based much of his material on an interview with Daudi Maina Kiraga, one of Alexander's theological students and later a very important independent churchman. A similar opportunity was unavailable to me since Kiragu died in May 1969, fourteen months before I began my field work.
12. *Oral Evidence*: Bernard Njoroge, February 5, 1971.
13. The Divine Liturgy of the African Orthodox Church, seen as DC/NYI 2/82, *KNA*.
14. Mugo Gicaru, *Land of Sunshine: Scenes of Life in Kenya Before Mau Mau* (London: Lawrence & Wishart, 1958), p. 79.
15. DC/NYI 2/82, Deposit 2, African Orthodox Church, Thika to DC, Fort Hall, September 11, 1936, African Orthodox Church, *KNA*.
16. Kiragu, *Kiria Giatumire Independent Igie*, p. 12.

17. John 13:5.
18. Oral Evidence: Johanna Gitau, May 22, 1971.
19. Kikuyu Independent Schools Association, Report and Constitution, p. 3.
20. Kiragu, Kiria Giatumire Independent Igie, p. 1.
21. For details see Welbourn, East African Rebels, p. 150, and Carl Rosberg and John Nottingham, The Myth of Mau Mau: Nationalism in Kenya (New York: Praeger, 1966),p. 130 and footnote.
22. Welbourn, East African Rebels, pp. 151-53.
23. "Kwamunuo Gwa Kanitha: [The Blessing of the Church] n.d. seen as DC/NYI 2/82, Deposit 2, KNA.
24. The geographic breakdown follows: Fort Hall 38: Kiambu 19: Nyeri 8: Kirinyaga 4: Embu 6: Meru 3: Rift Valley 31: Nairobi and Mombasa, one each. Kiria Giatumire Independent Igie, pp. 24-26.
25. Oral Evidence: Johanna Gitau, June 9, 1971.
26. Kiragu, Kiria Giatumire Independent Igie, p. 23.
27. PC/DC NYI/2/68 AIPC Thiku to Provincial Commission, Nairobi, July 24, 1948, African Independent Church, KNA.
28. Ed 1/3284, AIPC to Government of Kenya, February 29, 1940, Education-Independent Schools, KNA.
29. Unless otherwise noted, the following section is based upon this Oral Evidence: Abraham Ruiri, February 1, 1971; Michael Mwanyika, May 4, 1971; Johanna Gitau, May 31, 1971; Evan Kahinya, January 29, 1971; Naphtali Mwangi, February 21, 1971; Johanna Mitaro, June 30, 1971; Jeremiah Kimone, June 11, 1971; Naphtali Mwangi, February 21, 1971; Daktari Samuel, March 23, 1971; Ezekiel Kamau, manuscript written for interview on January 4, 1971.
30. KISA . . . connected with the African Independent Pentecostal Church, Report and Constitution, p. 4.
31. Kiragu, Kiria Giatumire Independent Igie, p. 14.
32. KISA . . . connected with the AIPC, Report and Constitution, p. 4.
33. For instance, see F.D. Corfield's comments in The Origins and Growth of Mau Mau, Kenya Government Sessional Paper No. 5 of 1959/60, pp. 174-75.
34. Dep. 1/4, D.C. Fort Hall to Education Department, Nairobi, May 8, 1928, Village Schools in Fort Hall District, KNA.
35. PC/CP 8/1/1, Church of Scotland Mission, Kikuyu, January 16, 1930, Female Circumcision 1928-30, KNA.
36. PC/CP 8/1/2, D.C. Fort Hall to Principal, AIM Githumu, November 10, 1930, Female Circumcision, 1930, PC/CP 4/1/2, Kikuyu Province Annual Report, 1930, KNA.
37. Oral Evidence: Justus Kang'ethe, January 20, 1971.
38. Oral Evidence: Ezekiel Kamau, manuscript written for interview on January 4, 1971.
39. The KISA Report and Constitution, implies that the Association was begun in 1929 but oral evidence from Gakarara and Gituamba place the date in 1933 or early 1934 during the meetings held alternately in both places. In fact,

Gakarara and Gituamba both claim to have been the site of the first KISA meeting. Oral Evidence: Ezekiel Kamau, January 4, 1971, and Ndungu, "Gituamba and Kikuyu Independency in Church and School," p. 135.

40. Oral Evidence: Paul Githagoge, December 28, 1970, and January 8, 1971; Titus Kiige, December 29, 1970; Simon Mwangi, October 31, 1970.

41. The section which follows on the building of Kaiiri is based upon oral evidence from Eli Ngugu, February 8, 1971, and the Kaiiri Independent School financial books. February, 1944, to December, 1950, a copy of which I have in my possession.

42. J.B. Ndungu, "Gituamba and Kikuyu Independency," p. 138.

43. Boxes of chalk, bibles, a wash basin, a set of carving knives and two unnamed gifts but described as "for girls at Kaiiri." Kaiiri Independent School Financial Books, p. 46.

44. Twice during the construction period, materials and labor costs had been greater than the balance in the Treasury and members of the community had to give loans to the school until more donations were made.

45. The extra money was quickly raised and construction for the dorm was begun in September 1950, in time for it to be available for students at the beginning of the school term in January 1951.

46. Oral Evidence: Jonah Karanja, January 1, 1971; Mwangi Wambicho, January 28, 1971.

47. PC/CP 4/3/1, Central Province Annual Report, 1935, KNA.

48. KISA Report and Constitution, p. 3.

49. Kiragu, Kiria Giatumire Independent Igie, p. 2.

50. Oral Evidence: Mwangi Wambicho, January 28, 1971; KISA Report and Constitution, p. 3.

51. PC/CP 4/3/1, Central Province Annual Report, 1937, KNA.

52. Ed. 1/3284, Director of Education to Chief Native Commissioner, January 2, 1940, Education-Independent Schools, KNA.

53. Ed. 1/3284, Secretariat to Executive Council Members-Draft Precis. May 15, 1940, Education-Independent Schools, KNA.

54. DC/FH 6/2, DC, Nyeri to Director of Education, August 6, 1938, Inspection of Schools, KNA.

55. PC/CP 4/4/1, Central Province Annual Report, 1939, KNA.

56. DC/FH 6/1, Director of Schools to DC, Fort Hall, February 25, 1941, Inspection of Schools, 1934-50, KNA.

57. Oral Evidence: Eli Ngugi, February 8, 1971; Oral Evidence: Bernard Njoroge, February 12, 1971.

58. The Origins and Growth of Mau Mau, p. 173.

59. DC/KBU 10/2, KISA to DC Kiambu, June 2, 1939, Private Schools-Kahunguini, KNA.

60. KISA Report and Constitution, pp. 4-6.

61. Oral Evidence: Mwangi Wambicho, January 28, 1971.

62. Only one of the independent schools inspected in 1938 had less than 200 students. DC/FH 6/2, Inspection of Schools, 1934-50, KNA.

63. Oral Evidence: Mwangi Wambicho, January 28, 1971, and Joseph Ruhiu, January 20, 1971; Oral Evidence: Amos Waweru, January 12, 1971.

64. Kaiiri Independent School Account Books.

65. Peter Mbiyu Koinange, The People of Kenya Speak for Themselves (Detroit, Michigan: Kenya Publication Fund), 1955, Chapters 4-6.

66. For more information see, Welbourn, East African Rebels, Chapter 8. Anderson has stated that since the building of Githunguri was the combined effort of KISA and KKEA the rift between the two associations so often mentioned by the government was imaginary. John Anderson, "Self Help and Independency: The Political Implications of a Continuing Tradition in African Education," African Affairs, 70, No. 278 (January, 1971), 14. It should be noted however that as late as 1963, Daudi Maina Kiragu, one of the founders of KISA had not forgiven KKEA for the promise it failed to keep to unite with KISA. Kiria Gratumire Independent Igie, pp. 10-11.

67. From January to October, 1939, 40,000 shillings ($6,000.00) was raised. A group of women organized in 1940, succeeded in raising an additional 85,000 shillings. Koinange, The People of Kenya Speak for Themselves, pp. 30-31, 50-51.

68. Oral Evidence: Mwangi Wambicho, January 28, 1971.

69. PC/CP 9/21/1, December 22, 1930, "Tenure of Church and School in Native Reserve," KNA.

70. Kiragu, Kiria Gratumire Independent Igie, p. 11.

71. Ndungu, "Gituamba and Kikuyu Independency in Church and School," p. 145.

72. Unless otherwise noted, the sections which follow are based upon this Oral Evidence: Mwangi Wambicho, January 28, 1971; Morris Gatiri, January 9, 1971; Samuel Wanjihia, June 11, 1971; Johanna Gitau, June 12, 1971; Jeremiah Kimone, December 9, 1970; Gideon Kamaja, June 19, 1971; Njugima Njoroge, February 13, 1971; Mwangi Wambicho, January 28, 1971; Moses Njau, February 20, 1971; Joseph Kang'ethe, June 16, 1971; Moses Thuo, March 10, 1971.

73. Statement written by Ezekiel Kamau for interview on January 4, 1971.

74. Kaiiri Independent School Financial Books, p. 17.

75. Harry Thuku, An Autobiography, with the assistance of Kenneth King (Nairobi: Oxford University Press, 1970), p. 60. Thuku discussed the personal and ideological reasons for the split in an earlier passage and ended with these words: "Soon there were two KCAs in Nairobi, and my ideas were becoming quite clear from theirs. I did not want violence, and I did not want to operate in darkness. I

wanted to do things constitutionally and not just hate people." Harry Thuku, An Autobiography, p. 56.

76. Oral Evidence: Gideon Kamanja, June 19, 1971.

77. Oral Evidence: Jeremiah Kimoni, June 11, 1971. Kimoni has saved all the letters he received as local KPA organizer from Harry Thuku. They give some insight into the organization, particularly its stand against Mau Mau. Kimoni Papers, 1936-57, copy in my possession.

78. CP/PC 4/3/2, Central Province Annual Report, 1940, AIM, New York.

79. A successful appeal was made in the 1940s to build a new KPA office in Nairobi, which may indicate a growing number of contributing members. Harry Thuku, An Autobiography, p. 61. Thuku's circular letters to rural KPA leaders also implies a growing membership. Kimoni Papers.

80. Metho is very circumspect about his role as oath adminis- trator: he does not deny it nor does he confirm it. He was detained by the government as an oath administrator, however. Oral Evidence: Ndegwo Metho, February 16, 1971, and Ndegwa Papers. The latter consists of his correspon- dence as KISA secretary, his detention warrant and his correspondence with the government while he was detained. For a discussion of oathing, see Rosberg and Nottingham, Myth of Mau Mau, pp. 243-48.

Chapter 7

The Arathi

In addition to the independents, a religious force consisting of people who had been "filled with the spirit" also grew out of Kikuyu experimentation and dissent of the 1920s. As we have seen, an early group of dissidents had been meeting at Gakarara in Fort Hall district since 1926. At one of their meetings, sometime prior to Muthirigu, Moses Thuo and several others present began to pray involuntarily, to groan or shout and to confess their sins aloud. Afterwards, they considered themselves to have been possessed or "filled with God's spirit." Later, they began to have dreams in which the spirit talked to them.(1)

A few miles south of Gakarara, in Kiambu district, Joseph Ng'ang'a, who lived near the GMS station at Ng'enda, had a similar experience. One evening in 1926, he set out for home after attending a beer-drinking party. But, too intoxicated to continue, he lay down by the roadside and went to sleep. An acquaintance of Ng'ang'a who learned later what happened, related the events of that night.

> In his sleep, he heard a voice calling him and though it stopped, he knew that it was God's. He went back to sleep. The strange thing about it was that the voice had called him Joseph and he was not yet baptized. In the morning, he looked for footprints but found none. He became conscious that it was God's call. He took the beer [which he was carrying] and gave it to others and also the apparatus [with which it was made.](2)

From the experiences of Thuo and Ng'ang'a, apparently quite independent of each other, a new religious force developed among the Kikuyu.(3) They called themselves Arathi after the Kikuyu diviners or prophets who professed to have had a close association with the creator god Ngai.(4) Another name they frequently used was Aroti, or dreamers, which reflected their dream experiences "with the spirit."

For a time, however, the Arathi were just a few individuals with a set of strange experiences. Their identity prior to the circumcision controversy was much the same as the other dissidents in the AIM and GMS. They shared a growing disgust for missions and a spiritual hunger, which found expression and satisfaction in continued Christian worship and fellowship. Moses Thuo began to gather around him a number of people who had had similar experiences "with the spirit." But they continued to meet with the dissidents at Gakarara. Ng'ang'a secluded himself after his experience to study the

Bible, meditate, dream and "groan" in communication with the spirit. Later he was joined by Gitao Mbembe and then three dissidents from the GMS station at Ng'enda--David Mukundi, Jerimiah Munyaka, and Charles Munene. They often worshiped together in each other's houses and occasionally attended the Sunday services with other dissident Athomi.(5)

During and after the female circumcision controversy, the Arathi cooperated with the independents, particularly with those in the Gakarara area in establishing their schools and churches. They made contributions to the new schools and helped in their building. The Arathi even sent their children to independent schools for awhile, and actively participated in Muthirigu singing, though they worshiped separately from the independents.(6)

But the very nature of their experience "with the spirit" eventually led them in quite a different direction. The spirit directed Arathi in both Ng'ang'a's and Thuo's groups, usually through dreams, to seek out other Kikuyu who had had similar experiences. Soon Arathi were discovered in the Kijabe area and later in the Rift Valley and around Mt. Kenya among the Embu and Meru peoples. Sometimes Arathi missionary tours to these areas attracted people to the Arathi movement. Occasionally these missionaries even found a group expecting their arrival with "dream news." One early Arathi missionary had this to say.

> Sometimes, when these voices came to a person, they told him to pass the message to another place. But when he arrived, he would find that people there had been informed about it [by the Spirit] and were waiting his coming.(7)

Joshua Ng'ang'a Kimani, who undertook many missionary tours outside Kikuyuland and is now an important Arathi leader in Kiambu, said he first became aware of the movement in a dream. This came shortly after he had dropped out of school because of a teacher's cruelty. He prayed about the dream and later two Arathi, whom he had never met, came to baptize him and gave him the name of Joshua. An increasing number of such contacts expanded the movement in the early 1930s, and Arathi began to forge an identity quite separate from the independents.

In fact, the Arathi and the independents slowly became estranged from each other. Moses Thuo said voices warned him against going to the AIM for baptism as some independents were doing prior to the arrival of Archbishop Alexander. He was irritated that Daudi Maina Kiragu and the other Gakarara independents were not "open to the Spirit," and did not emphasize the revelations of the spirit in church. Thuo said that just as he had felt "half a Christian" in the AIM, now because the independent church did not emphasize the spirit, it was something less than fully Christian as well.

Another difference that grew between the two groups was the critical attitude of the Arathi toward all aspects of western civilization. All foreign-made articles were thought to interfere with the worship of the spirit. Such everyday things as shoes, money, kerosene and all metal articles were to be abandoned. The Arathi also gave up western clothes and took to wearing the Kanzu, a long, white Swahili gown and a white turban.(8)

Many also believed in the millenarian idea that a new order of things was near. As this was to happen in the fore-seeable future, some stopped working to watch and pray. In 1931 a Murathi from the AIM station at Mataara predicted the world would end in two weeks. He and his wife shut themselves up in their house to prepare for the end. Others preached more generally of a coming doom, unsure of specific details of time. One Murathi had a recurring dream of a diseased, hungry, and impoverished country. He said he could "feel" something was going to happen, though he did not know when.(9)

The Arathi, therefore, rejected the goals of the indepen-dent churches and schools which, like the missions, attempted to prepare young people for the western-oriented world of the future.

The Arathi antagonized the non-Christian community as well. The strong feeling which Arathi had against witchcraft caused them to search out and destroy all charms and amulets and to ridicule the Kikuyu who possessed them.(10) They also preached against Kikuyu sacrifices to Ngai, the creator god and to Ngoma, the ancestral spirits. Arathi taught that proper contact with the spiritual world was to face Mt. Kenya and to pray aloud with uplifted arms.(11) They also desired to make changes in patterns of everyday life. Erastus Warii, a Kiambu Murathi, had a dream in which the spirit directed him to inform a local woman that she was not to work in her garden on Sunday. Another man was not to cook arrowroots on Sunday in prepara-tion for market the following day. When each objected, they were warned to stop their activity or be in danger of God's wrath. This attitude that the non-Christian community should conform to Arathi ideas met with resistance and resentment. The same was true when Arathi told independents that the only true Christians were those who had been "filled with the spirit."

The Arathi also became the subject of government concern. Beginning in 1930, government officers in Central Province began to take notice of the Arathi and to record their activi-ties. They were thought to be a group of "pseudo-religious fanatics" who made strange noises, participated in "supersti-tious practices" and had a "less elevated code of ethics."(12) The latter referred to one or two Arathi groups, in which the male and female members were on sexually intimate terms. As the government gathered more information, they became increas-ingly concerned about the political aspects of the Arathi movement, having learned that Joseph Ng'ang'a was instructed in

dreams to pray for the freeing of the Kikuyu from their colonial rulers. In some Arathi prophecies, God was to sweep aside
the Europeans and usher in a Kikuyu golden age. In one a
"yawning pit" was to appear just outside Nairobi into which
first the governor then all other Europeans would fall.(13) The
government was uneasy about the prophecies, while Arathi participation in singing Muthirigu, and alleged connections with
the KCA seemed to confirm suspicions.(14)

Alarm increased when the Arathi began to arm themselves
with bows, poison arrows and simis (short double edged swords).
Some Arathi maintained that carrying weapons symbolized arming
oneself against evil. One Murathi explained to police that he
had been directed in a dream to make arrows:

> One night last year the voice gave me the
> following text from the 7 Psalms 'God Judgeth
> the righteous and God is angry with the wicked
> every day.
> If he turn not he will whet his sword; he
> has bent his bow and made it ready.
> He has also prepared for him the instruments
> of death, he ordaineth his arrow against the
> persecutors.'
> On that occasion I saw a vision of a man
> in my heart. He seemed to be European and was
> dressed in long white garment like a Kanzu. I
> woke up but as I did so he vanished from the
> hut though the door was securely closed.
> The next night I saw the man again, this
> time he was dressed in Khaki clothes and I
> could not see his face clearly. He stood by my
> bed and then sat down on the floor of the hut
> and started working at something. I watched him
> and saw that he was making an arrow on which he
> put poison.
> When he had finished he took me into the
> forest and showed me a tree and told me how to
> make the poison.
> I woke then and he vanished with the
> arrow. I found myself lying in bed in my hut.
> Before I woke up I heard a voice saying make
> what I have shown you.
> In the morning I remembered how to make
> poison for arrows. You cut a branch from a
> small tree called Muricho in (Kikuyu) and chop
> it into small pieces. Then put the fragments
> into an earthenware pot with a little water and
> boil for about six hours. By that time most of
> the water has boiled and the juice of the wood
> is mixed with what is left forming a black
> paste which can be smeared when cool on the
> arrows.

> From that time, although I had never done
> so before, I made arrows. I do not know the
> purpose for which they are intended but I had
> been told to make them. So I had to do so. I
> have made a great number, some poisoned and
> some not, and have put them all aside. . . (to
> keep). In due course I should doubtless have
> been told what to do with them.(15)

Other Arathi speculated that the weapons may have been for protection against ill-treatment received at the hands of other Kikuyu and the government. Evidence exists to support this interpretation. Some Kikuyu disowned Arathi relatives, and many reported suffering physical abuse while attempting to preach among fellow Kikuyu.(16) By 1934 the government had infiltrated several Arathi groups and then imprisoned a number of Arathi for holding their meetings which the government had prohibited. Some said that in detention, they had been beaten.(17)

The Ndarugu forest incident of 1934 brought Arathi arming to a climax. While searching for Njoroge wa Mukono, a Kikuyu wanted for murder, a police patrol encountered a number of armed Arathi. In the skirmish that followed, two Arathi were shot dead, one of whom was Joseph Ng'ang'a, and another was fatally wounded.(18)

As a result, many independents not only saw the Arathi as peculiar but viewed them as a liability, both because they had alienated non-Christians, and because the government regarded them as dangerous. The Ndarugu forest affair was felt to have discredited the independency movement so severely that some independents gathered information on the Arathi for the government.(19)

The feeling was mutual, for those Arathi who had remained associated with the independents felt their religious and social ideas were not accepted, and their milenarian prophecies were scorned. In Fort Hall district, Moses Thuo and his group no longer met with the independents at Gakarara. In Kiambu, the Arathi took their children out of the independent schools which they had been attending. Though there continued to be some ties between them,(20) by 1934 the Arathi had become quite distinct from the independents.

The government remained apprehensive as rumors circulated that all Arathi had taken an oath to forcibly resist any government attempts at arrest.(21) Administrative and police reports for the decade reveal that the government kept track of Arathi activity. They record that a large Arathi meeting was held at Rucho, near Gakarara in 1934. Nearly 200 attended, coming from Kiambu and Fort Hall districts, more than half of them armed as if to challenge the government. Prayers were offered for the souls of those killed at Ndarugu forest, and Moses Thuo preached on the need for obedience to Arathi beliefs and on the fast-approaching end of the world. At the end of the year a similar meeting was held at Githumu which drew Arathi from all parts of Central Province. In 1937 many Arathi were repatriated by the government to the Kikuyu reserve from the Rift Valley, where their presence was "having disturbing effect upon labor." In the same year, some Arathi were preaching that a messiah was coming that would liberate the Kikuyu from their colonial masters. In 1943, a number of Arathi were fined and imprisoned for refusing to be vaccinated against smallpox. The following year some Arathi allegedly broke into a GMS school to hold a religious meeting. In 1946, Arathi disrupted an AIM worship service, and the police had to be called to intervene.

But these incidents, however worrying to the colonial administration, do not accurately reflect Arathi activities during the 1930s and 1940s. Ng'ang'a's death and the prison sentences for holding meetings seem to mark a change in the movement. The number active, estimated to be 400 in Fort Hall district in 1929-31, had decreased significantly by 1936.(22) Several informants in Kiambu had said that when Arathi from the Ng'enda area returned from prison, they shaved off their beards and announced that they were no longer Arathi.(23) In 1938, the superintendent of police in Kiambu noted other changes,

> None of the fanatical tendencies of past years
> are apparent and arrow making and the carrying
> of weapons have not been indulged in. The cult
> is consequently a missing [sic] a far less
> serious aspect than was formerly the case and
> does not seem to be spreading to any
> degree.(24)

Generally the Arathi became less aggressive.

Some accommodation was even achieved with the government. After a number of Arathi from Moses Thuo's group had been repeatedly fined and imprisoned, they applied to the Fort Hall District Commissioner for permission to hold their meetings. According to Thuo, the D.C. gave his permission because he had been struck by the meek and humble nature of the men he had previously imprisoned.

At the same time, Arathi attempted to coordinate their activities. A number of leaders attended a meeting held at Moses Thuo's home at Kaguthi (25) on September 9, 1933. They sought to knit together a common set of beliefs from the disparate practices that had developed independently in the various Arathi groups, and to take steps to correct questionable activities.

One of the first points taken up was when white garments should be worn. All Arathi believed that God had instructed them to wear white, but some felt it necessary only for worship. It was decided, however, that white clothes were to be worn at all times because--". . . God is not a fool when he tells you to wear white clothes. He knows that what is in the heart is reflected by the body."

Baptism, confirmation, and the number of days women should remain secluded following their child's birth were also discussed. The differing practices that had grown up between the various _Arathi_ groups were now regularized.

In response to some _Arathi_ cutting their hair and shaving off their beards, those present at the meeting reiterated the belief that God had specifically instructed all _Arathi_ to let their hair grow and that obedience to this command should continue.

The leaders at the Kaguthi meeting also decided that a council of twelve elders should be appointed within each _Arathi_ group. They would be charged with enforcing the rules and also reviewing the questionable behavior of some _Arathi_. The leaders agreed that it was imperative to obey God's commands, and they built that central idea into their worship service with the opening response:

> Our Father Who Art in Heaven (repeat 3 times)
> Oh Father, I will be answering
> Your voice when you call
> Through the name of the Holy Ghost
> and your will (repeat 3 times), Amen.(26)

But they all felt that certain excesses had taken place which should not be permitted in the future, and they resolved that commands of the spirit must be consistent with the Bible and with the commands God had given to others. Two specific matters had caused problems. A number of _Arathi_ had seduced young women. When questioned about their conduct they said that God had instructed them in dreams to take these women as their wives. The other problem involved unauthorized missionary tours outside the district. Apparently, some _Arathi_ had decided to go to certain places contrary to the general wishes of their group. Now it was proposed that both of these matters should be decided by the local councils of twelve.

The other major resolution to come out of the meeting dealt with a leader's responsibility to his group and to the _Arathi_ in general: ". . . they must fulfill their duties and look after the flock of the Lord, and anyone from any of the churches who will not fulfill these things, shall not stay in the _Arathi_ church."(27) During the next two decades, this skeleton of _Arathi_ beliefs and practices was expanded. Though leadership was discussed in terms of responsibility at the 1933 meeting, a hierarchy of specialization soon developed. By the 1940s, the top _Arathi_ leaders were known as high priests. The rest of the leadership hierarchy consisted of _Atumuo_--local church leaders who conducted the weekly services and the rites of baptism and confirmation, _Ahunjia_--missionary evangelists and _Arutiani_--teachers of _Arathi_ traditions. In each case, the spirit chose the person for the job by revealing the matter in a dream, either to him or to a colleague. In the case of high priests and local church leaders, ordination was necessary by public rite as described below:

> God says that he would like someone ordained for a certain job. We put the person involved on a choir and the one to whom God gave the message gets up and rests his right hand on the candidate's head and raises his left hand to pray for him asking God to do with him what he intends to. The man then shakes hands with the candidate three times and he is ordained.(28)

Evangelists and teachers did not need to be ordained but could take up their duties with the general approval of the local Arathi group.(29) The position of high priest was clearly paramount to all others. He prays, blesses and comforts his people, advises the other leaders and has final control over all church matters including baptisms, confirmations, weddings and preaching, even though these can be attended to by the local church leaders also.

The specialization of leadership that began to develop was reinforced as baptism, confirmation and wedding rituals became more elaborate. For baptism the key event was still the dream in which the spirit called the candidate by his new baptismal name. This was part of Joseph Ng'ang'a dream-experience in 1926:

> He heard a voice calling his name and he realized that it was God's voice. The surprising thing was that the voice called him by his baptismal name, but he was not baptized at that time.(30)

The dream still remained central to the ritual, but by the late 1930s it usually came after a candidate had become interested in the Arathi rather than "out of the blue" as with Ng'ang'a and some of the other Arathi founders. A procedure developed in which an inquirer attached himself to an Arathi group, received instruction, and then had the "naming dreams." Occasionally, the baptizer or someone else in the group had the dream, and this was considered a legitimate substitute. The baptism service recognized the candidate as a Murathi and welcomed him or her officially into the group, as described in the following testimony:

> When we are all gathered on Sundays, the candidates kneel in the space between the rows of benches and the baptizer shakes hands with each three times. He says that he has baptized them in the name of the Father, Son and Holy Spirit. After him comes the one who confirms

laying hands on the candidates and praying God
to keep the new name firm and he then shakes
hands with each three times.(31)

These Arathi could now wear white clothes, though some groups
demanded that they make public confession of their sins before
the clothes be put on.

Baptism names were normally taken from the Bible, although
some Arathi groups preferred to retain their Kikuyu name as
they considered Biblical names to be European and unattractive.
New members who had previously been baptized by the mission or
independent churches were not always re-baptized by the Arathi;
the high priest made decisions on an individual basis.

Marriage was also carefully arranged among Arathi. After
the suitor had made his intentions known to the bride's father,
the father informed the church elders and the high priest. The
latter then prayed together to see if it would be a good match.
If no obstruction was found, they called together the man and
his intended bride. If both agreed to the marriage, arrangements continued. The whole congregation assembled for the
wedding and the following rite took place in their midst.

We have new white clothes for the bride and
bridegroom and after washing [the clothes] we
take [Bride and Groom] to the house of God and
pray for them. Then the women take the girl's
clothes and go to put them on. We then have
them kneel in the space between the benches and
we let them hold each other's arms. However,
we do not put rings on them since God in the
Bible did not command us to do so. We pray to
God, and the women take the bride away and the
bridegroom goes out through another door. When
they come back we take them home with songs,
and on taking them home we bless them.(32)

It was possible for a Murathi to marry someone outside his
faith. But the fact that Arathi did not believe in bride-
wealth exchanges was a great hindrance to such unions.(33)

In the two decades following the 1933 meeting other patterns of belief developed or were elaborated upon; these can be
observed through the life and teaching of Joshua Ng'ang'a
Kimani. Following his introduction to Arathi beliefs and his
baptism in 1931, Kimani accompanied his baptizers on a missionary tour to Meru. Upon his return the next year, he spent some
time under Moses Thuo's influence at Kaguthi. Thereafter, he
worked to establish Arathi churches in various parts of the
Rift Valley and in Fort Hall until 1947. During that time, he
returned in 1939-41 to his home area of Kiganjo, Kiambu and
again in 1944-46 to be taught by Thuo at Kaguthi. After 1947,
he returned to Kiganjo as high priest of the congregations he

had established at Kiganjo and Fort Hall and to those in the Rift Valley. He continues to act in that capacity to this day.

Throughout this time he firmly believed in God's communication with him through dreams. He began to keep a record of all his dreams and he encouraged his followers to do the same. Each morning he and his group would assemble to share their dreams and to discuss what action if any should be taken.

Through dreams and his contact with Thuo and other Arathi, he systematized, elaborated upon and established a set of Arathi practices of his own. He said that God ordered him to record these beliefs which he did on March 3, 1950. This record, together with an undated account of how his ideas developed and the problems he encountered while teaching them to others, are contained in the first two appendices which appear at the end of the text.(34)

At the heart of Kimani's theological beliefs was the idea of good and evil, as illustrated in the following passage:

> There are two types of things that concern the Aroti [Arathi] church: The good spirit and the bad spirit. The bad spirit explains traditional [Kikuyu] things while the good spirit is the teacher of all good or godly things, not connected with tradition or the body.(35)

To maximize the good and to keep evil at bay, Kimani and other Arathi sought to sweep away Kikuyu tradition and construct society along lines which they considered more suitable. To achieve this, the Kikuyu concept of Thahu or ritual uncleanliness (36) was adapted to Hebrew laws taken mainly from the Old Testament. The result was a series of rules for Arathi society, the transgression of which would result in Thahu.(37) Many of the Thahu read like the following which discusses the uncleanliness resulting from death.

> If anyone touches or buries a dead body, touches or steps on a human bone, and stays unclean for seven days, he must stay in a separate place and purify himself on the first, third and seventh days. After that he must go to the house of God to be prayed for so that he may become clean.(38)

The various other Thahu mentioned deal with such things as: (1) the seclusion of women during their menstrual period, (2) childbirth and the cleansing process which follows, (3) sexual abstinence in preparation for worship and prayer, (4) nocturnal emission, (5) blood diseases and leprosy, (6) prohibitions against eating certain kinds of meat slaughtered according to Kikuyu custom, (7) conduct in church, (8) conduct on the

Sabbath day, (9) prohibition against adultery, cutting ones
hair, alcoholic drinking and (10) the wearing of white clothes.
Greeting people by shaking hands was prohibited since one
could also contract <u>Thahu</u> by touch and be cutoff from God as a
result.(39)

> It is not right to greet any one you meet on
> the way because people usually have <u>Thahu</u> of
> different kinds like adultery and eating sacri-
> ficial foods which a Christian should not
> touch, and on greeting him you both share those
> things that have <u>Thahu</u>. . . and you cannot pray
> to God as the <u>Thahu</u> in your midst separates you
> from Him.(40)

Bodily cleanliness was considered of great importance too;
one could be cut off from God if he were not clean. On Wednes-
days and Saturdays all <u>Arathi</u> were to wash themselves and their
clothes in preparation for worship on Fridays and Sundays. Two
weeks prior to each of the special prayer months of January,
July and December, <u>Arathi</u> were to keep themselves particularly
clean.
The laws met with some opposition within <u>Arathi</u> ranks.
Kimani recorded that the rules he preached set him in conflict
with some of his followers. Some were opposed to the prohibitions:

> Enmity with the elders was created and they
> sent me out of their villages and they wrote me
> a letter. . . saying that I was spoiling their
> faith.(41)

The multiplicity of rules bothered others:

> . . . they called mine a religion in which
> people washed many times and so it was a reli-
> gion of the Pharisees while they wanted a reli-
> gion of the Apostles without the rules of
> <u>Thahu</u>.(42)

Upon Kimani's return from the Rift Valley in 1947, he preached
against those <u>Arathi</u> who practiced polygamy. God had revealed
to him that having more than one wife was wrong and he was not
persuaded to change his mind by arguments that the Hebrews of
the Old Testament practiced polygamy.

> Those people [<u>Arathi</u>] who would like to emulate
> people of the Old Testament. . . like Abraham
> and Jacob for having many wives . . . should
> know that they were hiding in bad deeds since
> they were not commanded by God [to practice
> polygamy] but they were directed by tradition

> . . . Those who would like to emulate righteous
> people of old should look at people like Isaac
> who did not marry many wives . . . and Joseph.
> . . .(43)

This teaching of reform caused a great deal of antagonism and in 1949 led to a split between Kimani and several other Arathi groups, particularly Moses Thuo's group.

An issue that caused more fragmentation was Arathi participation in politics. The initial Arathi message was quite political. A number of Arathi had been active in the Kikuyu Central Association, and some continued to participate. Though estranged from independents, Arathi leaders continued to support the independent movement and adopted their stand on female circumcision by encouraging all Arathi to make up their own minds on the issue. The Arathi even prayed for the success of the independents, hoping their prayers would give the movement strength. Moses Thuo said true religious convictions only came to him when he was involved with the KCA. He was convinced that the church was the right place for political discussion because only there would people speak freely and frankly. In the late 1940s, however, Kimani said that God commanded Arathi never to join any association, and he spoke against people like Moses Thuo for their political involvement: "They mixed Godliness with politics but they never rhyme since each has its own foundation."(44)

Some attempts have been made toward reconciliation. Bildad Kaggia called all Arathi leaders to a meeting at Weithaga in Fort Hall district in 1948. Not very many accepted the invitation, however, and the proposed unity did not take place. Kimani has tried on several occasions to unite with other Kiambu and Fort Hall groups, but differences of beliefs have kept them apart. Kimani even hoped that the Mau Mau oaths that many Arathi took in the 1950s would bind them together after the rebellion, but the religious freedom guaranteed by the Kenya Government since independence in 1963 has fostered even more Arathi groups.(45)

The Arathi have also remained divided from the rest of Kikuyu society. The Arathi are critical of all other belief systems. They consider all non-Arathi to be living in a permanent state of Thahu and according to Kimani, this makes the Arathi as different from these Kikuyu as they are from other ethnic groups. There are also strong prohibitions against participating fully in the ebb and flow of rural and urban Kikuyu life. Any form of trade or commerce is prohibited and Arathi only agree to market their coffee through a cooperative if no bargaining over price is involved. Self-help projects such as day care centers, schools and water schemes are supported only if no profit is involved. Despite Kenya independence, Kimani and other Arathi leaders have instructed their followers to abstain from any political involvement, including voting in

elections. The Arathi have sought to create their own community, and have remained largely separate from the rest of
Kikuyu society.

By 1950 the Arathi had departed rather dramatically from
their origins twenty-five years earlier. Then, the Arathi
pioneers had been among the larger group of Kikuyu dissidents
who had protested against both mission and government. The
Arathi had been active supporters and many times members of the
KCA, and they had participated in the Aregi separation from the
AIM. But, by the mid-1930s, with an enlarged membership, the
Arathi had begun charting a different course, quite different
from the Aregi independents in both structure and philosphy.
They had rejected the independents' society with its emphasis
on schooling and Kikuyu led churches. They also rejected many
values traditional to the Kikuyu. In their place, the Arathi
had constructed a secluded community modeled on dream revelations and Old Testament Hebrew Laws.

END NOTES

1. Unless otherwise cited, this chapter is based upon the Oral Evidence: Moses Thuo, August 4, 1970, February 1971, March 10, 1971; Joshua Ng'ang'a Kimani, February 17, 1971; March 9, 1971, April 4, 1971.

2. Oral Evidence: Joshus Ng'ang'a Kimani, February 17, 1971.

3. The group that developed around each of these men assert their independent origin and I have found no evidence that links Thuo and Ng'ang'a prior to their experiences with the Spirit.

      Jocelyn Murray states that Joseph Ng'ang'a is the recognized Arathi originator but she bases this opinion entirely on Kiambu evidence: "The Kikuyu Spirit Churches: An Introductory Account," Journal of Religion in Africa, 5, No. 3 (1974), 198-234. I wish to thank Ms. Murray for allowing me to read an early draft of this article and for conversations with her that have helped me to interpret my own Arathi material more clearly.

4. John Middleton, The Central Tribes of the North-eastern Bantu (London: International African Institute, 1953), p. 65; Jomo Kenyatta, Facing Mt. Kenya (1938 rpt. New York: Vintage, 1962), p. 263.

5. Oral Evidence: Ng'enda interviews, April 10, 1971.

6. PC/CP 4/1/2, Kikuyu Province Annual Report, 1930, KNA; Oral Evidence: Ezekiel Kamau and Ndegwa Metho, April 11, 1971.

7. Oral Evidence: Moses Thuo, March 10, 1971.

8. Kenyatta, Facing Mt. Kenya, Chapter eleven. Kenyatta calls this chapter on the Arathi, "The New Religion in East Africa," and bases its content on meetings he had with them upon his return from Europe in 1930.

9. Oral Evidence: Paul Mugo, August, 1970, NCCK-Limuru Archives.

10. PC/CP 4/1/2, Kikuyu Provincial Annual Report, 1930, KNA.

11. Kenyatta, Facing Mt. Kenya, p. 264.

12. PC/CP 4/1/2, Kikuyu Province Annual Report, 1930, KNA.

13. PC/CP 4/1/2, D.C. Fort Hall to P.C. Nyeri, March 30, 1931, False Prophets, KNA.

14. The government had no definite proof of KCA linkages but considered all Arathi characteristics to be "distinct signs that it [Arathi] was allied with the Kikuyu Central Association," DC FH 1/1, KNA. In actual fact, such early Arathi as Moses Thuo and his associates around Gakarara were all supporters of the KCA. Oral Evidence: Ezekiel Kamau and Ndegwa Metho, April 11, 1971.

15. PC/CP 8/7/3, Police Report, Nakuru to Commissioner of Police, Nairobi, May 21, 1934, Political Unrest, 1934-52, KNA.

16. DC/FH 1/4, Statement made to CID, February 17, 1970.

17. PC/CP 8/7/2, CID, Nairobi to Provincial Commissioner, Nyeri, D.C. Fort Hall and D.C. Kiambu, March 17, 1934, Political Unrest 1934-52, KNA.

18. PC/CP 4/3/1, Central Province Annual Report, 1934, KNA. The police may have mistaken the Arathi for Njoroge wa Mukone and his gang and fired upon them. Ng'ang'a and the other Arathi may well have lashed out at the police patrol. As a reaction to the past government actions of prohibiting their meeting from taking place and imprisoning the offenders several Arathi have stated that Ng'ang'a anticipated his death, saying that it had been revealed to him in a dream. Oral Evidence: Elijah Kinyanjui, March 15, 1972, seen in Jocelyn Murray, "Kikuyu Spirit Churches: An Introductory Account," Journal of Religion in Africa, 5, No.3 (1974), 198-234.

19. One informer, while spying on Moses Thuo, was given overnight lodging by Daudi Maina Kiragu, the independent leader at Gakarara. PC/CP 8/7/2, CID Nairobi to D.C. Fort Hall, March 17, 1934, Political Unrest 1932-34, KNA.

20. Daniel Nduti, now an Arathi leader in the Githumu area, has said that while he and several others became Arathi in 1931, they remained associated with and contributed materials, money and labor to the independent church and school at Kiangare until 1940 when they finally left to begin their own Arathi group. Oral Evidence: Daniel Nduti, December 29, 1970.

21. This paragraph is based upon the following files: DC/FH 1/4, False Prophets 1934-60; PC/CP 8/7/23, Political Unrest 1932-52; CP/PC 4/3/2, Central Province Annual Report, 1943-44; PC/CP 8/7/3, Director of Intelligence to Superintendent, KNA.

22. DC/FH 1/4, AIM THika (Githumu) to CID Fort Hall, December 24, 1936, False Prophets, KNA.

23. Oral Evidence: Ng'enda group interview, April 10, 1971.

24. PC/CP 8/7/3, District Police Headquarters, Kiambu, January 4, 1938, Political Unrest 1934-52, KNA.

25. All information concerning this meeting comes from Joshua Ng'ang'a Kimani, who was a participant. He consulted a diary for a record of the points discussed and then elaborated upon them from memory. Oral Evidence: Joshua Ng'ang'a Kimani, April 1, 1971.

26. Oral Evidence: Joshua Ng'ang'a Kimani, April 1, 1971.

27. Ibid.

28. Ibid.

29. Apart from an early prophetess named Debra, there have been no Arathi women in leadership positions. Oral Evidence: Moses Thuo, March 10, 1971.

30. Oral Evidence: Joshua Ng'ang'a Kimani, February 17, 1971.

31. Ibid., March 9, 1971.

32. Ibid.

33. PC/CP 8/7/3, D.C. Kiambu to P.C. Nyeri, June 15, 1943, Political Unrest 1934-42, KNA.

34. Kimani permitted me to copy both documents which I now have in my possession. Appendix I and II are English translations from these Kikuyu copies. The translations have retained the style and the repetition of the originals.

35. Joshua Ng'ang'a Kimani, "Things to be observed by all Godly People," n.d., Appendix II.

36. See Middleton, _Central Tribes of the Northeastern Bantu_, pp. 15-65.

37. These rules along with other comments on morality, by Kimani, "Rules Written on March 3, 1950," Appendix I.

38. Ibid.

39. Some _Arathi_ have a more optimistic view of _Thahu_ then Kimani and feel that it is alright to shake hands with other _Arathi_. _Oral Evidence:_ Daniel Nduti, December 29, 1970.

40. Appendix I.

41. Ibid.

42. Ibid.

43. Appendix II.

44. Ibid.

45. For details see David B. Barrett, et.al., (eds.), _Kenya Churches Handbook_ (Kisumu: Evangel Publishing House, 1973), Part IV, "Directory of Churches in Kenya," pp. 229-51.

Chapter 8

The _Kirore_ Revolt

After _Muthirigu_, the AIM tried to rebuild its mission
system among the Kikuyu. Only a few adherents remained--the
Kirore; they were located at Kijabe and Githumu, the remaining
two central stations, and at a few out-stations scattered
between them. Generally, there were not more than a half
dozen adherents left at any of these stations; Kinyona, a large
and very active station in the 1920s, had only seven in
1931.(1)
But during the 1930s the AIM did manage to attract some
Kikuyu to their stations. AIM statistics for 1932 reveal
increases from their 1929-30 low point in all categories of
mission work, including church membership, attendance at church
services, and demand for medical services. By 1934, a large
catechumen's class met weekly at Githumu, and the class at
Kinyona had risen from six to forty. Between 1934 and 1937,
the AIM conducted three evangelistic conferences among the
Kikuyu; all of them attracted larger numbers than the mission
had expected. One for women held in 1935 was attended by more
than two hundred.
School attendance also began to rise. The provincial
commissioner mentioned in his annual report for 1932 that "the
station schools at Githumu and Kijabe [had] somewhat
increased." A year later, he noted that attendance at Githumu
had risen fifty percent. The seven students attending school
at Kinyona in 1931 had risen to 125 by 1936. In the same year,
Githumu's out-stations had risen in number to sixteen; in 1940
the AIM estimated their entire school attendance among the
Kikuyu to be as much as one thousand.(2)
There can be no denying that AIM attendance rose in the
1930s following the mass exodus from the mission in 1929-30.
The actual figures quoted were probably inflated, but attendance did rise. The missionaries and the _Kirore_ accounted for
the increase of adherents in spiritual terms: "The stronghold
of the devil" was being pierced, the "evil" days of the female
circumcision controversy were over, the "enemy" was being
attacked, and a revival was sweeping Kikuyuland.
These increases could be accounted for from a more secular
point of view as well. Certainly after the intimidation of
Muthirigu was over and the threat of reprisals had diminished,
Kikuyu who had been afraid to declare their sympathy to the AIM
returned to the mission in the 1930s. When the head assistant
of Theodora Hospital at Kijabe came to inquire about his job,
he was immediately reinstated. This return was credited to
spiritual rebirth; however, one might speculate that he simply
wanted his job back. Several years later when the Kijabe girls'
school was revived, two Kikuyu girls sought admittance after
walking seventy miles to get there. The girls were praised for

having chosen Christianity over their parents' wish that they
marry "old heathen men." The writer fails to consider the
possibility that the mission was providing a refuge for defiant
daughters.

The increase in school attendance can be explained by the
Kikuyu interest in education. In the early 1930s the Kikuyu did
not have many educational alternatives. The long promised
government school for Fort Hall District was not built until
1932, and then it was located to the north in Nyeri district
and enrollment was limited.(3) Independent schools, though
very popular, were still in embryo form and were crowded. It
is not surprising then, that some Kikuyu should have either
returned to AIM schools or joined them when reaching school
age. Of course, it was now much easier to attend an AIM
school, for under the missions' concessions following
Muthirigu, one did not have to become a Kirore to remain in
school.

With all of this apparent success, however, the AIM was
not doing very well. Education department inspection reports
indicate that AIM schools were poor in quality and were
steadily deteriorating. As early as 1933, the provincial commissioner wrote, "The chief educational problem which has confronted the authorities during the year, has been the backward
conditions of mission schools."(4)

Contributing to this condition was the poor quality of
teaching found both among mission and African teachers in AIM
schools. Few teachers had become Kirore and remained with the
mission during the 1929 exodus; those that did remain often had
little education. The AIM did not begin a teacher training
center of its own until 1949, and even then few Kikuyu teachers
were trained. The AIM, therefore, had to depend totally upon
other missions and the government for teachers. As the competition for these teachers was great, particularly by the new
KISA schools, the AIM was not able to attract very many. As a
result, the government school inspectors frequently noted that
AIM schools were understaffed. They also found that the
teachers employed were unqualified, often having failed their
certificate examinations, and that their teaching was
"amateurish." Several times the mission resorted to bringing
Kamba teachers from its stations in Ukambani, but this brought
little appreciable change.(5)

Critical comments could also be directed toward the missionary teachers. From the time of Muthirigu until 1935, none
of the missionary teachers were trained and after that only
one was.(6) Furthermore, the mission supervisor of schools
lived fifty miles away at Kijabe, which resulted in few inspections. The government school inspector in 1940 noted when
visiting Gikomora, an AIM out-school, that the last entry in
the visitors' book was August 3, 1937, when Mr. Kendall the AIM
supervisor had last been there.(7)

From the mission's lack of a serious educational program,
the government recommended the withdrawal or the reduction of

the educational grants made to four AIM out-schools. In the late 1930s the government closed several of the AIM out-schools for lack of teachers and adequate supervision. By 1942, the total AIM out-school network around Githumu had fallen from sixteen to twelve.(8)

In addition, attendance dropped in several AIM schools located on the fringes of AIM territory. The people of Muthithi had for some time tried to get the Church of Scotland Mission (CSM) to sponsor a school in their area. Several local teachers had been trained by the CSM. This connection, together with the good reputation the CSM had for its educational pro-gram, motivated the request. In 1940 the CSM, though reluctant at first, finally built a church and school at Muthithi.(9) Even after the facility was moved some distance away at AIM insistence, to limit competition, the church and school contin-ued to siphon off adherents from the surrounding AIM out-stations.(10)

A similar situation existed at Gathera, another AIM out-station. Speaking of that out-station a government inspector recorded in 1935, "The school was well attended, well kept up and pupils clean."(11) On the surface, the mission seemed to have had a successful school. This was not the case, however, for a long-standing dispute existed between the Gathera Kirore and the independents. Though the independents had built a temporary school and church nearby, they claimed Gathera as their own. In 1939, the two groups literally came to blows over the disputed school and church; several people required hospitalization and one independent was convicted and sentenced to six months hard labor.(12) After that incident, the mission lost the sympathy of almost all local people. Farmers owning the land surrounding the school planted their crops right up to the classroom walls. The good teachers were hired away by the independents, leaving only less motivated and untrained person-nel for the mission. Attendance radically dropped, from 106 in April, 1940, to eighteen by March, 1942.(13) The AIM realized that they could not compete with the independents. When the school inspector recommended that the government grant be with-drawn in 1942, the mission did not protest. Two years later the independents successfully took over the school and church building without any AIM or Kirore resistance.(14)

Many of the AIM's adherents recruited during the 1930s then had left the mission by the early 1940s. This group had been largely composed of non-Christians. When they found AIM schools deficient, they sought education elsewhere.

The Kirore remnant remained with the mission as they had in 1930. Their numbers had grown a little and their lives were a good deal more peaceful a decade after Muthirigu, but they, too, were now discontented. They struggled under the burden of an inadequate AIM educational system. A few Kirore with courage sent their children to independent schools where a better education was available, but the AIM usually disciplined such people by refusing to make them church elders.(15) The Kirore

at Kinyona established some separation from their missionary
overseers at nearby Githumu when they found the mission largely
unconcerned with them. By 1932 the Aregi-Kirore conflicts at
Kinyona had stabilized with the independents clearly dominant.
The independents were building a new school, and they had
recruited several fine teachers. Non-Christians in the area
were attracted and school and church attendance for the independents was steadily growing. The Kinyona Kirore wanted to
compete with the independents for the non-Christian population.
They proposed to the Githumu missionaries that the AIM build
them a new church and school and send them experienced
teachers. The missionary reply was predictable. They carefully
instructed the Kirore to concentrate on evangelism. Repeated
attempts over the next two years brought the same reply until
finally in 1934, the Kinyona Kirore stated that they would
build their own school and church and the AIM should henceforth
stay out of their way.(16) The schism, though real, was not
official, and this enabled the AIM to claim later that Kinyona
was the mission's first self-governing congregation! Over
further missionary objections, the Kirore at Kinyona began to
raise money for their new school by holding sports days and the
various bazaars associated with such events. As a faith mission, the AIM was officially against soliciting funds; they
also spoke out against the Kinyona sports days because they
felt the Kirore were copying the independents' way of raising
money.(17) Nevertheless, the school was built and government
inspection reports record that the Kirore school did quite
well.(18)

The attitude grew at Kinyona and elsewhere among Kirore
that the AIM did not have their interests at heart. The AIM
continued to refuse communion to Kirore under church discipline
just as they did to other church members. Many Kirore felt
that the abuse they had suffered during the Muthirigu period
entitled them now to special consideration; when this was not
forthcoming, some Kirore left the AIM for "lack of fellowship"
with the missionaries.(19) While the Church of Scotland and
Church of England missions were encouraging a self-governing
African church, most Kirore felt the AIM was deliberately
denying them positions of responsibility. Even after 1932,
when the AIM took up the formal training of pastors and evangelists at the Kijabe Bible School, it was a long, slow process.
Those enrolled in the pastor's course undertook three years of
classroom work to obtain a license to preach and administer
the sacraments. Then they spent a number of years in a parish
before returning for a final year of classroom work and ordination.(20) Many Kirore felt totally defeated by what they considered to be an outrageously long course of study. Some
speculated that the AIM never really wanted to ordain any
Kikuyu, but simply established the Bible school to pacify the
Kirore and perhaps to out-maneuver the independents who were
also making arrangements to have their clergy ordained at that
time. This point of view became more popular among Kirore by

1939 when there still was not one ordained African clergyman in the AIM!(21)

The _Kirore_ and other AIM Kikuyu were also deliberately excluded from the mission's governing board. The Kikuyu area was divided among several AIM districts in Kenya. Each district had a missionary committee which in turn had representation on the AIM field council in Kenya. This group of missionaries, under a director, actually ruled the AIM in Kenya, even to the extent that the general council in North America was sometimes subordinate to their field council on local matters. In 1941, when the AIM formally established an indigenous church organization, the African Inland Church (AIC), control over church power was still held by the missionaries. The church offices were filled with Africans, but the power to make all important decisions was still vested in the Kenya Field Council. The AIC remained tightly in missionary hands until 1971; at that time the AIM reluctantly handed over some power to the AIC and then only at the threat of deportation by the Kenya government.(22)

The fact that the AIM had failed to transfer meaningful responsibility to Africans was apparent to the _Kirore_ of the Gospel Mission Society (GMS) as well. In the early 1940s, the GMS was in a state of collapse. The single congregation in New Britain, Connecticut, which supported this mission, was no longer able to do so. As the Knapps, who were pioneer GMS missionaries, grew older, they urged their adherents to affiliate with the AIM, from whom the GMS had originally separated in 1911. The GMS adherents were reluctant to do so for the Knapps had given them a great deal of responsibility over the control of their churches and they did not wish to surrender it to the AIM.(23) The AIM was hoping at least to take control of the nearby and flourishing GMS station at Kihumbuini. But these hopes were dashed after the death of the Knapps. GMS members had noted the powerless AIC and in 1944 they voted to affiliate with the Church of Scotland Mission.(24)

Throughout this time, the AIM refused to make any changes or even to acknowledge _Kirore_ grievances. In 1939 the mission boldly stated its educational policy again. It was moved and carried:

> 1. That we restate our position taken in 1924, namely, that we do not agree to accepting any grants-in-aid which would obligate the mission to maintain a certain standard in the schools, or to furnish a specially [sic] qualified staff of teachers, or to erect and maintain better buildings.
> 2. That we authorize the Field Council to approach Government and state that we can not meet demands for better qualified teachers, grade requirements and buildings; that it is

>   impossible for us to make any promise whatso-
>   ever in this respect. . . .
>   3. That we suggest to the Kenya Field
>   Council that the educational standard in our
>   schools be limited to Standard IV. . . .(25)

A few missionaries and mission personnel in the United
States pointed out that the AIM could not hope to staff its
own schools with people who had only a Standard IV education.
It would be the American equivalent of sending fifth or sixth
graders back into the classroom as teachers after having completed a two-year teacher training course.(26) Others thought
that with this half-hearted attempt at education, perhaps the
AIM should get out of education altogether among the
Kikuyu.(27) On one occasion, the Kenya Field Director actually
proposed that the AIM hand over to another mission all of its
work among the Kikuyu.(28) Nothing came of this, however, and
the vast majority of AIM missionaries were quite satisfied with
the mission's policies and pursuits among the Kikuyu.

The inability to understand or to sympathize with Kikuyu
needs and aspirations eventually led to another and final
exodus from the AIM. In 1947, all _Kirore_ left the mission and
began their own autonomous organization: The African Christian
Church and Schools (ACC&S). Not surprisingly, the issue that
sparked the walkout was education.

Kirore pressure had finally moved a sympathetic missionary
at Githumu to add two advanced years to the meager four year
primary school program offered there. The Mission initially
agreed to this plan because they had weakly resolved several
years earlier that some advanced education might be useful at
Githumu because it would enable candidates for Bible School to
enter at a more advanced level;(29) the new classrooms cost the
mission nothing either as they were constructed by the adherents at their own expense.

At the end of 1946, when Kendall, the resident Githumu
missionary went on leave, his replacement from headquarters had
orders to close down the extra classes. The AIM felt that
Kendall had come too much under the influence of the Githumu
Kirore and that as the advanced primary graduates were not
going on to Bible School training but rather were seeking
government employment, the school was not fulfilling its purpose and should be closed. Propst, the replacement, not only
closed the classes in mid-term, but he tore down a hostel the
students had been using, and confiscated and later sold the
beds, mattresses and other furniture of the students.(30)

The students, their parents (most of whom were _Kirore_),
and AIM adherents in general were outraged. Their response was
swift; within a few days there was a boycott of the entire
Githumu school, the church and all other religious meetings and
activities. All patients left Githumu hospital, and all mission employees left their work. In addition, all personnel

at Githumu Mission were refused services at the market and shops in Githumu town.(31)

From the spontaneity of the boycott, there emerged a group of Kirore who began to meet and discuss what steps to take next. In fact, for several months prior to the boycott, these men had been meeting together for worship and discussion each Sunday instead of attending the AIM service at Githumu.(32) They were all friends who had grown up together in the AIM. Most of them had been adherents before Muthirigu, and they had remained loyal Kirore since that crisis. They elected Elijah Mbatia, head teacher at Githumu, their leader for, as one of the group stated, "Mbatia was a good Christian man, intelligent and educated, and he wouldn't lead us astray."(33) One of the first things Mbatia did was to send two letters of explanation to the AIM. These letters clearly show that just as the mission prohibition of female circumcision was not the only cause for the development of the earlier Kikuyu independency movement, so also, the inadequacy of AIM education was only one of several underlying issues that led to the formation of the ACC&S.

The first letter, dated November 25, 1947, is quite short and it takes up the topic of faulty AIM leadership.(34) Mbatia writes, "After all these years we have been with you, we have thought and understood that we shall never get anywhere under this mission leadership . . . your leadership has been a failure." He cites as an example "the decline of African Christianity under the AIM," and the falling off of church membership. The letter continues with a brief examination of the lack of Kikuyu progress under AIM, and then Mbatia closes by saying that among the Kikuyu a motto states that "leadership is everything" and as the AIM has little leadership to offer, "the church members of Githumu ask you AIM very anxiously to leave Githumu District for good, and work somewhere else as it pleases you as we are fed up with you."

The second, and much longer letter (35) continues to explore the lack of AIM leadership. According to this letter, there has been no continuity of mission staff at Githumu, and no comprehensive plan of development has been apparent. Mbatia states,

> We do not quite understand your [sic] AIM because when a Mission leader comes at Githumu station, he tries to alter and spoil the former missionaries' work whether good or bad. So, you mislead us and we do not know who is right or wrong. Because of this confusion, we go back instead of moving ahead.

Mbatia continues to discuss the consequences of this lack of leadership.

> You left us to lead ourselves in the work of
> the Lord before we are ready to guide our-
> selves. You ought to have given us time to be
> prepared and also to have given us a notice,
> but you did not do so.

Finally, this missionary neglect has produced a very weak
church.

> Githumu Church is very weak and nobody is
> interested to go to Bible School at Kijabe from
> here. . . . The young ones have become so
> disinterested that no one likes to join the
> church. The most important reason is that the
> European missionaries refused to give us help
> before we were strong enough to support our-
> selves. . . .

The reference to support not only involved mission personnel but also financial assistance. An AIM directive several
years earlier announced that because of financial problems, all
money raised in the future would have to be used for the support of missionaries, and all adherents who received financial
aid for their education or their Bible School training would no
longer be getting any.(36)
    The letter also took up what Mbatia considered a concerted
AIM effort to deny the Kikuyu access to information or to
organizations that would help develop their maturity. For one
thing, the Kirore felt that they had not been properly taught
the Bible.

> You have not taught us as the Bible says it
> ought to be taught. For example, in the church
> we have no full pastor although you have worked
> here for over forty years. Moreover you tell us
> that you came to teach the Gospel, and we seem
> to know very little of the Bible.

They also felt that the AIM had not fostered the right
relationship with the Kenya government so the two could cooperate to the advantage of the AIM adherents. In particular,
the Kirore said the AIM had purposely kept them uninformed
about government financial assistance. Where other missions
and their adherents had prospered through government grant-in-
aid money, the AIM had continually refused such funds for their
adherents.
    Finally, Mbatia raised the issue of the AIM's hostility
toward other missions. Throughout its tenure in Kenya, the AIM
remained exclusive and antagonistic to other missions. This
attitude contributed to at least two break-away mission groups,
the Gospel Mission Society (GMS) and the Gospel Furthering
Fellowship, both described above. Mbatia felt that this

inability to see the good in other mission societies worked to the disadvantage of the AIM adherents. "Another example which shows that you do not worry about the Africans' progress is how you refuse to unite with the other missionary bodies in this [sic] matters which concern the progress of the African." Mbatia lists three specific groups: The Alliance Mission, The African Christian Council and the Advisory Council on African Education. It may be well to note here that shortly after the formation of ACC&S, they joined the Christian Council of Kenya, successor to the African Christian Council, as its first independent church member.(37)

Only after these religious issues had been thoroughly discussed were the educational grievances brought up. Mbatia prefaces this section with a general comment on AIM educational failings:

> You annoy us very much because you tell us every now and then, that you did not come to teach the African education, but that you came to teach the Gospel only, and we Africans (like any other nation) like the Gospel as well as education.

The indictment is that the AIM has failed to serve the whole person. The Mission has seen the Kikuyu only as people in need of evangelism and not as people with other legitimate needs.

The letter then moved on to detail the inadequacies of the AIM's educational program: the schools lost to the independents, the poor teaching, the failure to apply for governmental educational grants until recently, the cancellation of grants because of low standards, and finally the most recent grievance concerning the closure of upper primary classes at Githumu. Mbatia finally stated that the AIM's deficient educational system did not happen by chance but resulted from planned neglect. He cited the case of the Githumu principal and school supervisor who had lived since 1943 at Kijabe, a station fifty miles away.

> He says that he can supervise being so far away, and every now and then he goes to Fort Hall Education Board to represent the Mission Schools while he himself knows almost nothing of what goes on at the different schools.

Mbatia went on to say that the excuse usually offered for this state of affairs was:

> that the missionaries are very busy at Kijabe, while we know that there are ten or more missionaries who are busily occupied in their own business which . . . do not concern the Africans.

146

These businesses concerned such things as the AIM press and publishing company, the cutting and selling of lumber from Kijabe forests and the raising and selling of vegetables and pyrethrum from Kijabe farms. The Mission chose to occupy itself in all of these concerns, Mbatia states, because there was great profit to be made; but such activities had little to do with Africans and in fact led to neglect in the Mission's school system.

The letter ended by anticipating the reaction it will receive from the AIM.

> We know that everyone of you will say that
> we are lazy and that it is [sic] why we are
> behind, but we kindly ask those who have mercy
> to try to be sympathetic [sic] and not to judge
> as [sic] wrongly. Because if we were lazy,
> there are many brothers who surround us and
> have progressed as their leaders have worked
> hard to raise them up.
> IN THESE CIRCUMSTANCES, the blame of the
> bad leadership must be placed on the past
> Leaders (The European Missionaries) and not on
> the ones to be led.

AIM headquarters in New York briefly acknowledged both of Mbatia's letters, saying that because of the distance, they would have to refer the situation back to the Kenya Field Council.

Both acknowledgments ended with the same uncompromising point:

> If there has been failure then let us look to
> the Lord to grant that it may be righted. Let
> us be certain, however, as to just where the
> failure is. Let us remember that it is not by
> might nor by power, and we might add nor by
> buildings, nor by education, nor by force, nor
> by many things which the world looks to, but by
> spirit, saith the Lord. There is always the
> danger that we may be granted the desires of
> our hearts, but with the leanness of our
> souls.(38)

The mission, although aware of the seriousness of the schism, refused to take any responsibility for what had happened. The General Secretary of the AIM in his report of the schism to the mission's officers, stated that none of the dissident leaders were members in good standing. This comment was obviously designed to cast doubt on the spiritual character of the movement. He went on to say that outside interference from the Kendalls was probably the "chief cause" for the schism.(39) There is some evidence that the Kendalls gave encouragement to the Kirore after the schism,(40) but it is naive and superficial for the mission to suggest that the Kendalls actually sponsored the separation itself. The report ended with the General Secretary urging that a strong hand be taken.

> Let us join hearts in prayer for the missionaries in Kenya, and ask God especially either to convict the signers of these letters and bring them into line, or give our men the grace to root them out and to proceed with the work.(41)

In December, 1947, the AIM sent Kenneth Downing, son of a Kijabe pioneer missionary, to Githumu to investigate the schism. He proceeded for several months to try to heal the break by ordering the Kirore back to church and school. He compared them to children having a temper tantrum when they could not have their own way. He said that the mission knew what was best for its adherents, and it was unthinkable that Africans should challenge the mission.(42)

Downing's insensitive approach convinced many adherents that they had been right to leave the AIM. He was about the same age as many of the Kirore; he had grown up with them on the mission field. Who was he to tell them what to do? They particularly resented the fact that Downing endorsed the idea of limited education for Africans when he himself had been sent off to the U.S.A. for both a complete high school and college education. To this day, Downing is not welcome at Githumu.(43)

The colonial government was anxious that the AIM and its adherents settle their dispute. They first suggested holding a plebiscite, because they thought that except for a few Githumu dissidents, the district would vote overwhelmingly to stay with the mission. But after Downing's stay at the mission, neither the AIM nor the government was certain that the vote would be in the mission's favor. As a result, the government suggested instead that a meeting be held on June 29, 1948 in the District Commissioner's office between the Kirore and mission leaders.(44)

As a gesture of goodwill, the government had persuaded the AIM to replace Downing with Mr. Devitt, a more popular Kijabe missionary.(45) However, the mission continued to insist that they knew what was best for their adherents.(46)

Many Kirore regarded this meeting as the point of no return. They came away feeling that the AIM was neither able nor willing to understand their point of view. The time had now come to make their separation from the AIM permanent,(47) and this happened in a rapid series of actions. The ACC&S was officially formed, by-laws and a constitution were written and work on ACC&S headquarters at Gituru was begun; ACC&S brought court action against the AIM to recover the investment the Kirore had made in the Githumu buildings;(48) ACC&S declared the seventeen AIM out-stations in the district now to be ACC&S schools and churches.(49)

Long range plans were also laid for the administrative structure of the ACC&S. This structure began in each congregation where the people chose a church committee and a school committee. The committees were encouraged to settle all local problems, but issues which could not be resolved were sent up the administrative hierarchy to the Parish Council. In this structure, which still exists, there are five parishes within the ACC&S, each with its own council composed of delegates from each congregation in the parish. If an issue cannot be resolved there, it moves on to the general council, the highest governmental group of the ACC&S. The congregational committees and the parish councils meet as often as needed, but the general council only meets annually. It is a large body with representatives elected from each congregation to three-year terms. The ACC&S president is elected at large for a three-year term also, and from within the general council a vice president and treasurer are chosen. Between the annual meetings of the large general council, the executive officers together with several appointed members look after ACC&S business throughout the year. To aid them, they have hired a general secretary, the only full time and salaried administrative employee.

The ACC&S constitution built in a number of safeguards to prevent the dominance the AIM had had over its adherents. Congregations and schools had a great deal of local autonomy. The parish councils and the general council had a broad representative base. Representatives could only be re-elected twice to the general council. Anyone could be removed from the general council by a seventy-five percent vote of that body.(50)

The ACC&S have remained theologically close to the AIM. Worship patterns and beliefs have remained the same and the ACC&S have rejected all Kikuyu customs, including female circumcision.(51) Unlike the AIM, however, they are anxious to have a trained African clergy. As there were no fully ordained clergy among the Kirore when they separated, the general council has elevated several men to that position. In the years since 1948, a few other men have received theological training and they, too have been ordained by the church.(52) In another about face from the AIM, the ACC&S has given full support to the cultivation of a person's mind, for they have said ". . . if a man's mind and body are weak, so also will be his spirit."(53) Indeed, the very name of the ACC&S was to emphasize the linkage between education and evangelism. The ACC&S was committed to serving whole people, not just their souls. Toward that end the ACC&S proposed to begin a number of medical dispensaries and to seek assistance for the vocational and technical training of its members.(54)

They believed that academic knowledge did not necessarily preclude one's belief in God, but that God could be served better by educated people. This gave impetus to the development of their educational system. The seventeen out-schools taken from the AIM continued to give three or four years of primary education. A new upper primary school was built at Gituru to provide four additional years of advanced education. The plan was for ACC&S students to begin their education in neighborhood schools and then if they wished, to continue preparatory work for secondary school at Gituru.

A successful financial appeal was made to all ACC&S members for the construction of Gituru school. In early 1949, 30,000 shillings was raised and this enabled the first buildings to be put up by mid-year.(55) With this accomplished, the ACC&S applied for a government grant to continue their building program. At the end of the year the Governor himself, Sir Evelyn Bearing, came to Gituru and presented ACC&S leaders with a 20,000 shilling check. A new stone section was added to the school with this money, consisting of six classrooms, four offices and an assembly hall.(56) A government inspection report in 1949 recorded that Gituru provided an excellent education and that its teachers and students were excited about learning. The only negative comment was that the attendance registers were not kept up to date: ". . . in some cases, the numbers present were in excess of the numbers given on the roll."(57) This can probably be explained by a very rapidly increasing enrollment.

The _Kirore_ never considered joining the independents. As one ACC&S leader said:

> During _Muthirigu_, they sang against us and so no one even thought of joining them at all . . . the question was never raised because everyone felt in their heart that they could not join the independents.(58)

Some accommodation with the independents at nearby Mariira was achieved, however, because all of the Githumu students were temporarily shifted to the KISA school there. They were taught separately from the other students, but they stayed at Mariira for two terms while the new ACC&S school at Gituru was being built.(59)

The ACC&S have grown and prospered since the separation from AIM in 1947: Gituru has become a large secondary school for both boys and girls; five KISA schools closed by the government have elected to come under ACC&S management since 1955; by 1970 ACC&S had a total of nineteen out-schools. The church has grown, too. The last statistics available record that in 1962, there were 14,000 adherents and 7,800 full baptized members worshiping in five parishes and twenty-three churches. By 1971, the number of adherents had nearly doubled to 25,000.(60) In the same year the ACC&S successfully attracted several Canadian missionaries to help with both church and school development.(61)

The AIM not only refused to acknowledge the success of the ACC&S but tried to prevent it. When the Kikuyu teachers boycotted Githumu school, the mission brought in Kamba teachers to keep the school open. Later the mission reversed its decision and added an upper primary section at Githumu.(62) This, of course, was exactly what the Kirore had wanted for so long, but the concession came too late and no one responded. The AIM next refused to hand over the out-school land certificates to the ACC&S, and hired a lawyer to fight the ACC&S suit for compensation on the Githumu mission buildings.(63) The AIM lost the case and was forced to pay 20,000 shillings compensation to the ACC&S. At the same time it had to officially hand over all out-schools to the ACC&S.(64)

The separation between the two groups was complete. Only three AIM adherents in Githumu district remained with the mission--two aged evangelists and a Kikuyu girl who had been adopted by one of the missionaries. Over the years a few ACC&S adherents have had second thoughts about the wisdom of the schism, among them an old and ailing Elijah Mbatia. But the vast majority of the ACC&S have remained confident that their decision was correct. The AIM refused to redress legitimate grievances and the Kirore, according to the official ACC&S history, had the right to seek another place "to feel at home."(65)

END NOTES

1. The section which follows is reconstructed primarily from articles found in <u>Inland Africa</u> (British Edition), 1931-1936, <u>AIM</u>, London.
2. Central Province Annual Report, 1936 PC/CP 4/3/1, <u>KNA</u>; Devitt to Campbell, April 2, 1940, Devitt File, <u>AIM</u>, New York.
3. Kikuyu Province Annual Report, 1932, PC/CP 4/1/2, <u>KNA</u>.
4. Kikuyu and Kamba Provincial Annual Report, 1933, PC/CP 4/1/2, <u>KNA</u>.
5. Inspection of Schools, 1934-50, DC/FH 6/2, <u>KNA</u>. See in particular the following dates for AIM school inspections: November 2, 1937, August 6, 1938, January 4, 1939, February 25, 1941, and March 12, 1941.
6. Central Province Annual Report, 1936, 1937, PC/CP 4/3/1, <u>KNA</u>.
7. Inspection of Schools, 1934-50, "Report to Githumu Inland Mission," November 2, 1937, "Inspection Report for Gi-Komora," April 3, 1940, DC/FH 6/2, <u>KNA</u>.
8. DC, Nyeri to Director of Education, Nairobi, January 4, 1959, Inspection of Schools 1934-50, DC/FH 6/2, <u>KNA</u>; Fort Hall District Annual Report, 1942, PC/CP 4/4/3, <u>AIM</u>.
9. A.R. Barlow CSM Tumu Tumu Mission to D.C., Fort Hall, May 27, 1938. Fort Hall and Naaro I File, <u>PCEA Archives</u>; <u>Oral Evidence:</u> Morris Gatiri, January 9, 1971.
10. <u>Oral Evidence:</u> Morris Gatiri, January 9, 1971.
11. Inspection Report 4/12/B6, Inspection of Schools, DC/FH 6/2, <u>KNA</u>.
12. Central Province District Annual Report, 1940, PC/CP 4/4/1, <u>KNA</u>.
13. Inspection of Schools, Gathera, April 2, 1940, and March 13, 1942, DC/FH 6/2, <u>KNA</u>.
14. Central Province Annual Report, 1942, PC/CP 4/4/2, <u>KNA</u>; Central Province Annual Report, 1944, PC/CP 4/4/2, <u>KNA</u>.
15. <u>Oral Evidence:</u> Philip Mutitu Ndegwa, August 25, 1970.
16. Hartsock to Campbell, Hartsock File, February 4, 1932, March 1, 1932, and May 3, 1932; Education Safari report for Githumu Out-Schools, August, 1932, <u>AIM</u>, New York.
17. "Education Policy in the Africa Inland Mission, Kenya Field": A memorandum submitted to the Annual Business Meeting of the Kenya Field, January, 1940, <u>AIM</u>, New York.
18. AIM Mission Schools Inspection Reports: February 25, 1941, and March 12, 1942, Inspection of Schools 1934-50, DC/FH 6/2, <u>KNA</u>.
19. <u>Oral Evidence:</u> Paul Githutha, January 6, 1971.
20. Ruth Recover, <u>Through Missionary Eyes: The Training of Pastors and Evangelists</u>, n.d., Recover file, <u>AIM</u>, New York.
21. <u>Oral Evidence:</u> Cleoper Gatiuka, January 9, 1971.

22. John Gration, "The Relationship of the Africa Inland Mission and Its National Church in Kenya Between 1895 and 1971," unpublished Ph.D. dissertation, School of Education, New York University, 1974; and private communication with John Gration whom I wish to thank for unstintingly giving of his time to answer my questions and for allowing me to read his dissertation while it was still in preparation.

23. CSM director, Tumu Tumu to Secretary, Mission Council, March 31, 1942, Kamrui I File, 1924-45, PCEA Archives.

24. Oral Evidence: Kambui group interview, June 4, 1971; Ngenda group interview, April 10, 1971.

25. "Education in Kenya" a memorandum presented to the Committee of Direction, August 9, 1939, AIM, New York.

26. "Education Policy in the AIM, Kenya Field," memorandum submitted at the annual business meeting; Kenya field, January 1940, AIM, New York.

27. Inspection Report for Ndakaini School, March 12, 1941, Inspection of Schools 1934-50, DC/FH 6/2, KNA.

28. Calderwood to Executive Committee of Council, Confidential Memorandum, February 28, 1939, Fort Hall and Naaro I File, PCEA Archives.

29. The minute reads that while a Standard IV education was sufficient in most places "at Central Stations more advanced education may be given in connection with Bible School training." Meeting of the Committee of Direction, August 9, 1939, AIM, New York.

30. Oral Evidence: Livingstone Mukunya, May 13, 1971.

31. Oral Evidence: Samuel Wanijihia, June 11, 1971. The other AIM central station, at Kijabe, did not participate in the boycott or the eventual formation of the ACC & S. There were fewer adherents around Kijabe though oral evidence reveals that apparently they had grievances against the AIM similar to those held by Githumu Kirore. When asked about ACC & S, Kijabe informants simply reply that it was a Githumu district affair and did not affect them. Apparently, Githumu Kirore never invited Kijabe adherents to join ACC & S either; Oral Evidence: Emma Mathys, November 19, 1970.

32. Blakeslee Prayer letter, August 31, 1947, Blakeslee File, AIM, New York.

33. Oral Evidence: Livingstone Mujunya, May 13, 1971.

34. Elijah Mbatia to AIM Field Director, Nairobi, and AIM Home Council, New York, November 25, 1947, "Githumu Affair" File, AIM, New York. All quotations in the following paragraph come from this letter.

35. Elijah Mbatia to the Aim Field Director, Nairobi, and AIM Home Council, New York, December 2, 1947, "Githumu Affair" File, AIM, New York. Unless otherwise cited, all material used in the following paragraphs comes from this letter.

36. Campbell, Director of AIM, to Woodley, November 15, 1930, Woodley File, AIM, New York.

37. Frederick Welbourn, <u>East</u> <u>African</u> <u>Rebels</u> (London: SCM
     Press, 1962), p. 155.
38. Ralph T. Davis, General Secretary, AIM to all members of
     the church of Githumu, December 18, 1947, and Davis to the
     Church Council, AIM Githumu, January 20, 1948, "Githumu
     Affair" File, <u>AIM</u>, New York.
39. Ralph T. Davis, General Secretary to Committee of Direc-
     tion, December 17, 1947, "Githumu Affair" File, <u>AIM</u>, New
     York.   Mr. and Mrs. Kendall were the AIM missionaries at
     Githumu who authorized the building of the advanced pri-
     mary classes and who were generally sympathetic to the
     Kikuyu desire for more education.   For this attitude, the
     Kendall's contract was not renewed, and after their leave
     in 1946, they returned to Kenya under the auspices of the
     Gospel Furthering Fellowship, a rival mission to the AIM.
     Fort Hall District Annual Report, 1947, PC/CP 4/4/3, <u>KNA</u>.
40. <u>Oral</u> <u>Evidence</u>: Joseph Muthungu, March 5, 1971; Kambui
     Mission to R.G.M. Calderwood, December 20, 1947, Kambui II
     File, <u>PCEA</u>.
41. Davis to Committee of Direction, December 17, 1947, <u>AIM</u>,
     New York.
42. <u>Oral</u> <u>Evidence</u>: Emma Mathys, February 2, 1971.
43. <u>Oral</u> <u>Evidence</u>: J. Ndiba, May 20, 1971; <u>Oral</u> <u>Evidence</u>:
     Emma Mathys, February 2, 1971; Elijah Mbatia interviewed
     by Samuel Mugo, August, 1965, <u>NCCK</u> <u>Archives</u>.
44. Fort Hall District Annual Report, 1948, PC/CP 4/4/3, <u>KNA</u>:
     Blakeslee Prayer Letter, September 17, 1948, <u>AIM</u>, New
     York.
45. Instructions to the Field Director and Confidential Notes
     from the Field Council Meetings, April 10-16, 1948, <u>AIM</u>,
     New York.
46. Fort Hall District Annual Report, 1948, PC/CP 4/4/3, <u>KNA</u>.
47. The people at Ndakaini had successfully boycotted the AIM
     in 1926; the mission finally let them appoint the teacher
     that they wanted.   Ndakaini and several other AIM out-
     stations viewed the 1947 boycott as a plot to get the
     mission to change.   But most AIM adherents never thought
     the mission would change. The boycott was just the begin-
     ning; now it was time to move on to the other steps toward
     final separation. <u>Oral</u> <u>Evidence</u>: J. Ndiba, May 20, 1971;
     Livingstone Mukunya, April 24, 1971; Joseph Muthungu,
     March 5, 1971.
48. Joel W. Kuria, "The Separated Brethren," unpublished
     honors paper, Kenyatta College, January 1969.
49. Fort Hall District Annual Report, 1948, PC/CP 4/4/3, <u>KNA</u>.
50. "Mawatho na Miturire ya ACC & S" [Constitution and by-laws
     of ACC & S] n.d., Mimeo, <u>NCCK</u> <u>Archives</u>.
51. <u>Oral</u> <u>Evidence</u>: Joseph Mutungu, March 5, 1971.
52. The first clergy ordained by ACC&S were men who had
     passed through the Kijabe Bible School program and were
     working in AIM parishes awaiting ordination.   To their
     credit, St. Paul's Theological College was the first

154

mission controlled seminary to take ACC & S candidates. More recently, several ACC&S candidates have received their theological education at the Lutheran Seminary in Arusha, Tanzania. Oral Evidence: Mugo Mwangi, April 22, 1971.

53. "Mawatho na Miturire ya ACC&S," p. 2.

54. Kuria, "The Separated Brethren," p. 10.

55. ACC&S appeal letter, n.d., kindly shown to me by Mugo Mwangi, General Secretary, ACC&S, from his personal file.

56. Oral Evidence: Elijah Mbatia interviewed by Samuel Mugo, August, 1965, NCCK Archives.

57. Report on visit to ACC&S school at Gituru by education officer, Nyeri, February 15, 1949, "Inspection of Schools, 1936-50, DC/FH 6/2, KNA.

58. Oral Evidence: Joseph Muthungu, March 5, 1971.

59. Oral Evidence: Daktari Samuel, March 16, 1971.

60. Kuria, "The Separate Brethren," p. 12.

61. Oral Evidence: Samuel Mugo Mwangi, May 19, 1971; Elijah Mbatia interviewed by Samuel Mugo, August, 1965, NCCK Archives.

62. Janet Wyngard to Joselyn Murray, October 13, 1966. Letter in my possession.

63. Davis circular letter 23 to Field Council members, September 27, 1948, AIM, New York.

64. Shapley, Barret, Allin & Co., Advocates to Rev. K.L. Downing, AIM, June 13, 1955, "Te S.C.C.C. Nol. 1952-1950-- Elijah Mbatia and Joseph Muthungu V. AIM," AIM, New York.

65. Kuria, "The Separated Brethren," p. 16.

Conclusion

The first five decades of this century have been marked by deep and sustaining religious divisions among the Kikuyu. Protest against mission authority, particularly as articulated by the AIM, and the need to establish institutions and structures that met their own needs had, by the mid-1930s, produced three identifiable groups: the Aregi independents or those who rejected AIM authority and seceded from the mission; the Kirore or those who remained local to the AIM (only to finally secede from the AIM twenty years later) and the Arathi or spirit people who rejected all things western as well as significant aspects of Kikuyu culture. In the years that followed, these rival groups regularly antagonized or shunned each other as they competed for adherents among themselves and within the larger pool of Kikuyu not associated with any group.

These divisions were particularly visible during the Mau Mau rebellion of the mid 1950s, and have been explored by scholars only in that context, when significant numbers of Kikuyu engaged the British in guerrilla warfare while others joined the Home Guard militia and fought against them. Scholars have generally attributed this emergence of nationalist and loyalist divisions in the 1950s to the differing political ideologies that developed among the Kikuyu.

This is the approach taken by Carl Rosberg and John Nottingham in their classic account of nationalism among the Kikuyu.(1) They argue that the Mau Mau rebellion was politically motivated and grew out of several decades of continuous political activity. According to them, this political activity prompted the development of several opposing groups, each with its own political beliefs. More recently, John Lonsdale has suggested that the political polarization found in the Mau Mau rebellion might be best seen as generational conflict in which the contemporary generation (1940s and 1950s) were seeking to usurp the power and influence of their elders.(2)

Other scholars have suggested that political ideology may not have solely determined the nationalist and loyalist groups of the rebellion. M.P.K. Sorrenson, the New Zealand historian, contends that

> . . . land lay at the bottom of much of the unrest in the Kikuyu reserve during the post-war years and which was to develop into the Mau Mau revolt. . . . Many grievances over land were in fact settled by the word during the Emergency.(3)

In D.W. Throup's "The Origins of Mau Mau," the polarization among the Kikuyu is also seen as economic. For Throup, there were two opposed and antagonistic groups in the reserve; the large commercial cultivators who were often times chiefs, and

the smaller, poor and middle peasants who were at their beck
and call.(4) Finally Greet Sluiter, in her study of fortified
villages during the Mau Mau rebellion concludes that the divisions which she witnessed had socio-economic roots as well.(5)

     While one cannot dismiss the political and economic polar-
ization that these authors have seen among the Kikuyu, especially in the 1950s, my own research suggests that neither
political ideology nor economic conditions adequately or completely explain these Kikuyu divisions. They were certainly a
contributing factor, but the origins of these divisions lie in
the arrival of Christianity and the Kikuyu encounter with it at
a much earlier date. I have argued that missionaries, Christianity and most especially Kikuyu Christians themselves
initiated and set in motion these divisions, through a whole
set of conflicts that were beginning to be visible as early as
the 1920s. At the heart of these conflicts were the differing
and increasingly antagonistic points of view that grew among
three groups: the Aregi who separated themselves from the AIM
over the issues of mission authority and control, and the
continuing role of culture in the lives of Kikuyu Christians;
the Kirore who remained loyal to the AIM and fought bitterly
with the Aregi over this loyalty; and the Arathi who despised
both groups and struck off on their own in defiance of western
and Kikuyu cultural conventions.

     This is not to say that politics played no part in the
origins of these groups. This study has shown that intrinsic
to the Kikuyu encounter with missionaries and Christianity, and
indeed, also with the colonial administration and government
chiefs was their growing dissatisfaction with all parties.
This dissatisfaction led to the formation of informal groups
throughout Kikuyuland, first visible in the 1920s, grievances
were discussed and action plotted against both government and
mission. The membership of these dissidents' cells drew
heavily from among all those who were to become Aregi, Kirore
and Arathi in the next decade. Membership in such discussion
groups and the topics discussed were very fluid. They did not
differentiate between the political and religious topics of
discussion; a recent speech by Harry Thuku or the return of
someone from a Kikuyu Central Association (KCA) meeting might
prompt a meeting just as often as a recent "run in" with a
missionary or growing AIM authority over a nearby outstation.

     Following Muthirigu and the rupture of relations between
the AIM and the Aregi, the association between the independents
and politics continued, particularly with the KCA. We have
seen how throughout the 1930s and 1940s, the Aregi sought
assistance from the KCA for fund raising, teacher training and
advice. In return, KCA membership often included Aregi independents and their church and school buildings were frequently
used for political meetings, including Mau Mau oathing in the
early 1950s. Indeed, the Aregi independents and the political
activists were closely linked groups and membership often
included the same people. The thread of association among

these people, which started in the 1920s, had continued right down to the beginning of the Mau Mau rebellion.

While _Aregi_ were often found to be members of the KCA and its later offshoot, the Kikuyu Progressive Association (KPA), it was unusual for either _Kirore_ or _Arathi_ to be found as members of these associations. This should not necessarily lead us to believe that they were unconcerned with the political issues that were being raised by these organizations. They were not any more insulated from the ills of living in a colonial society than were the _Aregi_. In the 1920s they had all been enthusiastic supporters of Harry Thuku and later the KCA. But a decade later, _Kirore_ and _Arathi_ support for the KCA had shrunk to almost nothing.

I think that at least a partial explanation for this paradox lies with the growing religious divisions among the Kikuyu. The explosion of ill feeling and the continuing antagonism among _Aregi_, _Kirore_ and _Arathi_ made it difficult for any of these groups to identify with the concerns sponsored by another, regardless of how sympathetic they might be to the political issues themselves. The fluidity of membership that was characteristic of religious and political dissent in the 1920s was almost completely absent in the 1930s and later. In this respect, the Kikuyu were quite different from the Shona of Zimbabwe who shifted freely among several identities, including mainline mission protestantism and African independency.(6) It was clear by the 1930s and 1940s that the Shona experience had not been duplicated among the Kikuyu. At that time, when the KCA and the KPA helped to promote church independency (often in rivalry to each other), they became associated with people who had been, and were continuing to be, adversaries of both _Kirore_ and _Arathi_. As a result neither of these groups could bring themselves to join or to continue their membership with the political associations of their rivals; the gulf that separated them was too great to cross.

Seen in this light the Mau Mau rebellion was a further expression of these religious divisions. I would suggest that a share of the people who took up arms against British colonial rule or who sympathized with those who did were _Aregi_ independents. They had long identified themselves with protest and action. Now their activities in support of Mau Mau, including those of oath administrator, flowed naturally from this earlier political and religious participation. In like manner, it was the _Kirore_ that often supported the government and joined the Home Guard, the militia formed to repel the forest fighters at the local level. Now it is not a coincidence that _Kirore_ and _Aregi_ were on opposite sides of the Mau Mau rebellion, though little scholarly attention has been given to this fact. The often cited rationale for _Kirore_ support of the colonial government has been their reluctance as Christians to embrace the violence of Mau Mau. In his comments on these loyalists, Bethwell Ogot has said that in being true to their faith, they had to reject Mau Mau.(7) Along the same lines, Mukaru

158

Ng'ang'a has suggested that the Christians of southern Murang'a
had become increasingly hostile toward the "terrorism and the
'heathen' way of the Mau Mau."(8) As convincing and as logical
as this may sound, it is not the whole story. What has not
been taken into account is that a large number of Christians in
this area were Kirore and this placed them on the side opposite
those associated with the rebellion, the Aregi. When for
instance, the African Christian Churches and Schools (ACC&S)
decided that they would support the colonial government against
Mau Mau, quite a number even joining the Home Guard in
Murang'a, it was not only because they abhorred violent methods
of resistance. It was primarily because the ACC&S was composed
exclusively of Kirore and by siding with the government against
Mau Mau, they were opposing their old rivals, the Aregi. Even
more than this, in becoming Home Guards, the Kirore were now in
a position to legally attack the people toward whom they had
felt such long-standing hostility and at whose hands they had
suffered in the past.

Time and the changing circumstances of post-independent
Kenya have not necessarily softened the antagonism among any of
these groups. The Arathi have continued to elicit an unsym-
pathetic reaction from all others and have kept to themselves.
The antagonism between the Kirore and the Aregi has continued
since the Emergency, but the Aregi have become more influ-
encial. Following the 1954 government ban on Kikuyu independent church activity, many independents handed their churches
over to the established missions, mainly the CSM and the CMS,
so that the structures would escape demolition. Others simply
joined these mission churches or stopped church worship altogether and waited for a better time. That time came after
independence in 1963 when the Kenyatta government granted freedom for all religious expression. This prompted an Aregi
exodus which Hastings had called the last big separation
phenomenon from mission churches (9) as the independents began
to rebuild their churches or reclaim the buildings that they
had given to the missions during the Emergency. This activity
has provided a new arena for bitterness and rivalry between
Kirore and Aregi. Kirore and their later converts were now
often in control of the very churches that the independents
handed over to the missions and now wished to reclaim. In the
1960s and 1970s, scenes reminiscent of the 1930s were again
acted out. Aregi and Kirore, and their full grown descendants
as well, clashed over a common claim to church plots, church
buildings and even church furniture. Court cases were
threatened and blows were exchanged in this long and continuing
dispute between the two groups. In one community the independents set about building their own church alongside the Kirore
church they had failed to reclaim. The Kirore came nightly to
impede the construction by filling in the trenches, stealing
the building stones and roofing sheets, and pulling down the
construction of the previous day. When finished the church was

so close to that one could disrupt a service in the other by simply shouting out of the window.(10)

Further rivalry and ill-feeling was generated between the two groups over the Kikuyu oaths of loyalty to President Kenyatta and his government which took place in 1969-70. Some _Aregi_ now claimed the right to be oath givers because they had administered oaths prior to and during the Mau Mau rebellion. They now used this opportunity to retaliate against their enemies, the _Kirore_, for it was in the oath-givers' power to punish people for past misdeeds when ratifying their pledge of loyalty to Kenyatta. Since many _Kirore_ had refused to take oaths during Mau Mau and had even fought against the rebellion as Home Guards, they were now fined large sums of money and even assaulted.(11) These latest reprisals by _Aregi_ against _Kirore_, though extreme, were only a continuation of the religious rivalry initiated in the first decades of the twentieth century.

For the Kikuyu, then, especially those of northern Kiambu and southern Murang'a, the encounter with Christianity and the AIM created deep religious divisions. These divisions had immediate and long lasting socio-political and religious implications. Kikuyu society was fundamentally changed. As Terence Ranger has so accurately commented on African Society: "We are nowhere dealing with single, homogeneous rural cultures or societies . . . they are complex and ambiguous."(12) These divisions have significantly influenced Kikuyu twentieth century history and must be taken into account even when discussing the Mau Mau rebellion and more recent events.

END NOTES

1. Carl Rosberg, Jr. and John Nottingham, _The Myth of Mau Mau: Nationalism in Kenya_ (New York: Paul Mall Press, 1966).

2. John Lonsdale, "Kikuyu Political Thought and Ideologies of Mau Mau," paper presented at the African Studies Association Annual Meeting, New Orleans, Louisiana, November 23, 1985.

3. M.P.K. Sorrenson, _Land Reform in the Kikuyu Country_ (Nairobi: Oxford University Press, 1967), 80.

4. D.W. Throup, "The Origins of Mau Mau," _African Affairs_ Vol. 84 (1985), 399-433.

5. Greet Sluiter, "Confidential on Migrant Labour and Connected Matters in Four Villages in Kiambu Reserve of Kenya," report for the Christian Council of Kenya, n.d. seen in the PCEA Archives, Nairobi.

6. Marshall Murphee, _Christianity and The Shona_ (New York, 1969, 187).

7. Bethwell A. Ogot, "Revolt of the Elders: An Anatomy of the Loyalist Crowd in the Mau Mau Uprising: 1952-56," _Hadith IV_ (Nairobi: EAPH, 1971), 134-148.

8. D. Mukaru Ng'ang'a, "Mau Mau, Loyalists and Politics in Murgang'a 1952-1970," _Kenya Historical Review_, Vol. 5, No. 2 (1977), 368.

9. Adrian Hastings, _A History of Christianity 1950-1975_ (London: Cambridge University Press, 78).

10. These scenes continued throughout the time I was conducting fieldwork in 1970-71.

11. _Oral Evidence_: Ndegwa Metho, April 22, 1971.

12. Terence Ranger, "Religious Movements and Politics in Sub-Saharan Africa," _African Studies Review_, Vol. 29, No. 2 (1986), 57.

Appendix I

Arathi Beliefs

"Rules Written on March 3, 1950"
by Joseph Ng'ang'a Kimani

Church Rules

This is the thinking that I, Joshua Mburu [known also as Joshua Ng'ang'a Kimani] was told by God to teach leaders [deacons or servants]. To choose from the Holy writings of god all that He has spoken and what He will speak later.

First Thahu--About Thahu

God has instructed us in the Holy Bible to separate ourselves from others when we have come in contact with Thahu.

For instance, in this church, when a woman or girl has Thahu during her monthly period, the rule is that she should stay by herself without coming into contact with other people for seven days. Her stool [or chair], clothes, bed or any other thing that she possesses cannot be touched. She cannot cook for people, and men cannot see her or sleep with her. This is God's and is found in the following scriptures: (Genesis 21:35-36, Leviticus 15:19, Ezekiel 18:6, 22:10 and 36:17, Mark 5:25, Luke 8:43).

Second Thahu--Giving
Birth and Being Cleansed

In this church, when a woman gives birth to a boy, she is unclean for 40 days and for 80 days if she has given birth to a girl. She cannot go to the Holy place like the house of God, and she cannot cook for holy [or clean] people. Her things cannot be touched by those who are praying to God until she goes to the house of God to be prayed for. She may stay with the one who is helping her with housekeeping for 14 days if a girl is born. If it is a boy, even if the 14 days are over and the mother is not clean, her helper can continue to stay with her until she is well, and she then can be left to serve herself for the remaining days until she becomes clean. When the helper leaves the mother, she stays for seven days in her house and then goes to the house of God to be prayed for: (Leviticus 12:1, Luke 1:59, 2:22).

162

Third Thahu--Husbands and Wives

The rule concerning husbands and wives in their home is that when they are trying to have children, they are not permitted to give clean or holy people food. If, however, they want to return to the house of God, they must purify themselves the first week and at the end of the second week go to the house of God: (Exodus 19:15 and 20:8, 1 Samuel 21:4, 1 Corinthians 7:5 and 6:18).

When a woman becomes pregnant, they must be careful not to spoil the baby before it is taken to the house of God to be prayed for: (Matthew 1:24-25, Joel 2:16).

Something Important

God spoke to Joshua telling him that people at home should purify themselves on Wednesday, so that they can be present in the house of God for service on Sunday. They should be careful not to give a baby Thahu by spoiling its milk: (Genesis 21:8, 1 Samuel 1-20 and 2-20, 1 Peter 2:2).

Fourth Thahu--Uncleanliness For Men Only

The rule in this church is that when a man gets Thahu during the night,[emits semen] he must wash himself with water. He must also wash all his clothes which he has in his bed and all other clothes that he may have. He also has to wash his chair, and none of those things can be touched before the sun sets: (Leviticus 15:16-22, Deuteronomy 23:10-15, Jude 1:23, Zachariah 3:3, Isaiah 6:6).

Fifth Thahu--Blood Disease and Leprosy

We members of this church believe that if one has Thahu from a blood disease or leprosy, he should stay separate from the others without coming into contact with them or touching the things to be used by people who are praying to God. Such a person cannot enter the house of God: (Numbers 5:2, Leviticus 15:2 and 22:4, 2 Samuel 3:29, Mark 5:15, Luke 8:43).

Sixth Thahu--Seeing or Burying a Dead Body

If someone touches or buries a dead body, touches or steps on a human bone or tomb, he stays unclean for seven days, and he must purify himself in a separate place on the first, third and seventh days. After that, he goes to the house of God to be prayed for so that he may become clean. One who enters a house which has a dead body or one who sleeps in it stays unclean for seven days and then must purify himself together with the house and everything in it: (Numbers 19:11, 5:2, 31:19, and 96:10, Leviticus 21:1, Ezekiel 44:5, Haggai 2:13).

Seventh Thahu--Thahu
of Eating

It is not good for any of God's people to eat blood
[eating meat from an animal whose blood was not drained
properly]. We do not eat blood because eating blood does
not please God: (Genesis 9:3-7, 7:26 and 28:4, 17:10-15,
and 19:26-27, Deuteronomy 12:15-17, 12:22-26, and 15:21-
23, Acts 15:19-21 and 21:25-26).

We do not eat meat from an animal that has died on
its own or has been killed by another animal: (Leviticus
11:7, 17:15 and 22-8, Numbers 22:31, Deuteronomy 14:3 and
32:38, Psalms 141:4, Isaiah 65:4 and 66:17, Hosea 9:3,
Acts 15:19-21 and 28:30).

We do not eat meat from a pregnant, sick or dead
goat. Nor do we eat meat sacrificed to the dead or anything offered to God which is not of truth, for example,
meat sacrifices offered by the Kikuyu during marriages or
after giving birth is food offered because of tradition,
and therefore not to be eaten.

It is Not Good for a Person of God
To Eat Sacrifices to Untrue gods

We do not eat sacrifices offered to untrue gods:
(Exodus 34:15, Numbers 25:2, Acts 15:20, 28:3, 21:25-26,
and 16:4, 1 Corinthians 8:1 and 10:19-28, Revelation 2:14-
18).

We do not eat the meat sacrifices offered when girls
are being married or the food offered by the Kikuyu during
marriages. We also do not eat the meat sacrifices offered
when women give birth, those offered when someone is
caught committing adultery in another man's home or those
offered when one has conceived a girl. We do not eat the
meat or any kind of food given for that nor do we take any
money given because God says that those who take such
things eat the body: (Numbers 25:2-10, Deuteronomy 23:17-
19, Leviticus 21:9 and 19:29, Acts 7:42, Revelation 2:14-
18, 1 Kings 14:24-27, 15:12-14, and 22:46-47, II Kings
23:7-9).

We Do Not Eat These Animals

Pigs, rabbits, camels and all things that have Thahu
because God does not hear those who eat them: (Leviticus
11:4-9, Deuteronomy 14:3-9, Isaiah 65:4-6, and 66:17-18,
Ezekiel 4:14, Acts 10:13, Romans 14:21).

The House of God

It is not good for shoes or any other articles of
Thahu to enter the house of God: (Exodus 3:5, Joshua
5:15, Exodus 38:8-9, Acts 7:22).

We wear white clothes while praying to God and even
put them on while working in our homes. That is what God

has taught us: (Leviticus 6:10 and 16:4, Exodus 39:27-29, Ezekiel 44:17, Revelation 19:14 and 4:4).

While building the house of God, we separate ourselves from any contact with women.

Other Laws
Baptism

When someone believes, we baptize him with the Spirit but not with water: (Isaiah 32:15, Jeremiah 31:31, Joel 2:28, Matthew 31:11-12, Acts 1:4-6).

If someone has been baptized elsewhere and he comes to our church, we lay hands on him if the Spirit gives him a name. We lay hands on all those that we baptize as the Lord has shown us: (Acts 19:4-7, II Timothy 1:6-7, Isaiah 56:5-6, I Corinthians 15:28-30).

Marriage
First-giving the dowry

When a man wants to marry, he comes to the church and tells the church elders. They pray to God to reveal the girl who ought to be married by that man, as Isaac the son of Abraham was married (Genesis 24:24 and 12:28). This is done because we never like our men or girls to marry people who are not of our church. They are like different tribes and we are told not to marry with tribes which are not believers of the word of God (Exodus 34:16, Genesis 6:2-4, Deuteronomy 7:3, Ezra 9:2).

When the man has promposed to a girl, the church calls her and asks whether she would agree to the marriage: (Genesis 24:57-60, 1 Corinthians 7:38-39).

When the girl agrees, they are given permission to go to her father, accompanied by one church elder to discuss the matter. The man must present himself and his faith to the girl's family and tell them that our church does not eat or offer sacrificial things asked for by the girl's father, like bags, calabash, strings, sacrificial meat or even beer. The girl also tells her parents that we do not give such things, because it is against the witness of our church: (1 Corinthians 10:19, Deuteronomy 32:16-18 and 7:25, Numbers 25:1, Joshua 23:7-8).

After the man has married, he gives only a token dowry because of the word of Moses, because it is not the custom of Christians to sell people like slaves. Our Lord Jesus came to release all people from the slavery of tradition and therefore, it is good for a Christian to give his daughter in marriage without asking for a dowry: (1 Corinthians 7:38-39, Genesis 2:18).

A Woman's marriage after the death of her Husband
     It is right that the woman should be married again
but not unless it is in the Lord 1 Corinthians 7:39-40).
For this reason, it is not acceptable that she should
marry one of her husband's brothers as is the Kikuyu
tradition, because he and his lineage may separate her
fro 'he church, claiming her for their property. They
take her for their wife, and then no church leader can say
anything about it since she becomes the property of
others. Although Moses told the Israelites to be marrying
widows, there was nothing bad in it since all had one
faith and were children of one God. We Christians and are
of the faith of Christ who came to release all people from
traditional customs. Therefore, it is not good for a
believer to ask for a dowry because the wife will then
live as a slave. Nor should the brother of the deceased
husband marry the widow. Rather, give your daughter to be
married in the Lord.

Marriage in the House of God
     When the man has paid the dowry, then he and his
bride are taken to the house of God to be married so that
they may be joined as wife and husband; he leaves father
and mother to be joined with his wife: (Genesis 2:24,
Malachi 2:14, Proverbs 5:14-20, Matthew 19:5-12, Ephesians
5:31, Hebrews 13:4).
     After marriage, they are commanded by God to stay
for three days praying for themselves without having
marital relations.

The Marriage Renewal of Husbands and Their Wives
     In this church, if the husband and his wife believe
both are baptized and married [marriage renewed]. It is
the word of God that said so because when they had lived
without a marriage [Christian] ceremony, they were
adulterers in the eyes of God as they had married
themselves without God's permission. Therefore, God sees
it as right for husband and wife who have become believers
to have their traditional marriage renewed in the church:
(Hebrews 13:4-6).

Giving Birth to Holy [Clean] Children
     In this church, Christians do not use the
traditional custom of naming their new born children after
members of the family.

Spirit's Command
     Soon after a baby is born, it should be said that an
Israelite has been born because early people of God did
not name their children but were given names by God:
(Genesis 17:19, II Samuel 12:25, I King 13:2-3, Matthew
1:21, Luke 1:13-23 and 1:57-65).

Our Resting Days
Sabbath Day on Sunday for All People
We rest on all Sabbath days of Sunday and we do no work such as collecting food from the garden, drawing water, selling in the market, going for a visit or cooking because we do not make fire. All of this is according to the fourth commandment: (Genesis 2:2, Exodus 16:23, 20:8 and 31:12, 32:21-22, and 35:2, Isaiah 56:2, and 58:13, Jeremiah 17:21, Nehemiah 13:15-22, Hebrews 3:7-16 and 4:4-8).

Friday Sabbath
We rest on all Friday Sabbaths in remembrance of the death of our Lord Jesus Christ: (Leviticus 16:29, 23:26, Hebrews 9:13).

Adultery or Fornication
If members of our church commit adultery or fornication, we send them out of our church forever because they have spoilt the Temple of God: (Matthew 5:27-33, I Corinthians 6:9-11, and 7:2-3, Revelation 21:8-9 and 22:15-16, Numbers 25:7-9 and 31:13-18).

Cutting of Hair or Beard
No one from our church male or female can have their hair or beard cut: (Leviticus 21:4-8, and 19:27, Judges 14:5-6, Numbers 6:5-6, Ezekiel 44:20).

Hand Greetings
It is not right to greet [by shaking hands] any person you meet on the way because people usually have Thahu such as having committed adultery, eating sacrificial foods which a Christian should not touch. As a result, on shaking hands, you are contaminated with his Thahu. Another may have come from eating pork, drinking beer, or from a tomb and after greeting him, you can not pray well to God. God has said, "Come from their midst and separate yourselves from them.": (II John 1:10, II Corinthians 6:17, Luke 10:4, Psalms 73:13, Isaiah 52:11).

The Right Greetings
Laying on of Hands
When one is being ordained as a preacher, baptizer or a church elder, he is greeted by the elders who are above him so that they may be of one fellowship. Those are the only correct hand greetings: (Galations 2:9-10, Numbers 27:18-23, Deuteronomy 34:9-10, Acts 13:3, 6:6, 8:17 and 19:4, I Timothy 4:14, II Timothy 1:6).

Appendix II

Arathi Beliefs

"Things to be Observed by all Godly People"

by Joseph Ng'ang'a Kimani

1. We went to help Eratstus Warii, Mark Ndonga and. other people who were not believers as they were building something in Khiriga. After the work, we sat down to eat and drink as is the custom.
2. On going back home from the work, we went to our place of worship and God spoke to us in the mouth of Mark Ndonga s/o Mwanja saying, "You have sinned very much because of eating sacrificial things since Kikuyus do no building work without eating food more impure by adultery or connected with improperly slaughtered animals. If you are asked again to help, do not eat or drink anything there."

The Sabbath

Erastus Warii and his family used to dig arrow-roots on Saturday and prepared with fire on that day in the garden. On the Sabbath, fire was made for them the whole day so that they could be sold on Monday in Giitwa Market. One day, he and his wife Martha Wambere went to sell the arrow-roots and on their way back, Erastus was bitten by Isaiah Kagwanja's dog called Ndege on the thigh and the thigh swelled very much. God said that he had caused the dog to bite him because of their cooking on Sabbath days. On another Sunday, his wife pounded maize for porridge and in the evening became sick. God then said that she became sick as she had worked on a Sunday.

Our house of worship was next to the garden of John Karuga's mother and as she came to get food from it, God told Erastus Warii to tell her not to come for food again or else God would beat her. She then said that she belonged to the group which worshiped round a stump and they had belief like that and so she would continue to get food from the garden as she used to. Warii told her that she would have to see. When she came to get green vegetables and maize from the garden and went home, she became sick and her son John Karaugu called us to pray for her. On arriving, God said that she could go to get maize from the garden on Saturday. Since it now was on a Thursday, she said that she would be very glad with God if she recovered. God was a true God for she recovered. On recovering, she said that she would go to the stump to ask Arathi to pray for her for the Thahu. However, she was

later taken by the disease again and she died because of
spoiling the sabbath.

Eating Sacrificial Things

God stopped me in Kahiriga at the time when Mark
Ndonga's sheep was pregnant. God said that it should not
be eaten. A pregnant sheep is bad even if slaughtered.
When we were in Ithiru in Kirigithu, four people were
asked for goats to be eaten by Deacons. One gave a pregnant she goat and God said that it should not be slaughtered.

In 1933, a girl called Ruth Njeri Kamau was conceived by a Mwaru called Njoroge and an ox was slaughtered
for her. Her father called the Deacons to go and eat the
meat. God said that the meat should not be eaten by His
Deacons because they come from a body.

In 1949, an ox was slaughtered in Gathumuri which
was meant for a feast. People said that it should be
slaughtered in the Arati way [drained of all blood] so
that all people could eat. After everyone had eaten, God
said that in the future meat offered on such occasions
could not become holy because of the way it was slaughtered, and should not be eaten.

Ayub Wanjaama

I was told that I am not liked on Ayub Wanjaama's
ridge because I eat meat from sacrifices.

God's voice told me that I have been seen eating
food at weddings in Cukari. Now I thought that everything
found there has been blessed by an ox offered as a sacrifice. But God said that there is nothing clean even if
cleansed by wisdom or prayer because the blood of Jesus
has not been trusted, only the blood of an ox.

What is Mixed With Kikuyu Tradition

In the west was a teaching that if a woman conceived
and then stayed for six months sleeping with her husband,
the babies [or children] were spoilt.

On giving birth, the woman would not eat until the
time when she was cleansed, and went to be prayed for on
that day. At that time the child "was made to grow" and
a goat for the baby was slaughtered. If any of the meat of
the slaughtered goat was eaten before the baby tasted it,
then the child would become bad. On that day, the wife and
husband hurried very much to go and be together so that
the woman cooking for them [helping] would not eat before
them and the child became a bad one [get sick or die].

This is not connected with Christianity even a bit
but is all traditional. There are two types of things in
Arati Church: good spirit and bad spirit. The bad spirit
explains traditional things while the good spirit is the
teacher of the good things of God and holy things which

are Godly and which are not connected with tradition and the body. That is why there cannot be agreement [or friendship] between people directed by the true Spirit and people directed by the bad spirit. So that Satan may not be seen, he connected his things with God's. Now we had a very big struggle and a big split.

Taking Two Wives

The bad spirit got a chance to get in amongst us when people said "it is right for leaders to marry two wives so that if one has Thahu, the other can still cook for her husband. However, this was not a good thing but something to corrupt our leaders so that the work of God's spirit could not be perfect.

I, Joshua Mburu, [known also as Joshua Ng'ang'a Kimani] opposed it and there was a conflict because God told me to stop this practice. Enmity with elders was created and they sent me out of their villages and they wrote me a letter saying that I should leave them because I was spoiling their faith. I stayed in Mbiga at Jonah Kabui's and some young men and girls found me there. They had been expelled because they had refused to pay a shilling for something they did not know about. Fearing that they might have to join a Kiama they did not know about, they had refused to pay. While we were still at Mbiga's, God told me, "I have been waiting for you to choose those things which you have heard God say should be followed. Collect them with those good writings in the Bible and put them in one basket to give me." I then collected them and Jonah told me that God had done good now for these young men and girls could now be taught the word of God because it is the one which is troubling them. I taught all those who wanted the word of God including old men, women, young men, girls and even children. I then took them to the house of God and we prayed, consecrating ourselves to God and separating ourselves for God to follow His ways and what He would teach us.

After praying, God spoke to Paul Daniel Thiongo telling him that not all who were taught spoke the truth for some turned their faces to God while others turned their backs to Him. This means that some have accepted the word of God while others have refused it. Rebecca Herina, a girl, was told to come and tell me that the basket in which I was told to put the word is the Holy Spirit of God.

After a time, I received a letter of prophecy from Safron Gichuki, telling me that those young men and girls who had come to me were not after the word but deceived Joshua and God. That thing came to pass as there emerged a religion of young men and girls calling themselves Apostles and was against what I had taught them as they called mine a religion where someone washed many times and so a religion of Pharisees and theirs a religion of Apostles with no Thahu. They said in their religion that each man should claim one girl and later to marry her so the religion became a bad one.

The Sin of the Old Men Who Contacted Thahu

The first shepherd in Murangi at Joseph's was Zedekia Kimwaki, and he went to Njoro with Naumi. While they were on the way, he told her to put on a sheet so that on arrival, they could say that they were married and therefore be allowed to stay together. On arrival, they were given a separate room and they had their chance to sleep together. On their way back to Murangi, God said that they had done something bad.

Safron and Hanah Warigia went to visit Safron's brother and were given a place to sleep. At night, Safron called Hanah and told her that he had already committed adultery with her in his heart, so they could now do it bodily. However, the girl refused, and Safron had Thahu and they left Njoro on the following morning. On another day, as he and his wife were lying together in a bed and Hanah was sleeping on the floor, he went to the floor and told her to fulfill the word of God, but the girl refused.

Adultery and Meat Which Has Not Been Well Slaughtered

The witness is David Macharia Kahirian, who was told by God that men would die for the sake of women [for liking them]. Secondly, unclean food is of three types: (1) meat which has not been well slaughtered, (2) having anything to do with idols or dead people (Acts 15:20, 15:28, 1:4), and (3) meat that has been forbidden by God.

The sin of Arathi guided by the bad spirit is to make a meeting unclean in two ways: (1) to attract leaders to worldly things and (2) to deceive others into thinking that they are the givers of the word of the Lord, thereby sinning because the spirit of Jesus does things of Jesus and not of the world. When Jesus was offered the world by Satan, he refused it. Even when given [the world] by Jews (John 6:15 and 18:36), he refused it. The Arathi started marrying as many wives as their heart pleased, taking the example of the old people who did it. It is sinful to marry two wives; the first example was Lamech of the tribe of Cain who was not blessed by God (Genesis 4:19-20). The other was Abraham, who was given Hagar by Sarah so that she could bear him children. This was following the custom of where they had come from and Abraham believed it because he was only young in the faith and the advice of God (Genesis 16:1-4). But this thing among people never became perfect because enmity developed between Sarah and Hagar until Sarah blamed Abraham for the cause of the bad feeling (Genesis 16:5-6).

This should be understood by everyone that Sarah
told Abraham that she gave Hagar her servant to him to put
on his bosom, but then Hagar turned against Sarah. Sarah
then said, "Now let God judge me with you whether it is
right for Hagar to be my fellow wife.
Abraham did not wait for God to judge the case but
believed in Sarah's reasoning and gave her Hagar to do
with her whatever Sarah wanted (Genesis 16:6-7). Hagar
left the home because of being hated by Sarah and escaped.
She was brought back by an angel of God and told to go and
humble herself before Sarah. Hagar was thus called by the
angel a ser ant but not a wife. She was called Sarah's
servant (Genesis 16:7).
This was done when Abraham and Sarah had become wise
[or had knowledge] in the word of God on His holiness
to know that people's sayings and God's are not the same.
God opened Sarah and she bore a boy called Isaac (Genesis
21:1-8). Sarah saw that Hagar hated Isaac so she told
Abraham to send [Hagar] away with her son, for the son
could not be a heir like Isaac (Genesis 21:9-11). Abraham
felt badly that he should lose his son, but God had to
come and judge him with Sarah because God had to judge
them whenever something was too difficult for them
(Genesis 21:11).

Emulating People from the Past

Those people who would like to emulate people of the
Old Testament like Abraham who sinned for having many
wives, and Jacob for many wives and putting up a stone for
sacrifice should know that they are hiding in bad deeds
since those people of old were not commanded by God but
hid and were hidden by the bad spirit together with Satan.
People who would like to emulate righteous people of old
should look at people like: (1) Isaac who did not marry
many wives for he knew himself as one of the covenant and
waited to be used by his owner rather than use himself
(2) Joseph, the son of Jacob, who told his master's wife
when she wanted to lie with him that he did not like to
sin against the People of God (Genesis 39:7-19). He
refused to commit adultery before he even thought of
having a wife because of the fear of God. Many people
committed fornication with prostitutes, people's wives and
even girls because they did not know when God would give
them a dream of the person which they were to marry.
Adultery and fornication today are very common since men
are not satisfied with their wives, and wives are not
satisfied with their husbands. Young men and girls do
not wait. Joseph refused the woman's offer because of
fearing God even though he did not know whether he
would get a wife. Deacons [servants] should not copy
Solomon; he was a ruler and rulers can do whatever they
like with women. Moreover, he did not please God. Let

them copy Joseph because when he became ruler over all of Egypt, he was given a girl to be his wife but he did not commit adultery nor did he marry another wife; he did no wrong in ruling either.

Joshua was the leader of all Israel and a leader of all battles and with no wife but he never degraded his rule by making himself unclean with wives of other people, harlots or girls. He was a leader with no wife like Jesus, Paul, or John (Joshua 1:1-10, 11:15-16). Joshua was righteous, and that is why God gave him power to defeat kingdoms even with much power.

Samuel, while both a judge and a ruler, did not spoil the work which he was given by God but was careful not to be bribed so as not to make himself bad before God and the people (1 Samuel 12:1-5). Those who connect themselves with the word before the coming of Christ should copy those servants Isaac, Joseph, Joshua and Samuel.

Now let us start talking about Jesus, who said "copy me because I am both the beginner and the one to turn people back to God in happiness" (Matthew 11:29). We now have learned to dedicate ourselves to God till we had no weakness and were like Him (Hebrews 1:12, 1 Peter 1:18). He never offered the blood of any other thing to beseech God. If Jesus did not offer any visible sacrifice, he who offers a visible sacrifice does not copy or follow Him.

What Jesus wants is for us to dedicate ourselves to Him. We assume that we do not exist just as Christ did, to demand not his will but the will of God so that Jesus can do His will in us (Romans 12:1-3, Ephesians 5:2-5).

The disciples of the Lord Jesus teach the followers of God to copy them because they copied Jesus. Paul told his disciples to copy him (1 Corinthians 11:1-2, 4:16-17). Peter, on advising doers of the work of the Church or in preaching, told them to do deeds which were good so that they could be followed by learners of Godly things. John told disciples that as Jesus lived here with us, Jesus wants us to live like that (1 John 3:17, 4:17-18). That is how we should copy Jesus and His disciples, who did as God wanted (1 Thessalonians 4:7-8).

Leaders of these days have not differentiated between the spirit of God and the spirit of the devil; that is the reason why our faith is being led by the bad spirit to the dirt of the things which cannot rhyme with God or the Spirit of God like that one of marrying more than one wife. That is not the spirit of Jesus.

Offering sacrifices and spilling blood or burning and having gold walking sticks for leaders conferences is the advice of the bad spirit because Jesus did not have such things and did not offer sacrifices for land bound- aries as they are doing these days. He did not consecrate a house before living in it by throwing Taatha [contents of an animal's stomach, considered powerful] on the land, for this is not following Jesus but another seed led by the bad spirit. The seed of the spirit of Jesus may get spoilt by such practices.

Israelites were forbidden to pray on mountains or under trees so as not to copy what other nations were doing. (Matthew 12:2, 16:21, Isaiah 57:5-7, 1:29, Jeremiah 3:6, 17:2, 1 Samuel 1:12).

But they stilled prayed on mountains, hills and under trees (Chronicles 6:25 and 1 Kings 3:4). When they stopped pleasing God, they made themselves unclean in His eyes (Psalms 78:58-60). When Jesus came, He built a new building pulling down the old one and said that God did not want to be prayed for on mountains or in villages. But a time will come when he will bear new seeds by the spirit those who will not need to pray on mountains or under beautiful trees but will be praying to God with the Spirit because God looks for those to be praying to Him (John 4:19-25, 2 Corinthians 3:17 and Ephesians 2:14-20). Now to go to heaven does not involve worship at the mountains and the sacred trees. There is no other blood which remained for cleansing Thahu or making a follower a worker of God perfect except that one of Jesus alone. Again He is the one who gives people His Spirit so that they might be really perfect to do His work. There is nothing like a lamb offering to the old men so they might remove their grudge or so that a newly married man may succeed in his new undertaking or for one who touches a corpse, or a delivered woman, a woman with a child just dead or if a woman is raped by rogues. All these are defeated by the blood of Christ and there is no other help needed.

Again about praying facing Mt. Kenya. We Arathi made the doors of our houses face that way. Those of the churches, burying a person facing Mt. Kenya or facing it during circumcision; in all these, we found that Jesus was not in them because he himself is all these. He said in John 4:21, 3:16, 3:35, 5:22, 6:39, that now there is no covenant in the Lord or church until God has penetrated the hearts, all hearts and spirits that tell lies and also those things which are done in secret (1 Corinthians 4:5-6).

Along the same line of teaching were these things: If the greatest part of the down [Kugurario] was not done and other things fulfilled according to Kikuyu customs, the girl would not fare well or deliver well. If a goat was not slaughtered before the marriage, the girl will not be good or feel settled throughout her lifetime. She was to face some difficulties since no blood was shed. Before a man got married he gave out an offering to the elders so that he might be regarded as an adult old enough to marry. He gave a lamb and if he failed to do this, the marriage was not perfect since no blood was shed.

In order to be married and considered adults, people must have their background traced so as to know whether they had entered the _Kiama_ or not. If they had not, they would be requested to, so that they may be regarded as adults.

It was a must that a goat be slaughtered. But this ordination was not good in front of God's eyes; it was for this tradition. Those who were ordained were of three kinds.

1. Muhoi
2. Preacher
3. Church elder who had the first seat.

God said these things in December of 1947 when Kenyatta came from England, and he said them at Jororoko too. If the servants of God refused to serve and obey him, then they should not disobey Kenyatta, the president. They would be taken to Kenyatta to serve him and be baptized by him. From thence, God's servants did not continue perfectly in serving Him. They mixed godliness with politics, but they never rhyme since each of these has its own foundation.

Versions of Muthirigu

I.(1)   If I were to say (repeat two times)
        Macana Kinungi would have his medals added
        Lamentation! this lamentation!
        You are lamenting over uncircumcised girls.

        Envious old man sit down with us
        I am 'of the aeroplane'(2) and so
        I can pass in the air
        Mwembe (muthirigu) which I saw in the path or way of
        native.

        The church you are liars
        The church you are liars
        You've cheated the governor and
        'we were singing with spears'
        Mwembe (muthirigu) which I saw in the path
        or way of native.

        If I were to say (repeat two times)
        This country of Kenya would never be
        settled by a foreigner
        Rather let me be arrested but let
        Muthirigu continue.

        If I were arrested today I would
        be taken to Murang'a
        Europeans at Murang'a are the arm-rings of Mbira
        Rather let me be arrested but let
        Muthirigu continue.

        Kikuyu you are foolish and it is no joke
        You lost the 'driller' because of 'matchbox'
        Mwembe! (muthirigu) which I saw in the path
        or way of native.

        We now have the Aeroplane, Ciachini Karanja
        Our native person will be the 'driver'
        Rather let me be arrested but let
        Muthirigu continue.

        If I were to say (repeat two times)
        Machana Kinungi could have his medals added

        Let me be beaten or be cut
        but these Mambo Leo(3) remain.
        Oh! dear! the song entered into

our veins
Seven days sleeping in the woods
Rather let me be arrested but let
Muthirigu continue.

Fifty-cents or a cent piece
So that when John [Kenyatta] comes,
he may take tea at hotel
Rather let me be arrested but let
Muthirigu continue.

The church you are liars
The church you are liars
You cheated the governor and
'we were singing with spears'
Sorry! Sorry my dear which is meaningless.

Stop saying this English and Swahili [nonsense]
I was brought up by being fed
with potatoes and lumps of bananas
Rather let me be arrested but let
Muthirigu continue.

The church you are clever
The church you are clever
"You ate a peeled potato
now you give it unpeeled"(4)
Rather let me be arrested but let
Muthirigu continue.

Father only brings grief
and Mother the same
I became disobedient to parents
and in danger of 'Kimuri'
Be beaten or even cut but let Muthirigu continue.

Girls of Kihumbu-ini
you're good in front of the eyes
But you are measured
in pounds like meat
Be beaten or even cut but Muthirigu continue.

II.(5)A. Kikuyu you are foolish
Kikuyu you are foolish
You left "Githegethi"(6) for match boxes
Arara, arara, arara, for match boxes

You Church elder
You ate an uncovered sweet potato
And when mine arrives
You tell me to eat it covered.

I am being told to marry a KIRUGU(7) with mbari (clan)
that have no "NGINME"
I will be giving "Mambura" [offering]

Kurinu I will never be a Christian
Kurinu I will never be a Christian
I became a Christian a long time ago
and I experienced loss rather than gain

Naitipu will be forgiven
Naitipu will be forgiven
because of revealing secrets
which have been concealed

Mother of a KIRIGU if we meet
Greet me and greet me with Mbembe [Muthirigu]

For I am not your "Muthoni" [inlaw]
Your Muthoni is "NGUI" [a bitch or conflict]

Give a cent or a fifty cent piece
When John comes back he will drink tea with Naitipu.

I will never travel in the Monday vehicle [train]
It sweeps away "Githana"(8) or "Ruhiri"(9)

B.   Haya, Haya, Haya
Doctor [Arthur] with Riki [Leakey]
You have conspired to make Kikuyu children
hit kokoto [small stones]

If you want to kill me,
kill me
And you will be killed by the sword
of Jehovah.

I will marry a KIRIGU for "Thiguku"
     (celebration or holiday)
to please IRII(10) with her.

Mother do not worry,
do not worry yourself
For I am a Kikuyu
and I cannot change religion.

IRIGU are not costly;
only seven dogs and you marry in the Church.

We want Githomo [education]
but where can we be schooling because of
the bad smell of IRIGU.

Naitipu if I had to give my opinion,
the people of union could
be buried speaking.

C. Haya, Haya, Haya, I will speak
Mene, Mene,(11) I do not live in a person's
home. I do eat Naitipu's
Mwere and Mukombi is Kikuyu's wheat.
And to know that it is really bad,
it (Kirigu) will urinate in the bed and say that
the bed had become cold.

You will marry but your mother is circumcised,
therefore where will you build for it [Kirigu].

I will sing with sorrow because of KIRORE
which we have been forced to put aside.

III.(12)Little knives
In their sheaths,
That they may fight with the Church,
The time has come.

I am going to break all friendships,
The only friendship I shall retain
Is between me and Jehovah.

I used to think Jesus was the son of God;
I have now found out
That he was an Indian. [in another version "Picture"]

He who signs(13)
Shall be crucified.

You elders of the Church.
You are fools.
Would you sell your lives for money?

Ten thousand shillings
Were given for Harry:
Now the same amount
Is offered for John.

When Johnstone shall return
With the King of the Kikuyu,
Philip and Koinange
Will don woman's robes.

The D.C. ---------------
Is bribed with uncircumcised girls,
So that the land may go.

```
        It [the "muthirigu dance"] has intoxicated us,
        We spend the night in the bush
        And go home in the morning.

IV(14)1.The Church you are stupid
        You abandoned your fire lighters
        for the sake of matches box

      2.The uncircumcised girl is ignorant
        She is asked for a tie
        And she brings a tether,

      3.You know they [uncircumcised girls] are stupid
        For Joseph Gathoga
        Has lost his head.

      4.I would not marry an uninitiated girl
        For an uninitiated goat
             [portion of ears and tail cut off]

      5.The Church, you say you are a helper
        Why does Kamuro son of Mutaro
        Wear tattered clothes.

      6.I drink beer and the Church punishes me
        But when a Church leader drinks
        He is forgiven.

V.(15)1.If  I  were  to say,  Koinange  and  Waruhui  [colonial
            chiefs]
        Would be buried alive.
        Land, Land, This Land
        Was left to us by Iregi [our ancestors].

      2.To be sure he is foolish, [Koinange]
        He went to tell the Governor about it.

      3.Koinange and Waruhui
        Is it the Kikuyu people
        That you are imprisoning.

      4.Koinange and Waruhui
        Koinange and Waruhui
        You will be buried alive.

      5.This Land you are betraying
        Was left to us by Iregi.

      6.The Governor said that,
        If Muthirigu stopped,
        He would not rule again.
```

7.We want people like Macharia,(16)
  Macharia Kinungi, Macharia Kinu,
  Who speaks with the D.C.

8.It was asked who and who
  were singing Muthirigu
  Macharia Kinungi put up his hands.

9.You say that it has been composed
  but it is not, for it is voicing things
  Which had been disturbing us in our minds for a long
  time
        Mountain Mountain
        This mountain you call Kenya
        Was called Kirinyaga.

10.Dance it well
   As we danced it
   In chief Kagori's location.

11.There is not a single place
   God for them (Iregu)
   For if they go to the West [Kisumu],
   Their teeth will
   Be taken off.(17)

12.They will all be circumcised
   But one will be left
   To keep the rule only.

13.It was asked who and who
   Were singing these things
   And I, a Kikuyu,
   Put up my hand.

14.And the mother of Rahiti
   Always mourns at the thought,
   That she would never
   Greet anything after her
   Daughter was converted.

15.You say it is forbidden
   You say it is forbidden
   Who read the forbidding letter,
   Smell, smell, smell
   I have smelt uncircumcised
   girls passing nearby.

16.They want wise people
   Like my Peter Gichura
   Who buys for them
   Half a donkey's body to eat.

17. Wallace(18) has given birth
    His wife has given also.
    They cried all the night
    Who is going to cook for them.

18. I will ask my father
    If my clan marries
    Uncircumcised girls.

19. I will buy one myself [an uncircumcised woman]
    Tinned milk is bankrupting me.

20. I will buy one
    For my Mother
    Who is old now.
    She can fetch firewood
    for her.

21. I will buy one to make me some stockings
    After making me the stockings,
    I will send her away.
    Smell, smell, smell
    I have smelt
    Uncircumcised girls
    Passing nearby.

22. Nickolas Kariuku has given birth.
    His wife has given birth also,
    They cried throughout last night.
    Who is going to cook for them.

23. It has taken us
    We spend the nights outside
    Singing and return to our
    Homes in the mornings.

24. Joseph Kimui has given birth.
    His wife also has given birth.
    They cried throughout last night.
    Who will go to cook for them.

25. To be sure that she is foolish.
    When I ask for a tie she brings,
    A rope instead.

26. I have been wandering.
    Like a bull-dog.
    But when I returned to my home,
    You brought to me a creature.
    With the worst characters.

27. To be sure that she is foolish.
    She gives a one-week-old baby maize.

28. To be sure she is naughty,
    Whichever home she goes
    She climbs castor oil trees.

29. To be sure she is naughty,
    She urinates in the bed,
    And says it is another kind of wetness.

END NOTES

1. Oral Evidence: recorded during an interview with Kamunja Karanja, February 15, 1971.
2. Kikuyu age-set, dated about 1918.
3. Government sponsored newspaper, published monthly in Swahili.
4. Church elders had married circumcised wives before the controversy began, but now they insisted that Christians marry only uncircumcised wives.
5. These verses were found in English in an unpublished paper by Mugo Mwangi "ACC & S Foundation and Early History," August 12, 1965, NCCK-Limuru Archives.
6. A fire making stick.
7   Uncircumcised girl--an insulting term.
8. A cow's first milk.
9. A cow which has not yet produced a calf.
10. Bit uncircumcised boy--an insulting term.
11. To speak frankly.
12. Recorded in CSM Memorandum on Female Circumcision, Appendix V.
13. Takes the "vow" against female circumcision.
14. Found in English in Joseph Ndung'u's field notes, n.d. NCCK-Limuru Archives.
15. Oral Evidence: Recorded at an interview with Simon Mwangi, October 31, 1970.
16. Local out-school leader in Kamunyaka--Giachuki area.
17. Reference to the Luo practice of removing the front teeth.
18. Wallace Njuguna married an uncircumcised woman to the great consternation of the local community.

BIBLIOGRAPHY

I. Oral Sources

A. Interviews
        My single most important set of data consists of 125
interviews which I conducted from June, 1970, to August,
1971. These interviews were helpful for virtually all the
areas investigated but also absolutely essential for
reconstructing the origins and development of rival groups
of adherents.

B. Student conducted interviews
        Approximately 200 interviews were conducted for me
by Kikuyu secondary school students.   These interviews
were helpful in locating knowledgeable informants which I
then interviewed myself; some of my best informants were
located in this way.

C. St. Paul's Theological Seminary at Limuru and the National
Christian Council of Kenya Research Project.
        Students at St. Paul's have conducted interviews on
the establishment and growth of Christianity in various
parts of Kenya since 1965.   The Rev. William B. Anderson
kindly made available to me transcriptions of the Kikuyu
interviews.

II. Archival Sources

A. Africa Inland Mission Archives--New York (AIM, New York)
        When I consulted these records in April, 1970, they
were somewhat haphazardly housed in the old mission headquarters in Brooklyn and the new headquarters at Pearl
River, New York.   Little care had been taken to preserve
them in an orderly way; there was no index or other
instrument with which to guide ones research.   Consequently, I had to begin work at one end of a long line of
filing cabinets and simply work my way through to the
other end.   The basic categories of the Archives are the
following, though these sets of data were often mixed
together, some-times within the same file: correspondence
from missionaries on the field to the AIM director;
minutes of district, regional and central committee
meetings;   candidate papers;   manuscripts and position
papers on various mission issues, e.g. education, AIM
origins,   recruitment;   prayer letters; correspondence
between AIM, New York and AIM, London; personal files for
each AIM missionary.   Missionaries' personal files provided the single most useful source of helpful information; prayer letters ranked second.

B. Africa Inland Mission Archives--London (AIM, London)
        Very few records have apparently survived several
    moves of the London headquarters.   I had access to the
    minutes of various councils, correspondence between London
    and New York, and a number of manuscripts. I was told that
    there was nothing else but missionaries' personal files
    which I was not permitted to see.

C. Kenya National Archives (KNA)
        It is possible to generally reconstruct a year by
    year account of what local, regional and national colonial
    officials thought was happening among the Kikuyu through
    Handing Over Reports, Annual Reports, Political Record
    Books, Minute Books and correspondence on a variety of
    topics such as female circumcision, political dissent,
    education and Watu wa Mungu (People of God).   While valu-
    able for learning about colonial government ideas and
    plans, and generally understanding the "European perspec-
    tive," these records reveal very little of what was
    actually happening between Kikuyu. Deposits from the
    Church Missionary Society and Ministry of Education were
    also consulted.

D. Rhodes House Archives--Oxford
        From this massive project which seeks to collect and
    to preserve non-official materials from the entire British
    Empire, I found a number of diaries and manuscripts. These
    I have listed below under VII, Unpublished Papers and
    Manuscripts.

E. Public Record Office (PRO)
        In this deposit for official British Colonial
    records, I consulted the correspondence and reports of the
    Imperial British East Africa Company and the Foreign
    Office for Machakos, Fort Smith and Dagoretti.

F. Presbyterian Church of East Africa Archives--St. Andrews
      Church Nairobi (PCEA)
        Only a small portion of the PCEA, [formerly Church
    of Scotland Mission], materials have been organized and
    catalogued; the vast majority are simply laying on tables
    or on the floor of a tower room in St. Andrews Church.
    Between August, 1970, and March, 1971, I worked my way
    through these files and piles of paper. Of particular
    interest was the CSM-AIM correspondence, records of AIM
    out-schools and churches that later came under the CSM
    control, discussion of the handing over of the Gospel
    Mission Society the CSM.

III. Private Papers

A. Autobiographies of Ezekiel Kamau and Ndegwa Metho
   Both men, early AIM adherents in the Gakarara area, wrote extensive accounts of their lives to 1950, in preparation for interviews with me.

B. Francis George Hall, Letters, Papers, and Diaries of a D.O. (with typed) calendar of correspondence 1880-1901. 10 vols. Seen in Rhodes House Archives as MSS Afr. S. 54-62.
   Agent of Imperial British East Africa Company at Machakos and Dagoretti and later employed by Kenya Colony as military commander of Fort Smith and Fort Hall (Mbiriri) until death in 1901.

C. Ndegwa Metho Papers
   These papers consist of two files: Metho's correspondence as Fort Hall District secretary of the Kikuyu Independent Schools Association 1945-1950 and letters and papers concerning his detention as an oath administrator during the Mau Mau rebellion.

D. Joshua Ng'ang'a Kimani Papers
   Kimani kept two notebooks: a book of Arathi doctrine which he says he received from God and an autobiographical account of his activities as an Arathi leader. Both documents appear as appendices I and II respectively.

E. Jeremiah Kimoni Papers
   Jeremiah Kimoni was Harry Thuku's main contact in the Githumu area for the Kikuyu Provincial Association (KPU). Kimoni's papers consist of correspondence with Thuku and other materials concerning the KPU.

F. Meinertzhagen, Richard, Diaries: India, Mountains, East Africa, Palestine, as military advisor, Colonial Office, 1899-1965, 76 vols. (Seen in Rhodes House Archives as MSS Afr. S).
   Led punitive expeditions against the Kikuyu, 1902-1904 as chief military commander in Kenya Colony. His diaries for those years have been abridged and form the basis for his book, Kenya Diary 1902-1906.

G. Johanna Mitaro Notebooks and A Short History of the Gospel Mission Society.
   Mitaro, Athomi leader at the GMS out-station of Kihumbuini from 1926, kept a series of notebooks in which he recorded major incidents at Kihumbuini together with his own comments, instructions from GMS missionaries, school and church accounts and drafts of letters which he wrote to the GMS, the colonial government and to others.

188

Mitaro's history of the GMS is largely an autobiographical
account of his life at Kambui, Ngenda and Kihumbuini.

IV. Other Documents

Africa Inland Mission. Diamond Jubilee 1895-1955. Kijabe:
    African Inland Mission Press, 1955.
Africa Inland Mission Marriage Register for Githumu District,
    1919-1971.
        Record of all church marriages performed by the AIM
    in their largest Kikuyu district. Information is recorded
    for each marriage under the following headings: name and
    age of bride and groom, date of marriage, dowry, address
    by chief and village, condition (spinster, widow, bach-
    elor) and dates when banns were published.
Church of Scotland Mission. "Memorandum on Female
    Circumcision," 1931. (See in KNA: as DC/FH 3/4).
        Written by CSM missionary, Dr. Arthur, this defense
    of the mission ban on female circumcision was supported
    and signed by the AIM.
Mawatho na Miturire ya [Rules and Constitution of the] African
    Christian Church and School Committee, n.d.
The Constitution of the African Christian Church and Schools,
    June, 1964.
        A longer, more detailed version of the ACC&S consti-
    tution showing the increasing elaboration of administra-
    tive structure.
Divine Liturgy of the African Orthodox Church. Church
    Headquarters, Bevionsfield, South Africa, rpt. Nairobi,
    1936. (Seen in KNA as DC/NYI 2/82 Deposit 2).
        Used by Archbishop Alexander when training Kikuyu
    Independent Church clergy at Gituamba.
Government of Great Britain. Kenya Land Commission, Evidence
    and Memoranda. 4 vols. Nairobi: Government Printer, 1933.
Government of Great Britain. Kenya Land Commission Report,
    Nairobi: Government Printer, 1933.
Government of Kenya. The Origins and Growth of Mau Mau
    [Cornfield Report]. Sessional Paper No. 5 of 1959-1960.
History of Mataara Mission and Growth of Gatunguru Independent
    Church, n.d.
        Prepared by and kindly shown to me by the elders of
    Mataara and Gatunguru churches.
Kaiiri Independent School Financial Books, February, 1944-
    December, 1950.
        A ledger-book showing all incoming and outgoing
    money and goods used for the building and upkeep of Kaiiri
    Independent School, often with comments on how money and
    goods were raised and why it was spent.
Kikuyu Independent Schools Association. Established 1929,
    Connected with the African Independent Pentecostal Church.
    Report and Constitution. Nyeri, Kenya: pub. by the

Executive Committee of KISA, 1938. (Seen in KNA as DC/EBU 4/5).

Kikuyu Provincial Association to His Excellency the Governor-in-Council, Through the Honourable the Provincial Commissioner, Central Province, Nyeri, December 23, 1943. A position paper written by Harry Thuku and sent to the Governor on the need for greater African representation in Kenya's Legislative Council.

Kugururwo Kwa Watho wa King Gikuyu uria Ithaka cia Andu Airu a Kenya uria ugwitwo [Results of the Carter Land Commission Report]. Kenya (Native Areas) Order in Council 1939.
    Distributed by Harry Thuku to KPA members.

Mutugo wa Kurathimaga Kanitha [The Blessing of the Church], n.d. (Seen in KNA as DC/NYI 2/82. Deposit 2).
    A record of the service which took place when the Kikuyu African Orthodox Church severed its connection with Archbishop Alexander's African Orthodox Church in South Africa.

Presbyterian Church of East Africa. Mahoya Ma Jubilee ya Kihumbuini [Prayers for the Kihumbuini Jubilee] n.d. Part I & II.
    A history of the GMS out-station at Kuhumbuini, written by Johanna Mitaro.

Rules and Regulations of the Kikuyu Provincial Association, n.d.
    The association's administrative framework and procedures.

V. Periodicals

A. Hearing and Doing [later Inland Africa]. 1895-
    This monthly AIM journal with almost identical American and British editions, is a rich source for learning what the AIM wanted others to know about their mission. Mission projects, growth in converts and financial need are given much attention in each issue. To 1940, when the wholesale reprinting of missionary letters was discontinued, it was also possible to learn a little about the problems missionaries faced among the Kikuyu.

B. Muigwithania [The Newsbearer]
    The Kikuyu Central Association Newsletter from 1928 to the early 1930s. Its major purpose was to knit the Kikuyu together as one people and raise their consciousness to the triple threat of the colonial government, white settlers and Christian missions. The twelve issues read (Vol. I, No. 3--Vol. II, No. 3, 1928-1929) were seen in the KNA as DC/MKS 10B/13/1.

190

VI.   Thesis and Dissertations

Gration, John.   "The Relationship of the Africa Inland mission
    and its National Church in Kenya Between 1895 and 1971,"
    Ph.D. Diss. School of Education, New York University,
    1974.
        An exellent account of the friction that developed
    between the AIM and its national church in Kenya with
    comparisons to AIM work in Tanzania and Zaire. Gration, a
    former AIM missionary, is sympathetic and sensitive to the
    point of view of the national church.
de Kiewiet, Marie. "History of the Imperial British East Africa
    Company, 1876-1895," Ph.D. Diss., University of London,
    1955.
McIntosh, Brian G. "The Scottish Mission in Kenya, 1891-1923,"
    Ph.D. Diss., Edinburgh University, 1969.   A mission-
    centered reconstruction of CSM work.
Muriuki, Godfrey. "An Oral History of the Kikuyuto 1904,"
    Ph.D. Diss., University of London, 1969.
        The only comprehensive and systematic collection of
    Kikuyu oral traditions and the basis for Muriuki's,
    History of the Kikuyu 1500-1900.
Teasdale, Charles W. An Evaluation of the Ecclesiology of the
    Africa Inland mission, unpub. M.A. Thesis Wheaton College,
    1956.

VII.   Unpublished Papers and Manuscripts

Anderson, William B.   "The Experiences and Meaning of Conver-
    sion for Early Christian Converts in Kenya." Paper pre-
    sented at the Workshop in Religious Research, University
    College, Nairobi, Kenya, December 27, 1967- January 12,
    1968.
        A digest of information from his students' inter-
    views by the person who pioneered the establishment of the
    Limuru-NCCK Archives at St. Paul's Theological College.
Colchester, Trevor Charles.
        Note on the association between death of Chief
    Waiyaki in 1893 and the Leakey sacrifice during the Mau
    Mau emergency.   (Read in Rhodes House Archives as MSS.
    Afr. S. 742).
Kibicho, Samuel G. "The Interaction of the Traditional Kikuyu
    Concept of God with the Biblical Concept," Theory and
    Practice in Church Life and Growth: Proceedings of an
    Interdisciplinary Workshop in Research on Religion in
    Africa, June 1966-1968, Nairobi, Kenya, 3 1-396.
Kuria, Joel W. "The Separated Brethren." unpub. honors paper,
    Kenyatta University College, January, 1969.
        Short, but accurate account of the origins and
    development of the ACC&S by one of its members.

191

Lonsdale, John, "Kikuyu Political Thought and Ideologies of Mau Mau," Paper presented at the African Studies Association Annual Meeting, New Orleans, Louisiana, November 23, 1985.

Macharia, Ephantus G. "Traditional Religion Among the Kikuyu," Seminar paper, Kenyatta University College, n.d.

Mathu, George W. "Gikuyu Marriage: Beliefs and Practices." Institute of African Studies Discussion Paper No. 17. University of Nairobi, March, 1971.

Mitugo Ya Agikuyu ya Tene [Ancient Kikuyu Customs]; Kuhitania Ya Agikuyu Ya Tene na Ya Mau Mau [Changes in Kikuyu Customs brought by Mau Mau]; Maundu Maria Magitagira Agikuyu Ta Kuuma Miaka 900 Ithirite [Kikuyu Problems over the last 900 years].

    Three manuscripts given to me by Johana Mitaro of Kihumbuini who claimed authorship.

Mwangi, J.H. "Worship of Ngai in Gikuyu." Seminar paper, St. Paul's Theological College, n.d.

Mwangi, Mugo. ACC&S: Foundation and Early History, n.d. (Read at Limuru-NCCK Archives).

    Interviews and field notes for research project by the ACC&S General Secretary when he was a student at St. Paul's Theological College.

Ndungu, Joseph. African Independent Church and School at Gituamba, Fort Hall. (Read at Limuru-NCCK Archives).

    The field notes and interviews upon which Ndungu wrote his article in Ngano.

Sluiter, Greet. "Confidential on Migrant Labour and Connected Matters in Four Villages in Miambu Reserve of Kenya." Department of Social Service, Training and Research of the Christian Council of Kenya, 1958. (Seen in PCLEA Archives).

    Contains an interesting chapter linking mission Christianity with Kikuyu socio-economic structure.

Watt, J.A. Stuart. Recollections of Kenya, 1895-1963, with copies of correspondence regarding Church Missionary Society activities in East Africa, 1877-1908, (Read in Rhodes House Archives as MSS. Afr. S. 391).

    AIM work described by the son of an early missionary and fruit farmer.

VIII. Books

Anderson, John. The Struggle For the School. Nairobi: Longmans of Kenya Ltd., 1970.

    A good, concise account of western education in Kenya with emphasis on the links between independent schools during the colonial period and self-help Harambee schools since Kenya's independence in 1963.

Baeta, C.G. Christianity in Tropical Africa. London: Oxford University Press, 1968.

Barrett, David B. (ed.). African Initiatives in Religion. Nairobi: East African Publishing House, 1971.
_____. Schism and Renewal in Africa. Nairobi: Oxford University Press, 1968.
Barrett, David B. et. al., (eds). Kenya Churches Handbook: The Development of Kenyan Christianity 1498-1973. Kisumu, Kenya: Evangel Publishing House, 1973.
Bennett, George, Kenya, A Political History, The Colonial Period. London: Oxford University Press, Students' Library, 1963.
Bewes, T.F.C. Kikuyu Conflict: Mau Mau and the Christian Witness. London: The Highway Press, 1953.
Blakeslee, Helen Virginia. Beyond the Kikuyu Curtain. Chicago: Moody Press, 1956.
        A long account glorifying the AIM and particularly her mission work from 1911-1954 among the Kikuyu.
Boyes, John. King of the Wa-Kikuyu. London: Methuen, 1911.
Buell, Raymond Leslie. The Native Problem in Africa. 2 vols. London: Frank Cass, 1965.
Cagnolo, Father C. The Akikuyu, Their Customs, Traditions and Folklore. Nyeri, Kenya: The Mission Printing School, 1933.
Capon, Martin G. Towards Unity in Kenya. Nairobi: Christian Council of Kenya, 1962.
        Records Protestant cooperation in Kenya and the unsuccessful attempt by Protestants to create a united African Church.
Delf, George. Jomo Kenyatta. London: Victor Gollanez, 1961.
Eliot, Sir Charles. The East African Protectorate. London: Edward Arnold, 1905.
Farson, N. Last Chance in Africa. London: Gollanez, 1949.
Fisher, Jean. The Anatomy of Kikuyu Domesticity and Husbandry. London: 1964. (Seen in the KNA as DC/FH 3/2).
Gicaru, Muga. Land of Sunshine: Scenes of Life in Kenya before Mau Mau. London: Lawrence & Wishart. 1958.
        Though much of the book describes the hardships of Kikuyu squatters on white settler farms in the Rift Valley, Gicaru does give information and insight into KISA schools where he received some of his education.
Handbook of Kenya Colony. Naval Staff: Intelligence Division, 1920.
Harlow, Vincent and E.M. Chilver (eds). History of East Africa, II. Oxford: Clarendon Press, 1965.
Hasting, Adrian. A History of Christianity 1950-1975, London: Cambridge University Press, 1979.
Hayward, Victor E. (ed). African Independent Church Movement. London: Edinburgh House Press, 1963.
Hobley, Charles Willham. Bantu Beliefs and Magic. London: H.F. & G. Witherby, Ltd., 1938.
_____. Ethnology of the Akamba and Other East African Tribes. Cambridge: University Press, 1910.
_____. Kenya From Chartered Company to Crown Colony. London; J.F. & G. Witherby, 1929.

Huxley, Elspeth. White Man's Country: Lord Delemare and the Making of Kenya. London: Chatto & Windus, 1953.

Huxley, Julian. African View. New York: Harper & Row, 1931.

Jackson, Sir Frederick. Early Days in East Africa. London: Edward Arnold & Co., 1930.

Kangethe, Joseph. Uria Kenyatta Atwarirwo Ruraya Ni KCA. [How Kenyatta was Sent to Europe by the KCA], Nairobi: Zahur Printers, n.d.

Keltie, J. Scott. The Partition of Africa. London: Edward Stanford, first edition 1898, 2nd edition 1895.

Kenyatta, Jomo. Facing Mt. Kenya. London: 1938 rpt. Vintage 1962.

Kiragu, D.M. Kiria Giatumire Independent Igie [Independent church origins] Nairobi: Regal Press, n.d.
     The "official" account of origins and growth of Kikuyu independent churches and schools by their unofficial though widely recognized leader.

Koinange, Mbiyu. The People of Kenya Speak For Themselves. Detroit, Michigan: Kenya Publication Fund, 1955.
     Chapters four, five and six give details on the building of the KISA "college" at Githunguri under the leadership of Koinange.

Lambert, H.E. Kikuyu Social and Political Institutions. London: Oxford University Press, 1956.

Leys, Norman. Kenya. London: Hogarth Press, 2nd ed. 1925.

Leakey, L.S.B. Kenya Contrasts and Problems. London: Hodder & Stoughton, 1938.

_____. The Mau Mau and the Kikuyu. London: Meuthen, 1952.

McDermott, P.L. British East Africa, A History of the Formation and Work of the Imperial British East Africa Company. London: Chapman & Hall, 1895.
     Official history of the company written by its secretary.

Macpherson, Robert. The Presbyterian Church in Kenya. Nairobi: Presbyterian Church of East Africa, 1970.
     Contains an interesting and accurate though brief chapter on the Gospel Mission Society which seceded from the AIM in 1911 and in 1944 joined the Church of Scotland Mission [later Presbyterian Church of East Africa].

Mbiti, John. African Religion and Philosophy. London: Heinemann, 1969.

Meinertzhagen, Richard. Kenya Diary 1902-1906. London: Oliver and Boyd, 1957.

Middleton, John. The Kikuyu and the Kamba of Kenya. Ethnographic Survey of Africa: East Africa, Part 5, London: The International African Institute, 1953.

Miller, Catherine S. Peter Cameron Scott, The Unlocked Door. London: Perry Jackson Ltd., 1955.
     Glowing account of the AIM founder by a British AIM missionary.

Muriuki, Godfrey. A History of the Kikuyu 1500-1900. Nairobi: Oxford University Press, 1974.

The only comprehensive and systematic collection and interpretation of Kikuyu oral traditions.

Neckebrouck, Valeer. Le Onzieme Commandement: Etiologie d'une eglise independante an pied du mont Kenya, Immensee, 1978.

_____. Le Peuple Afflige: Lew Determinants de la Fissiparite dans un Nouveau Mouvement Religieux an Kenya Central. Immensee, 1983.

Oliver, Roland. The Missionary Factor in East Africa. London: Longmans, 1952, 2nd ed. 1965.

Oliver, Roland and G. Mathew. History of East Africa. I. Oxford: Clarendon Press, 1963.

Perham, Margery (ed). The Diaries of Lord Lugard. 4 vols. London: Faber & Faber, 1959.

Philip, H.R.A A New Day in Kenya. London: World Dominion Press, 1936.

Rawcliffe, D.H. Struggle For Kenya. London: Gollanez, 1954.

Richardson, Kenneth. Garden of Miracles: A History of the African Inland Mission. London: Victory Press, 1968.
The official history by a former AIM missionary to the Congo; written for readers sympathetic to the mission; no footnotes or bibliography. Useful for understanding the Who's Who of AIM missionaries. Little is said about African people.

Robinson, Ronald and John Gallagher with Alice Denny. Africa and the Victorians. New York: St. Martin's Press, 1961.

Roelker, Jack R. The Genesis of African Protest: Harry Thuku and the British Administration in Kenya, 1920-1922. Syracuse University: Program of E.A. Studies, Occasional Paper No. 41, n.d.

Rosberg, Carl G. Jr. and John Nottingham. The Myth of "Mau Mau": Nationalism in Kenya. New York: Frederick A. Praeger for the Hoover Institution on War, Revolution and Peace, 1966.
The Mau Mau rebellion accurately shown to be a political movement rather than a return to religious atavism. But little attention given to the religious motivations that led some Kikuyu to be loyalists and others to be forest fighters.

Ross, W. McGregor. Kenya From Within. London: Allen & Unwin, 1927.

Routledge, W. Scoresby. With a Prehistoric People. London: Edward Arnold, 1910.

Smith, Edwin W. The Christian Mission in Africa. London: The International Missionary Council, 1926.

Sorrenson, M.P.K. Origins of European Settlement in Kenya. Nairobi: Oxford University Press, 1968.

_____. Land Reform in Kikuyu Country. Nairobi: Oxford Undersity Press, 1967.

Strayer, Robert W. The Making of Mission Communities in East Africa: Anglicans and Africans in Colonial Kenya 1875-1935. London: Heinemann, 1978.

195

Thomson, Joseph. _Through Masailand_. London: Sampson, Low, Marston, Searle & Rivington, 1885.
Harry Thuku, _An Autobiography_, with the assistance of Kenneth King. Nairobi: Oxford University Press, 1970.
    Dictated in English by Thuku shortly before he died, this book gives insight into the urban life of the Kikuyu educated elite and Thuku's change from a radical protestor to a moderate.
Stuart-Watt, Rachel. _In the Heart of Savagedom_. Glasgow: Pickings & Inglis, 3rd ed. n.d.
    Trials and tribulations of missionary life from 1893-1914 among the Kamba by an independent missionary and the fruit farmer whose work was taken over, at his death, by the AIM.
Von Hohnel, Lieut Ludwig. _Discovery of Lakes Rudolf and Stefanie_. London: Longmans, 1894.
Welbourn, Frederick B. _East African Christian_. London: Oxford University Press, 1965.
    .__East African Rebels_. London: SCM Press, 1961.
    Second half of book is pioneer account of the origins and development of Kikuyu Independent churches and schools.
Weller, Henry Owen. _Kenya Without Prejudice_. London: East Africa Newspaper, 1931.
Wiseman, E.M. _Kikuyu Martyrs_. London: Highway Press, 1958.
    A collection of eleven 1-3 page accounts of Kikuyu who were either killed or who narrowly escaped martyrdom for refusing to be oathed during the Emergency.
    An excellent portrayal of the cleavages between some Kikuyu Christians.

IV. Articles

Anderson, John. "Self Help and Independency: The Political Implications of a Continuing Tradition in African Education in Kenya." _African Affairs_, 70. No. 278 (January 1971), 9-22.
Austin, H.H. "The Passing of Waiyaki." _The London Times_, November, 1922.
Barlow, A.R. "Kikuyu Land Tenure and Inheritance." _The Journal of the East Africa and Uganda Natural History Society_, No. 45-46 (April-July 1932), pp. 56-66.
Beech, M.W.H. "A Ceremony at a Mugumo or Sacred Fig-Tree of East Africa. _Man_, 13, No. 51 (1913), 86-89.
    ."Kikuyu System of Land Tenure." _Journal of African Society_, 17, (1917), 46-59, 136-144.
    . "The Sacred Fig-Tree of the A-Kikuyu of East Africa." _Man_, 13, No. 3 (1913), 4-6.
    . "Suicide Amongst the A-Kikuyu of East Africa." _Man_, 13, No. 30 (1913), 56-57.

196

Bewes, T.F.C. "The Work of the Christian Church Among the Kikuyu." International Affairs, 19 No. 3 (July, 1952), 316-25.

Dundus, C. "The Organization and Laws of Some Bantu Tribes in East Africa (Kamba, Kikuyu, Tharaka)." Journal of the Royal Anthropological Institute, 45 (1915).

Hall,, B.E.F. "How Peace came to Kikuyu: extract of letters from F.G. Hall." Journal of the Royal African Society, 37, 432-448.

Hobley, C.W. "Kikuyu customs and beliefs. Thahu and its connection with circumcision Rites." Journal of the Anthropological Institute, 40 (1910), 428-52.

Horton, Robin. "African Conversion." Africa, 41, No. 2, (April 1971), 85-108.

Kenyatta, J. "Kikuyu Religion, Ancestor Worship and Sacrificial Practices." Africa, 10 (1937), 308.

Kibicho, Samuel G. "Theory and Practice in Church Life and Growth." Proceedings of an Interdisciplinary Workshop in Research on Religion in Africa, June, 1966-1968, Nairobi, Kenya, pp. 381-94.

Lawren, William L. "Masai and Kikuyu: An Historical Analysis of Culture Transmission." Journal of African History, 9, No. 4 (1968), 571-83.

Leakey, L.S.B. "The Economics of Kikuyu Tribal Life." The East African Economics Review, 3 (1956), 165-80.

_____. "The Kikuyu Problem of the Initiation of Girls." Journal of the Royal Anthropological Institute, 61, (1931), 277-85.

_____. "Some Problems arising from the part played by sheep and goats in the life of the Kikuyu." Journal of the African Society, 33 (January 1934), 70-79.

Lonsdale, John. "Some Origins of East African Nationalism." Journal of African History, 9, No. 1 (1968), 119-46.

_____. "European Attitudes and African Pressures: Missions and Government in Kenya Between the Wars." Race, 10, No. 2 (October, 1968), 141-51.

Mungeam, G.H. "Masai and Kikuyu Responses To the Establishment of British Administration in the East Africa Protectorate." Journal of African History, 11, No. 1 (1970), 127-43.

Muriuki, Godfrey. "Kikuyu Reaction to Traders and British Administration 1850-1904." Hadith I (Proceedings of the Annual Conference of the Historical Association of Kenya, 1967). Nairobi: East African Publishing House, 1968, pp. 101-18.

Murray, Jocelyn. "The Kikuyu Spirit Churches." Journal of Religion in Africa, 5, No. 3 (1974), 198-234.

Ndungu, Joseph B. "Gituamba and the Kikuyu Independency in Church and School," Ngano, Brian G. McIntosh (ed.), Nairobi: East African Publishing House, 1969.

Ng'ang'a, D. Mukaru. "Mau Mau, Loyalists and Politics in Murang'a, 1952-1970." Kenya Historical Review, Vol. 5, No. 2, 1977, 358-377.

Ogot, Bethwell. "Revolt of the Elders: An Anatomy of the Loyalist Crowd in the Mau Mau Uprising: 1952-56." Hadith IV, Nairobi: EAPH, 1971.

Ranger, T.O. "African Attempts to Control Education in East and Central Africa 1900-1939." Past and Present, 32 (December 1965), 57-85.

_____. "Missionary Adaptation of African Religious Institutions. The Masai Case." T.O. Ranger and I.N. Kimambo (eds.). The Historical Study of African Religion, Berkeley, 1972, 221-51.

_____. "Religious Movements and Politics in Sob-Saharan Africa." African Studies Review, Vol. 29, No. 2 (June, 1986), 1-69.

Savage, Donald C. and J. Forbes Munro. "Carrier Corps Recruitment in the British East African Protectorate 1914-1918." Journal of African History, 7, No. 2 (1966), 313-42.

Throup, D. W. "The Origins of Mau Mau." African Affairs Vol. 84 (1985), 399-433.

Welbourn, F.B. "Keyo Initiation." The Journal of Religion in Africa, 1, No. 3 (1968), 212-32.

INDEX

African Christian Church and Schools: separation from AIM, 142-147; leadership of, 148; schools, 149-150; _Kirore_ membership in, 137-142.

African Independent Penecostal Church: early development, 104; belief system and literary, 105-106; compatability with Kikuyu, customs, 106; connection with Kikuyu independent schools, 113; connection with Kikuyu political movement, 113-115

African Inland Church, 141

African Inland Mission: origins, 17-20; expansion of, 20; Kijabe headquarters, 20; early problems of, 21-25; candidate selection, 22; philosophy of evangelism, 23-24, 53-54; education and schools, 23-24, 39-40, 53-54, 138-139; refuge for Kikuyu, 39-40; Kikuyu boycott of, 87-88; land owners, as, 32, 51; attack on Kikuyu customs, 52; church discipline, 54-55; _Kirore_ unhappiness with, 138-141

African Orthodox Church of South Africa, 101

African Orthodox Church, 103

Ainsworth, John, 19

Alexander, Archbishop Daniel William, 101-103

Alliance of Protestant Missions, 51, 73

anti-mission aggression, 41

Arathi: definition of, 121; early development, 121-122; estranged from independents and community, 122-123, 125; westernization, critical of, 123; prophicies, 123, 124; trouble with government, 123-126; Ndarugu forest incident, 125; specialization of leadership, 127-128; importance of dreams, 121, 124-125, 128, 130; _Thahu_, beliefs in, 130-131; Mau Mau, _Arathi_ participation in, 132

Aregi independents, 88ff.

Athomi, definition of, 37

Beauttah, James, 101

Carrier Corps, 38

Chiefs: colonial appointment of, 16; conflict with Chrstians, 41, 50-51; support of ban on female circumcision, 79

Church Missionary Society, 51, 59, 100

Clan or _Mihiriga_, 9

Clitoridectomy--see Female Circumcision

CMS _Memorandum_, 75, 93

color bar, 25

Downing, Kenneth, 147

East African Association, 55

Education: AIM schools, 23-24, 39-40, 53-54, 138-139; _Aregi_ indepedent schools, see Kikuyu Independent Schools Association; _Kirore_ schools, see African Christian Churches and Schools

1. Grave of Peter Cameron Scott, founder of AIM,
   with the graves of two other pioneer missionaries

2. Chief Njiiri, as he appeared for interview with author

3. Joseph Muthungu, one of the first AIM adherents at Kinyona

4. Joseph Kang'ethe and Jeremiah Kimoni, early critics of the AIM

5. Typical Kikuyu countryside near Githumu Mission

6.   "A Kikuyu Village Scene," about 1900